# SAS® Macro Language

## Course Notes

*SAS® Macro Language Course Notes* was developed by Jim Simon. Additional contributions were made by Hunter McGhee, Bill Powers, Warren Repole, and Kari Richardson. Editing and production support was provided by the Curriculum Development and Support Department.



**SAS® Macro Language Course Notes**



Book code E70160, course code MACR, prepared date 22Jun06. MACR_003

1-59994-173-2

# Table of Contents

## Course Description

This instructor-based course is for experienced SAS programmers who want to build complete macro-based systems using the SAS macro facility.

This two-day course focuses on the components of the macro facility and how the macro language affects the normal processing of SAS programs. Emphasis is on designing macro systems and debugging techniques.

### To learn more…

SAS Education

A full curriculum of general and statistical instructor-based training is available at any of the Institute's training facilities. Institute instructors can also provide on-site training.

For information on other courses in the curriculum, contact the SAS Education Division at 1-800-333-7660, or send e-mail to training@sas.com. You can also find this information on the Web at support.sas.com/training/ as well as in the Training Course Catalog.

SAS Publishing

For a list of other SAS books that relate to the topics covered in this Course Notes, USA customers can contact our SAS Publishing Department at 1-800-727-3228 or send e-mail to sasbook@sas.com. Customers outside the USA, please contact your local SAS office.

Also, see the Publications Catalog on the Web at support.sas.com/pubs for a complete list of books and a convenient order form.

# Prerequisites

Before selecting this course, students should be able to

- write and submit SAS programs on your operating system
- use LIBNAME, FILENAME, TITLE, and OPTIONS statements
- use a DATA step to read from or write to a SAS data set or external data file
- use DATA step programming statements such as IF-THEN/ELSE, DO WHILE, DO UNTIL, and iterative DO
- use character functions such as SUBSTR, SCAN, INDEX, and UPCASE
- use the LENGTH and RETAIN statements
- use SAS data set options such as DROP=, KEEP=, AND OBS=
- form subsets of data using the WHERE clause
- create and use SAS date values, including SAS date constants
- execute base SAS procedures such as SORT, PRINT, CONTENTS, MEANS, FREQ, TABULATE, and CHART.

# General Conventions

This section explains the various conventions that may be used in presenting text, SAS language syntax, and examples in this book.

## Typographical Conventions

You will see several type styles in this book. This list explains the meaning of each style:

|  |  |
|---|---|
| UPPERCASE ROMAN | is used for SAS statements and other SAS language elements when they appear in the text. |
| *italic* | identifies terms or concepts that are defined in text. Italic is also used for book titles when they are referenced in text, as well as for various syntax and mathematical elements. |
| **bold** | is used for emphasis within text. |
| `monospace` | is used for examples of SAS programming statements and for SAS character strings. Monospace is also used to refer to variable and data set names, field names in windows, information in fields, and user-supplied information. |
| **select** | indicates selectable items in windows and menus. This book also uses icons to represent selectable items. |

## Syntax Conventions

The general forms of SAS statements and commands shown in this book include only that part of the syntax actually taught in the course. For complete syntax, see the appropriate SAS reference guide.

**PROC CHART** DATA = *SAS-data-set*;<br>
    **HBAR** | **VBAR** *chart-variables* </ *options*>;<br>
**RUN**;

This is an example of how SAS syntax is shown in text:

- **PROC** and **CHART** are in uppercase bold because they are SAS keywords.
- DATA= is in uppercase to indicate that it must be spelled as shown.
- *SAS-data-set* is in italic because it represents a value that you supply. In this case, the value must be the name of a SAS data set.
- **HBAR** and **VBAR** are in uppercase bold because they are SAS keywords. They are separated by a vertical bar to indicate they are mutually exclusive; you can choose one or the other.
- *chart-variables* is in italic because it represents a value or values that you supply.
- </ *options*> represents optional syntax specific to the HBAR and VBAR statements. The angle brackets enclose the slash as well as *options* because if no options are specified you do not include the slash.
- **RUN** is in uppercase bold because it is a SAS keyword.

# Chapter 1 Introduction

# 1.1 Purpose of the Macro Facility

## Objectives

- State the purpose of the macro facility.
- View examples of macro applications.

3

## Purpose of the Macro Facility

The *macro facility* is a text processing facility for automating and customizing flexible SAS code.

The macro facility supports

- symbolic substitution within SAS code
- automated production of SAS code
- dynamic generation of SAS code
- conditional construction of SAS code.

4

## Purpose of the Macro Facility

The macro facility enables you to

- create and resolve **macro variables** anywhere within a SAS program
- write and call **macro programs** (*macros*) that generate custom SAS code.

5

The macro facility is a tool for customizing SAS and for minimizing the amount of program code you must enter to perform common tasks.

## Substituting System Information

Example: Include system information within SAS footnotes.

```
proc print data=perm.all;
title "Listing of PERM.ALL Data Set";
footnote1 "Created 10:24 Wednesday, 25AUG2004";
footnote2 "on the WIN System Using Release 9.1";
run;
```

**Automatic macro variables,** which store system information, can be used to avoid hardcoding these values. → OS, date

6

## Substituting User-Defined Information

Example: Include the same value repeatedly throughout a program.

```
proc print data=perm.schedule;
   where year(begin_date)=2004;
   title "Scheduled Classes for 2004";
run;
proc means data=perm.all sum;
   where year(begin_date)=2004;
   class location;
   var fee;
   title "Total Fees for 2004 Classes";
   title2 "by Training Center";
run;
```

**User-defined macro variables** enable you to define a value once, then substitute that value as often as necessary within a program.

7

## Conditional Processing

Example: Generate a detailed report on a daily basis. Generate an additional report every Friday, summarizing data on a weekly basis.

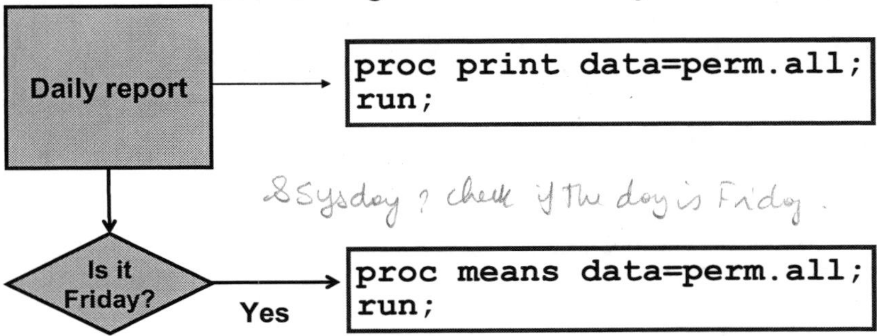


Macro programs can **conditionally** execute selected portions of a SAS program based on user-defined conditions.

8

## Repetitive Processing

Example: Generate a similar report each year from 2003 to 2005.

```
proc print data=perm.year2003;
run;
```

```
proc print data=perm.year2004;
run;
```

```
proc print data=perm.year2005;
run;
```

The macro facility can **generate SAS code repetitively**, substituting different values with each iteration.

9

## Data-Driven Applications

Example: Create a separate subset of a data set for each unique value of a selected variable.

```
data Boston Dallas Seattle;
   set perm.schedule;
   select(location);
      when("Boston") output Boston;
      when("Dallas") output Dallas;
      when("Seattle") output Seattle;
      otherwise;
   end;
run;
```

The macro facility can **generate data-driven code**.

10

## Developing Macro-Based Applications

If a macro-based application generates SAS code, use a four-step approach.

Step 1:

- write and debug the desired SAS program without any macro coding
- make sure the SAS program runs with hardcoded programming constants on a fixed set of data.

Steps 2-4 will be presented later.

11

Beginning the development process in this manner enables rapid development and debugging because syntax and logic at the SAS code level is isolated from syntax and logic at the macro level.

## Efficiency of Macro-Based Applications

The macro facility can reduce program

- development time
- maintenance time.

SAS code generated by macro techniques

- does not compile or execute faster than any other SAS code
- depends on the efficiency of the underlying SAS code, regardless of how the SAS code was generated.

12

# 1.2 Program Flow

## Objectives

- Identify the tokens in a SAS program.
- Describe how a SAS program is tokenized, compiled, and executed.

14

## Program Flow

A SAS program can be any combination of

- DATA steps and PROC steps
- global statements
- SAS Component Language (SCL)
- Structured Query Language (SQL)
- SAS macro language.

When you submit a program, it is copied to a location in memory called the *input stack*.

15

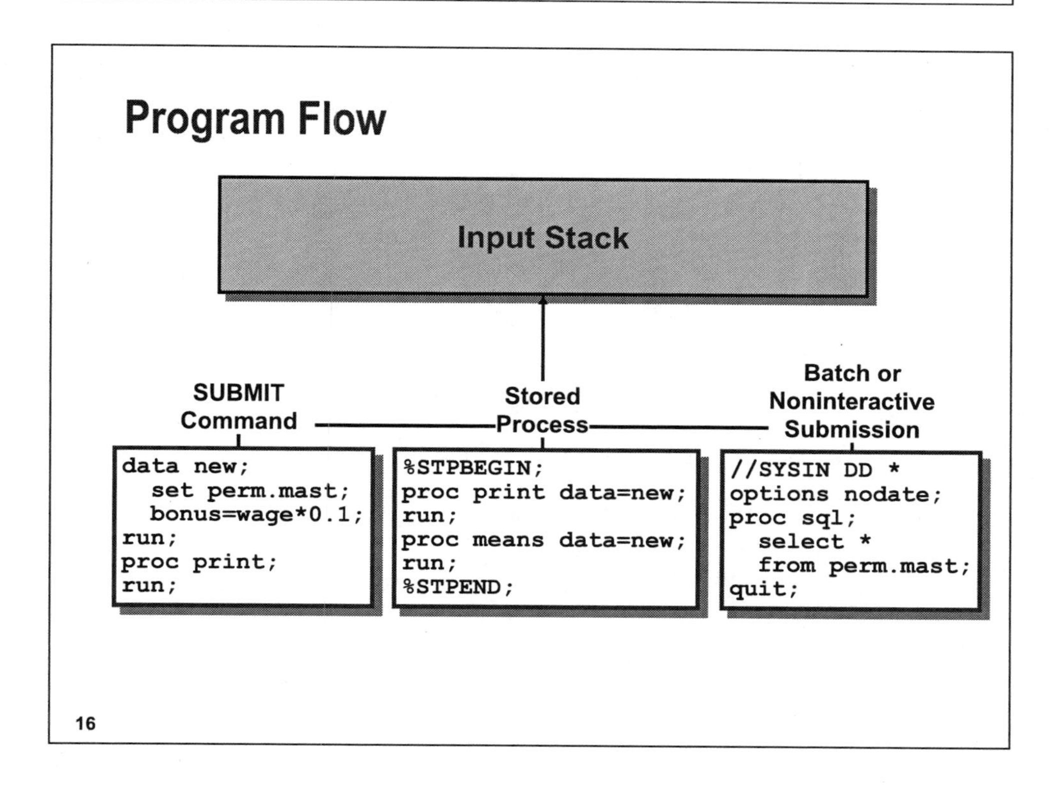

## Program Flow

Once SAS code is in the input stack, a component of SAS called the *word scanner*

- reads the text in the input stack, character by character, left-to-right, top-to-bottom
- breaks the text into fundamental units called *tokens*.

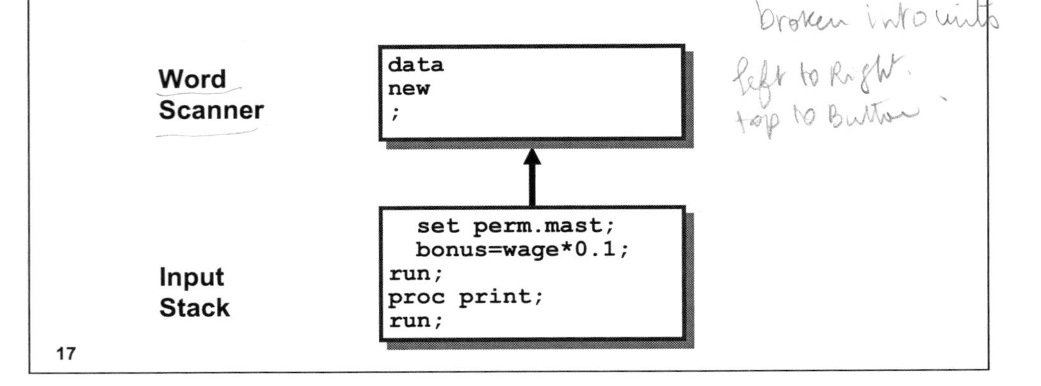


17

## Program Flow

The word scanner passes the tokens, one at a time, to the appropriate compiler, as the compiler demands.

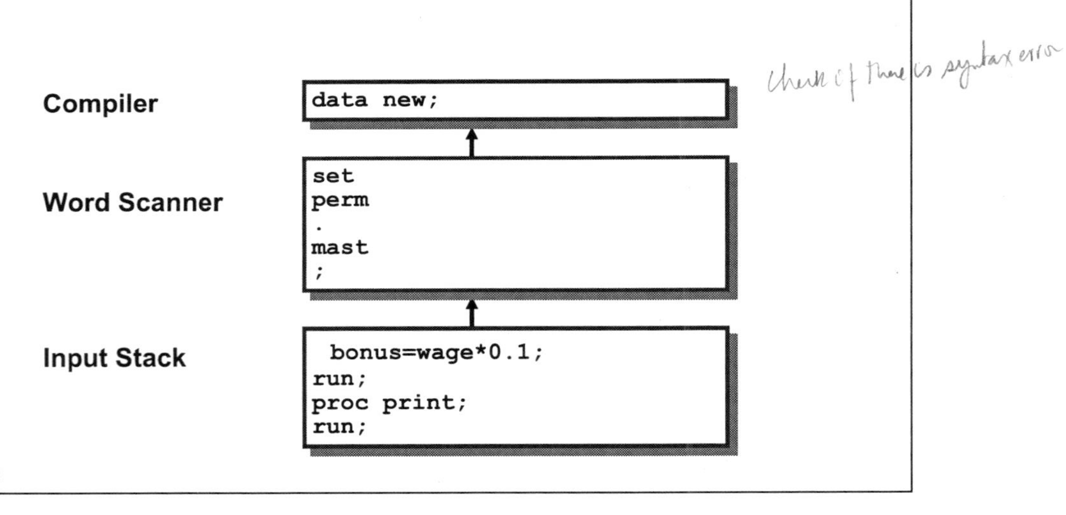


18

## Program Flow

The compiler

- requests tokens until it receives a semicolon
- performs a syntax check on the statement
- repeats this process for each statement.

SAS

run, quit or proc or data step.

- suspends the compiler when a step boundary is encountered
- executes the compiled code if there are no compilation errors
- repeats this process for each step.

19

## Tokenization

The word scanner recognizes four classes of tokens:

- literal tokens
- number tokens
- name tokens
- special tokens.

20

## Literal Tokens

A *literal token* is a string of characters enclosed in single or double quotes.

Examples: 'Any text'
"Any text"

The string is treated as a unit by the compiler.

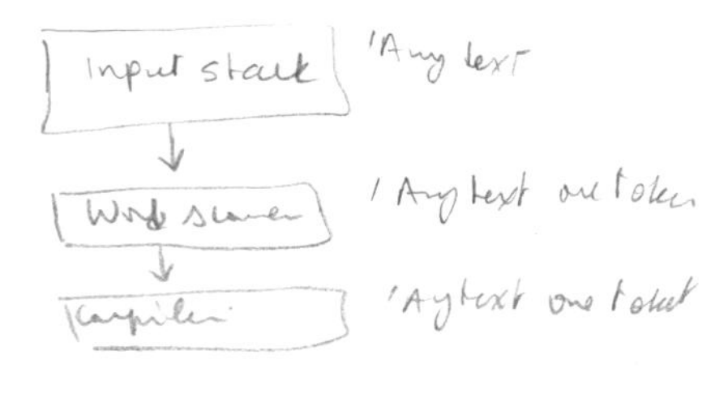

21

## Number Tokens

*Number tokens* can be

- integer numbers, including SAS date constants
- floating point numbers, containing a decimal point and/or exponent.

Examples: 3
3.
3.5
-3.5
'01jan2002'd
5E8
7.2E-4

22

## Name Tokens

*Name tokens* contain one or more characters beginning with a letter or underscore and continuing with underscores, letters, or numerals.

Examples: infile

_n_

item3

univariate

dollar10.2

Format and informat names contain a period.

23

## Special Tokens

*Special tokens* can be any character, or combination of characters, other than a letter, numeral, or underscore.

Examples: * / + - ** ; $ ( ) . & % @ # = ||

24

## Tokenization

A token ends when the word scanner detects

- the beginning of another token
- a blank after a token.

Blanks

- are not tokens
- delimit tokens.

The maximum length of a token is 32,767 characters.

25

## Example

**Input Stack**

```
var x1-x10                    z       ;
```

**Tokens**

1. var
2. x1
3. -
4. x10
5. z
6. ;

26

## Example

**Input Stack**

```
title 'Report for May';
```

**Tokens**

1. title
2. 'Report for May'
3. ;

27

## Question

How many tokens are present in each of these statements?

```
input @10 ssn comma11. name $30-50;
```

```
bonus=3.2*(wage-2000);
```

```
plot date*revenue='$'/vref='30jun2001'd;
```

28

## Answer

How many tokens are present in each of these statements?

```
input @10 ssn comma11. name $30-50;
```

11

```
bonus=3.2*(wage-2000);
```

10

```
plot date*revenue='$'/vref='30jun2001'd;
```

11

29

## Processing Tokens

flow1

By executing the program below, one token at a time in the Program Editor, you can observe in the SAS log which tokens trigger SAS to compile and execute code.

```
proc
options
;
proc
print
;
run
;
```

1. Which token triggers execution of the PROC OPTIONS step, displaying the current settings of system options in the SAS log?

   proc. print.
   ______________________________

2. Which token triggers an error message in the log window indicating that no data set is available to be printed?

   ; Could not find the data set because print. (data = set)
   ______________________________

3. Which token triggers a note indicating that the SAS System stopped processing the step?

   ; You complete the step.
   ______________________________

each token is compile

## The %INCLUDE Statement

The %INCLUDE *statement*

- copies SAS statements from an external file to the input stack
- is a global SAS statement
- is not a macro language statement
- can be used only on a statement boundary.

Input Stack

```
%include 'pgm1.sas';
proc print;
run;
```

External File: pgm1.sas

```
data new;
   set perm.mast;
   bonus=wage*0.1;
run;
```

31

## The %INCLUDE Statement

The contents of the external file are placed on the input stack. The word scanner then reads the newly inserted statements.

Input Stack

```
data new;
   set perm.mast;
   bonus=wage*0.1;
run;
proc print;
run;
```

External File: pgm1.sas

```
data new;
   set perm.mast;
   bonus=wage*0.1;
run;
```

32

...

## The %INCLUDE Statement

The %INCLUDE statement retrieves SAS source code from an external file and places it on the input stack.

General form of the %INCLUDE statement:

```
%INCLUDE file-specification < / SOURCE2 >;
```

| | |
|---|---|
| *file-specification* | physical name or *fileref* of the file to be retrieved and placed on the input stack. |
| SOURCE2 | requests inserted SAS statements to appear in the SAS log. |

33

If SOURCE2 is not specified in the %INCLUDE statement, the setting of the SAS system option SOURCE2 controls whether the inserted SAS code is displayed.

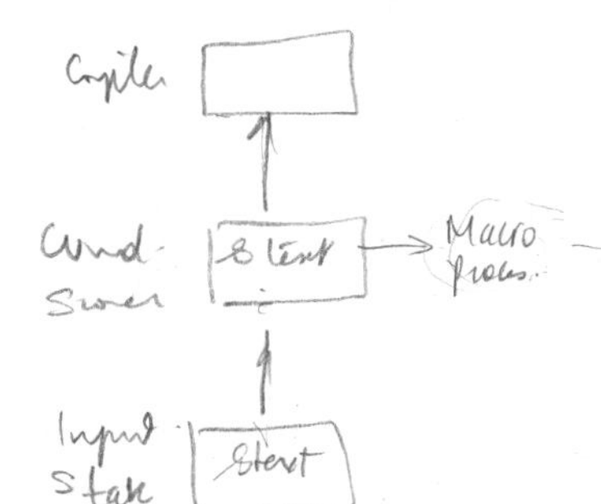

## Macro Triggers

During word scanning, two token sequences are recognized as **macro triggers**:

- *%name-token* a macro statement, function, or call
- *&name-token* a macro variable reference.

The word scanner passes macro triggers to the **macro processor**, which

- requests additional tokens as necessary
- performs the action indicated.

34

## Macro Statements

Macro statements

- begin with a percent sign (%) followed by a name token
- end with a semicolon
- represent **macro triggers**
- are executed by the **macro processor**.

35

## The %PUT Statement

The %PUT statement

- writes text to the SAS log
- writes to column one of the next line
- writes a blank line if no text is specified
- does not require quotes around text
- is valid in open code (anywhere in a SAS program).

General form of the %PUT statement:

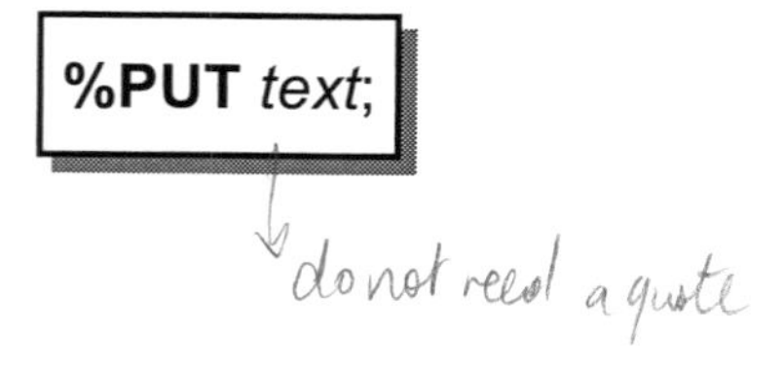


36

## The %PUT Statement

Example: Use a %PUT statement to write text to the SAS log.

Partial SAS Log

```
12 %put Hi Mom!;
Hi Mom!
```

37

## Program Flow

The %PUT statement is submitted.

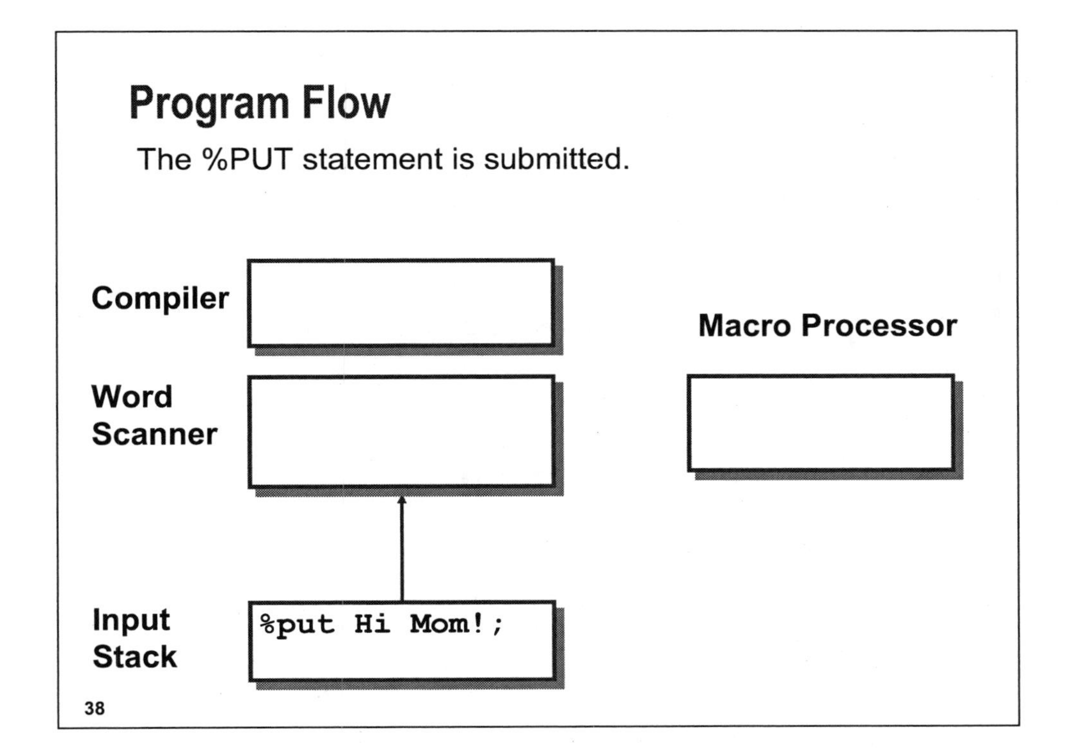


38

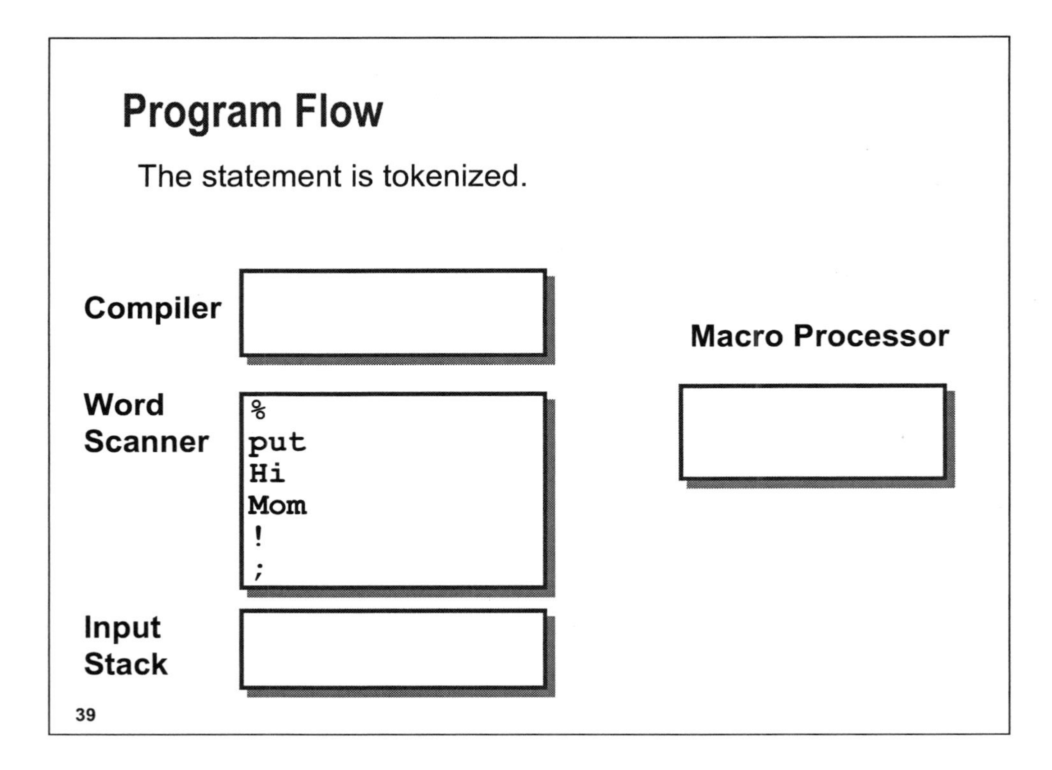
Program Flow
The statement is tokenized.
Compiler
Macro Processor
Word Scanner
%
put
Hi
Mom
!
;
Input Stack
39

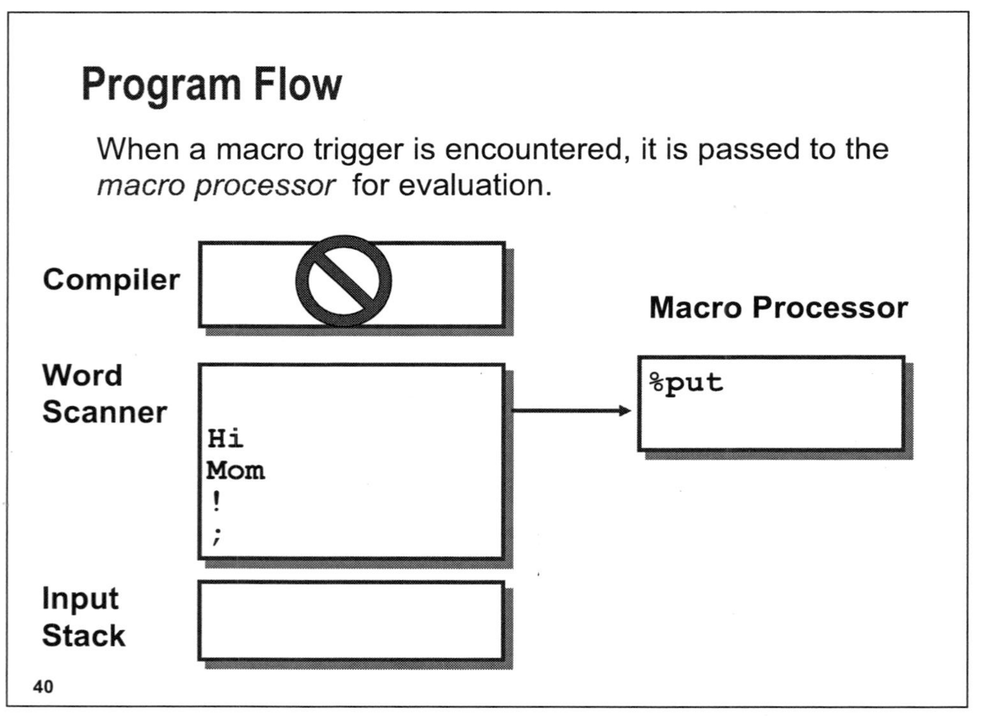
Program Flow
When a macro trigger is encountered, it is passed to the macro processor for evaluation.
Compiler
Macro Processor
Word Scanner
Hi
Mom
!
;
%put
Input Stack
40

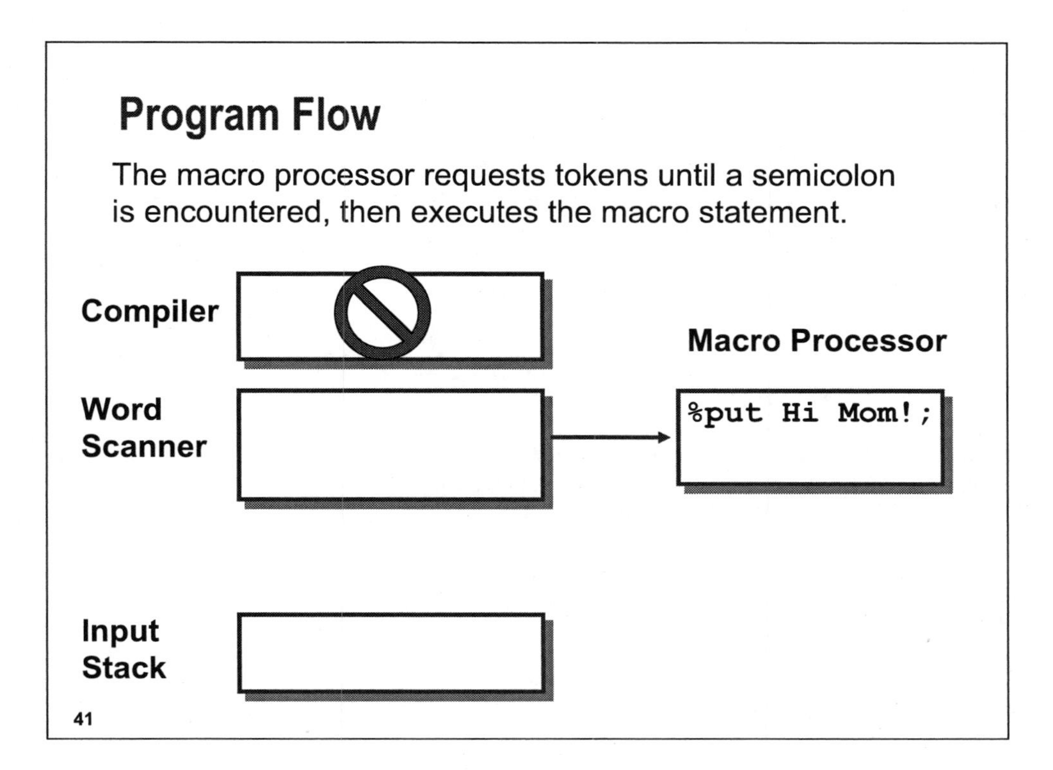
Program Flow
The macro processor requests tokens until a semicolon is encountered, then executes the macro statement.
Compiler
Macro Processor
Word Scanner
%put Hi Mom!;
Input Stack
41

# Exercises

Issue a LIBNAME statement to assign the **perm** libref to the SAS data library according to instructions provided by the instructor.

### 1. Insert Code with the %INCLUDE Statement

The program below is stored in a file named **printnum**. It creates a list of students enrolled in a specific course. Execute the **printnum** code directly using a %INCLUDE statement.

```
proc print data=perm.all label noobs n;
   where course_number=3;
   var student_name student_company;
   title "Enrollment for Course 3";
run;
```

### 2. Write Text to the SAS Log with the %PUT Statement

Submit a %PUT statement which writes your name to the SAS log.

## Solutions to Exercises

### 1. Insert Code with the %INCLUDE Statement

```
%include 'printnum.sas';
```

### 2. Write Text to the SAS Log with the %PUT Statement

```
%put Jane Doe;
```

# 1.3 Course Data

## Objectives

- Describe the data used in the course examples and workshops.

44

To demonstrate features of the macro facility, this course uses course registration data from a company specializing in computer training.

The company presents its courses in cities (Boston, Dallas, and Seattle) around the United States.

The company is developing a registration and reporting system.

Data for October 2004 through March 2006 are documented in the following data sets:

| **SAS Data Set** | **Description** | **Number of Observations** |
|---|---|---|
| `courses` | contains information about courses with one observation per course. | **6** |
| `schedule` | contains information about each course with one observation per course at a particular location and date. | **18** |
| `students` | contains information about students with one observation per student. | **207** |
| `register` | contains information about students registered for a specific course with one observation per student for a particular course. | **434** |
| `all` | joins all data files with one observation per student per course. | **434** |

These data sets are stored in a SAS data library with a libref of **`perm`**.

## The COURSES Data Set

```
                              The CONTENTS Procedure

Data Set Name        PERM.COURSES                 Observations          6
Member Type          DATA                         Variables             4
Engine               V9                           Indexes               0
Created              Tuesday, May 30,             Observation Length    48
                     2000 04:21:30 PM
Last Modified        Monday, June 12,             Deleted Observations  0
                     2000 10:39:41 AM
Protection                                        Compressed            NO
Data Set Type                                     Sorted                NO
Label
Data Representation  WINDOWS_32
Encoding             Default


                 Engine/Host Dependent Information

Data Set Page Size          4096
Number of Data Set Pages    2
First Data Page             1
Max Obs per Page            84
Obs in First Data Page      6
Number of Data Set Repairs  0
File Name                   C:\workshop\winsas\macr\courses.sas7bdat
Release Created             8.0000M0
Host Created                WIN_NT


             Alphabetic List of Variables and Attributes

#   Variable       Type   Len   Format     Informat   Label

1   Course_Code    Char     4                         Course Code
2   Course_Title   Char    25                         Description
3   Days           Num      8   1.         1.         Course Length
4   Fee            Num      8   DOLLAR5.   DOLLAR5.   Course Fee
```

```
                      Listing of PERM.COURSES
            Course_
     Obs     Code     Course_Title                Days     Fee

      1      C001     Basic Telecommunications     3      $795
      2      C002     Structured Query Language    4     $1150
      3      C003     Local Area Networks          3      $650
      4      C004     Database Design              2      $375
      5      C005     Artificial Intelligence      2      $400
      6      C006     Computer Aided Design        5     $1600
```

## The SCHEDULE Data Set

```
                                        The CONTENTS Procedure

Data Set Name          PERM.SCHEDULE       Observations          18
Member Type            DATA                Variables             5
Engine                 V9                  Indexes               0
Created                Monday, July 12,    Observation Length    56
                       2004 04:29:52 PM
Last Modified          Monday, July 12,    Deleted Observations  0
                       2004 04:29:52 PM
Protection                                 Compressed            NO
Data Set Type                              Sorted                NO
Label
Data Representation    WINDOWS_32
Encoding               wlatin1  Western
                       (Windows)


               Engine/Host Dependent Information

Data Set Page Size          8192
Number of Data Set Pages    1
First Data Page             1
Max Obs per Page            145
Obs in First Data Page      18
Number of Data Set Repairs  0
File Name                   C:\workshop\winsas\macr\schedule.sas7bdat
Release Created             9.0101B3
Host Created                XP_PRO


          Alphabetic List of Variables and Attributes

  #  Variable       Type  Len  Format  Informat  Label

  4  Begin_Date     Num     8  DATE9.  DATE7.    Begin
  2  Course_Code    Char    4                    Course Code
  1  Course_Number  Num     8  2.      2.        Course Number
  3  Location       Char   15                    Location
  5  Teacher        Char   20                    Instructor
```

```
                         Partial Listing of PERM.SCHEDULE

      Course_  Course_                Begin_
Obs   Number   Code     Location       Date        Teacher

  1     1      C001     Seattle     26OCT2004   Hallis, Dr. George
  2     2      C002     Dallas      07DEC2004   Wickam, Dr. Alice
  3     3      C003     Boston      11JAN2005   Forest, Mr. Peter
  4     4      C004     Seattle     25JAN2005   Tally, Ms. Julia
  5     5      C005     Dallas      01MAR2005   Hallis, Dr. George
  6     6      C006     Boston      05APR2005   Berthan, Ms. Judy
  7     7      C001     Dallas      24MAY2005   Hallis, Dr. George
```

## The STUDENTS Data Set

```
                                   The CONTENTS Procedure

Data Set Name          PERM.STUDENTS            Observations          207
Member Type            DATA                     Variables             3
Engine                 V9                       Indexes               0
Created                Tuesday, May 30,         Observation Length    85
                       2000 04:21:31 PM
Last Modified          Monday, June 12,         Deleted Observations  0
                       2000 10:39:11 AM
Protection                                      Compressed            NO
Data Set Type                                   Sorted                NO
Label
Data Representation    WINDOWS_32
Encoding               Default


                  Engine/Host Dependent Information

Data Set Page Size            8192
Number of Data Set Pages      4
First Data Page               1
Max Obs per Page              95
Obs in First Data Page        80
Number of Data Set Repairs    0
File Name                     C:\workshop\winsas\macr\students.sas7bdat
Release Created               8.0000M0
Host Created                  WIN_NT


             Alphabetic List of Variables and Attributes

         #    Variable            Type    Len    Label

         3    City_State          Char     20    City,State
         2    Student_Company     Char     40    Company
         1    Student_Name        Char     25    Student Name
```

```
                              Partial Listing of PERM.STUDENTS

Obs   Student_Name                Student_Company              City_State

  1   Abramson, Ms. Andrea        Eastman Developers           Deerfield, IL
  2   Alamutu, Ms. Julie          Reston Railway               Chicago, IL
  3   Albritton, Mr. Bryan        Special Services             Oak Brook, IL
  4   Allen, Ms. Denise           Department of Defense        Bethesda, MD
  5   Amigo, Mr. Bill             Assoc. of Realtors           Chicago, IL
  6   Avakian, Mr. Don            Reston Railway               Chicago, IL
  7   Babbitt, Mr. Bill           National Credit Corp.        Chicago, IL
  8   Baker, Mr. Vincent          Snowing Petroleum            New Orleans, LA
  9   Bates, Ms. Ellen            Reston Railway               Chicago, IL
 10   Belles, Ms. Vicki           Jost Hardware Inc.           Toledo, OH
 11   Benincasa, Ms. Elizabeth    Hospital Nurses Association  Naperville, IL
 12   Bills, Ms. Paulette         Reston Railway               Chicago, IL
```

## The REGISTER Data Set

```
                                            The CONTENTS Procedure

Data Set Name         PERM.REGISTER           Observations          434
Member Type           DATA                    Variables             3
Engine                V9                      Indexes               0
Created               Tuesday, May 30,        Observation Length    40
                      2000 04:21:31 PM
Last Modified         Monday, June 12,        Deleted Observations  0
                      2000 10:39:54 AM
Protection                                    Compressed            NO
Data Set Type                                 Sorted                NO
Label
Data Representation   WINDOWS_32
Encoding              Default


                  Engine/Host Dependent Information

Data Set Page Size          4096
Number of Data Set Pages    6
First Data Page             1
Max Obs per Page            101
Obs in First Data Page      68
Number of Data Set Repairs  0
File Name                   C:\workshop\winsas\macr\register.sas7bdat
Release Created             8.0000M0
Host Created                WIN_NT


              Alphabetic List of Variables and Attributes

  #   Variable         Type   Len   Format   Informat   Label

  2   Course_Number    Num      8   2.       2.         Course Number
  3   Paid             Char     1                       Paid Status
  1   Student_Name     Char    25                       Student Name
```

```
                  Partial Listing of PERM.REGISTER
                                           Course_
         Obs    Student_Name               Number     Paid

           1    Albritton, Mr. Bryan          1         Y
           2    Amigo, Mr. Bill               1         N
           3    Chodnoff, Mr. Norman          1         Y
           4    Clark, Mr. Rich               1         Y
           5    Crace, Mr. Ron                1         Y
           6    Dellmonache, Ms. Susan        1         Y
           7    Dixon, Mr. Matt               1         Y
           8    Edwards, Mr. Charles          1         N
           9    Edwards, Ms. Sonia            1         Y
          10    Elsins, Ms. Marisa F.         1         Y
          11    Griffin, Mr. Lantz            1         Y
          12    Hall, Ms. Sharon              1         Y
```

## The ALL Data Set

The program used to create the PERM.ALL data set is shown below.

```
proc sql;
   create table perm.all as
      select students.student_name,
             schedule.course_number,
             paid, courses.course_code,
             location, begin_date,
             teacher, course_title, days, fee,
             student_company, city_state
         from perm.schedule, perm.students,
              perm.register, perm.courses
         where schedule.course_code =
               courses.course_code and
               schedule.course_number =
               register.course_number and
               students.student_name =
               register.student_name
         order by students.student_name,
                  courses.course_code;
quit;
```

## The ALL Data Set

```
                                 The CONTENTS Procedure

Data Set Name        PERM.ALL                     Observations          434
Member Type          DATA                         Variables             12
Engine               V9                           Indexes               0
Created              Friday, July 23,             Observation Length    184
                     2004 02:53:26 PM
Last Modified        Friday, July 23,             Deleted Observations  0
                     2004 02:53:26 PM
Protection                                        Compressed            NO
Data Set Type                                     Sorted                YES
Label
Data Representation  WINDOWS_32
Encoding             wlatin1  Western (Windows)


                     Engine/Host Dependent Information

Data Set Page Size          16384
Number of Data Set Pages    6
First Data Page             1
Max Obs per Page            88
Obs in First Data Page      76
Number of Data Set Repairs  0
File Name                   C:\workshop\winsas\macr\all.sas7bdat
Release Created             9.0101B3
Host Created                XP_PRO

                Alphabetic List of Variables and Attributes

   #   Variable           Type   Len   Format     Informat    Label

   6   Begin_Date         Num      8   DATE9.     DATE7.      Begin
  12   City_State         Char    20                          City,State
   4   Course_Code        Char     4                          Course Code
   2   Course_Number      Num      8   2.         2.          Course Number
   8   Course_Title       Char    25                          Description
   9   Days               Num      8   1.         1.          Course Length
  10   Fee                Num      8   DOLLAR5.   DOLLAR5.    Course Fee
   5   Location           Char    15                          Location
   3   Paid               Char     1                          Paid Status
  11   Student_Company    Char    40                          Company
   1   Student_Name       Char    25                          Student Name
   7   Teacher            Char    20                          Instructor


                          Sort Information

                  Sortedby       Student_Name Course_Code
                  Validated      YES
                  Character Set  ANSI
```

## The ALL Data Set

Partial Listing of PERM.ALL

| Obs | Student_Name | Course_ Number | Paid | Course_ Code | Location |
|---|---|---|---|---|---|
| 1 | Abramson, Ms. Andrea | 10 | Y | C004 | Dallas |
| 2 | Abramson, Ms. Andrea | 6 | N | C006 | Boston |
| 3 | Alamutu, Ms. Julie | 14 | N | C002 | Seattle |
| 4 | Albritton, Mr. Bryan | 1 | Y | C001 | Seattle |
| 5 | Albritton, Mr. Bryan | 5 | Y | C005 | Dallas |

| Obs | Begin_ Date | Teacher | Course_Title |
|---|---|---|---|
| 1 | 16AUG2005 | Tally, Ms. Julia | Database Design |
| 2 | 05APR2005 | Berthan, Ms. Judy | Computer Aided Design |
| 3 | 06DEC2005 | Wickam, Dr. Alice | Structured Query Language |
| 4 | 26OCT2004 | Hallis, Dr. George | Basic Telecommunications |
| 5 | 01MAR2005 | Hallis, Dr. George | Artificial Intelligence |

| Obs | Days | Fee | Student_Company | City_State |
|---|---|---|---|---|
| 1 | 2 | $375 | Eastman Developers | Deerfield, IL |
| 2 | 5 | $1600 | Eastman Developers | Deerfield, IL |
| 3 | 4 | $1150 | Reston Railway | Chicago, IL |
| 4 | 3 | $795 | Special Services | Oak Brook, IL |
| 5 | 2 | $400 | Special Services | Oak Brook, IL |

# Chapter 2 Macro Variables

# 2.1 Introduction to Macro Variables

## Objectives

- Understand macro variables.
- Describe where macro variables are stored.
- Identify the two types of macro variables.

3

## Macro Variables

Macro variables store text, including

- complete or partial SAS steps
- complete or partial SAS statements.

Macro variables are referred to as *symbolic variables* because SAS programs can reference macro variables as symbols for additional program text.

4

## Global Symbol Table

Macro variables are stored in an area of memory called the *global symbol table.* When SAS is invoked, the global symbol table is created and initialized with **automatic macro variables**.

| | Global Symbol Table | |
|---|---|---|
| | . | . |
| | . | . |
| **Automatic Variables** | SYSTIME | 09:47 |
| | SYSVER | 9.1 |
| | . | . |
| | . | . |

5

## Global Symbol Table

**User-defined macro variables** can be added to the global symbol table.

| | Global Symbol Table | |
|---|---|---|
| | . | . |
| | . | . |
| **Automatic Variables** | SYSTIME | 09:47 |
| | SYSVER | 9.1 |
| | . | . |
| | . | . |
| **User-defined Variables** | CITY | Dallas |
| | DATE | 05JAN2004 |
| | AMOUNT | 975 |

6

## Macro Variables

Macro variables in the global symbol table

- are global in scope (available any time)
- have a minimum length of 0 characters (*null value*)
- have a maximum length of 65,534 (64K) characters
- store numeric tokens as character strings.

7

## 2.2 Automatic Macro Variables

### Objectives

- Identify selected automatic macro variables.
- Display automatic macro variables in the SAS log.

9

### Automatic Macro Variables

Automatic macro variables

- are system-defined
- are created at SAS invocation
- are global (always available)
- are assigned values by SAS
- can be assigned values by the user in some cases.

10

## System-Defined Automatic Macro Variables

Some automatic macro variables have fixed values that are set at SAS invocation:

| Name | Description |
|---|---|
| SYSDATE | date of SAS invocation (DATE7.) |
| SYSDATE9 | date of SAS invocation (DATE9.) |
| SYSDAY | day of the week of SAS invocation |
| SYSTIME | time of SAS invocation |
| SYSSCP | abbreviation for the operating system: OpenVMS, WIN, HP 300, and so on |
| SYSVER | release of SAS software being used. |

11

## System-Defined Automatic Macro Variables

Some automatic macro variables have values that change automatically based on submitted SAS statements:

| Name | Description |
|---|---|
| SYSLAST | name of most recently created SAS data set in the form *libref.name*. If no data set has been created, the value is _NULL_. |
| SYSPARM | text specified at program invocation. |

12

## Automatic Macro Variables

Example: Write the names and values of all automatic macro variables to the SAS log using the _AUTOMATIC_ argument of the %PUT statement.

```
%put _automatic_;
```

13

## Automatic Macro Variables

Partial SAS Log

```
12   %put _automatic_;
AUTOMATIC AFDSID 0
AUTOMATIC AFDSNAME
AUTOMATIC AFLIB
AUTOMATIC AFSTR1
AUTOMATIC AFSTR2
AUTOMATIC FSPBDV
AUTOMATIC SYSBUFFR
AUTOMATIC SYSCC 3000
AUTOMATIC SYSCHARWIDTH 1
AUTOMATIC SYSCMD
AUTOMATIC SYSDATE 05FEB04
AUTOMATIC SYSDATE9 05FEB2004
```

The macro variables SYSDATE, SYSDATE9, and SYSTIME store character strings, **not** SAS date or time values.

14

# 2.3 Macro Variable References

## Objectives

- Understand how macro variable references are handled by the word scanner and macro processor.

16

## Macro Variable Reference

Macro variable references

- begin with an ampersand (&) followed by a macro variable name
- represent macro triggers
- are also called *symbolic* references
- can appear anywhere in your program
- are passed to the macro processor.

When the macro processor receives a macro variable reference, it

- searches the symbol table for the macro variable
- resolves the macro variable by substituting its value
- issues a warning to the SAS log if the macro variable is not found in the symbol table.

17

## Macro Variable Reference

Example: Write the day of the week to the SAS log.

Partial SAS Log

```
12   %put Today is &sysday;
Today is Tuesday
```

18

## Substitution within a Macro Statement

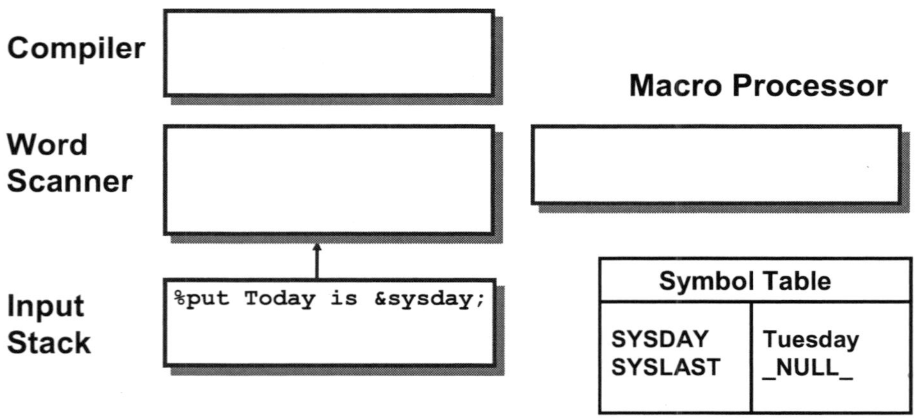

Compiler

Word Scanner

Input Stack

```
%put Today is &sysday;
```

Macro Processor

| Symbol Table | |
|---|---|
| SYSDAY | Tuesday |
| SYSLAST | _NULL_ |

19

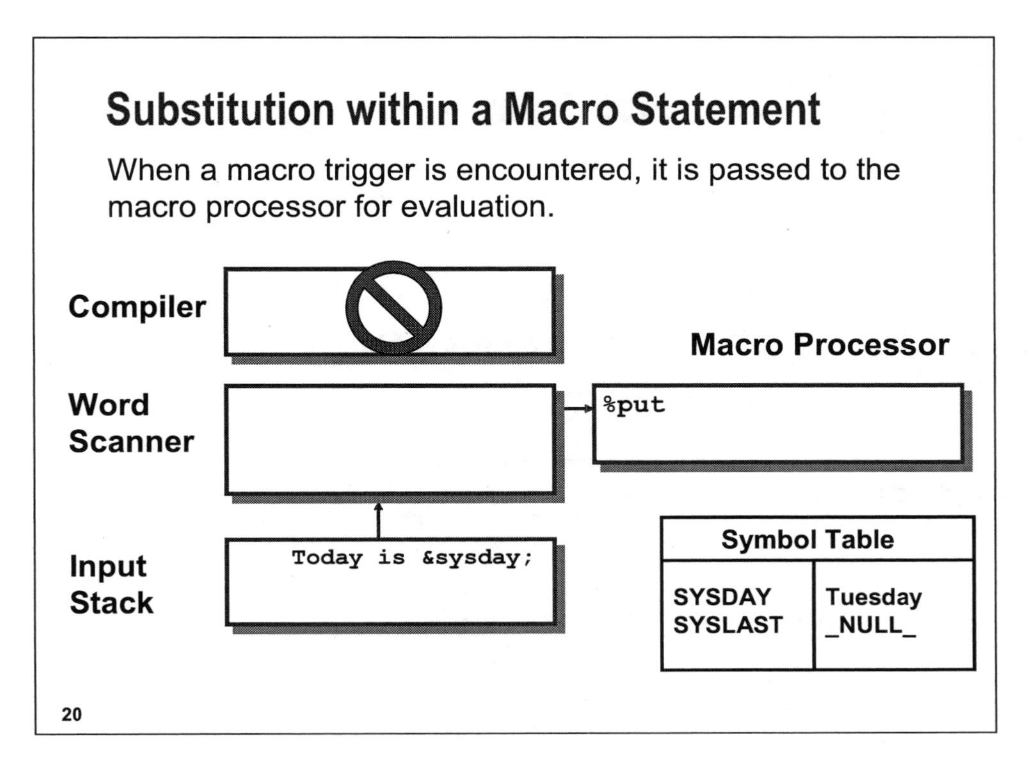
Substitution within a Macro Statement
When a macro trigger is encountered, it is passed to the macro processor for evaluation.
Compiler
Macro Processor
Word Scanner
%put
Input Stack
Today is &sysday;
Symbol Table
SYSDAY
SYSLAST
Tuesday
_NULL_
20

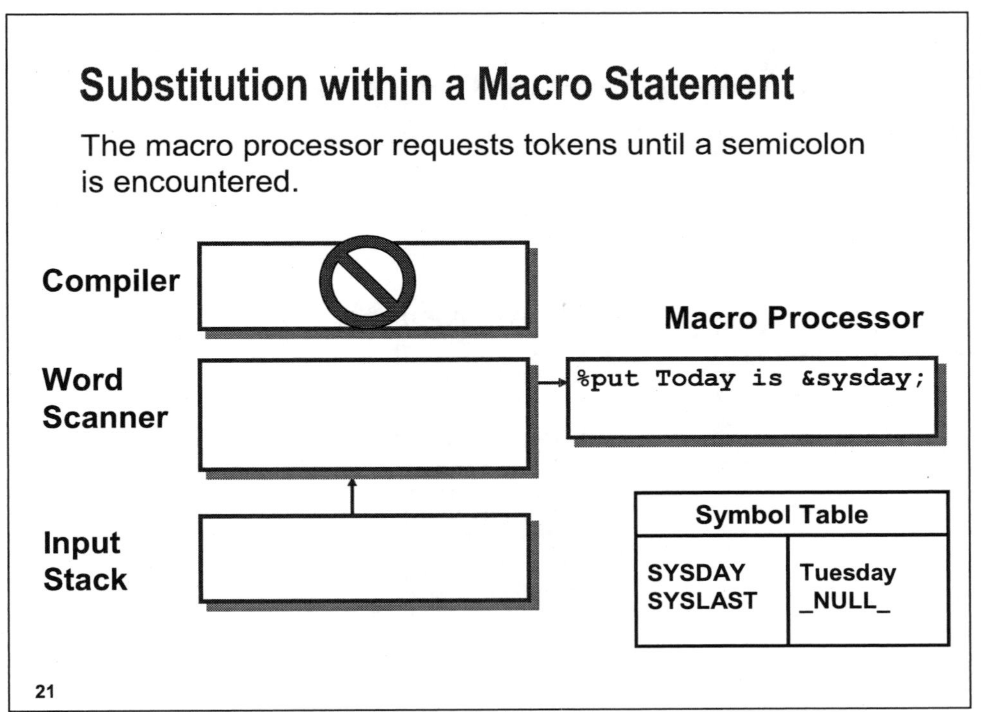
Substitution within a Macro Statement
The macro processor requests tokens until a semicolon is encountered.
Compiler
Macro Processor
Word Scanner
%put Today is &sysday;
Input Stack
Symbol Table
SYSDAY
SYSLAST
Tuesday
_NULL_
21

## Substitution within a Macro Statement

The macro variable reference triggers the macro processor to search the symbol table for the reference.

Compiler

Word Scanner

Input Stack

Macro Processor

```
%put Today is &sysday;
```

| Symbol Table | |
|---|---|
| SYSDAY<br>SYSLAST | Tuesday<br>_NULL_ |

22

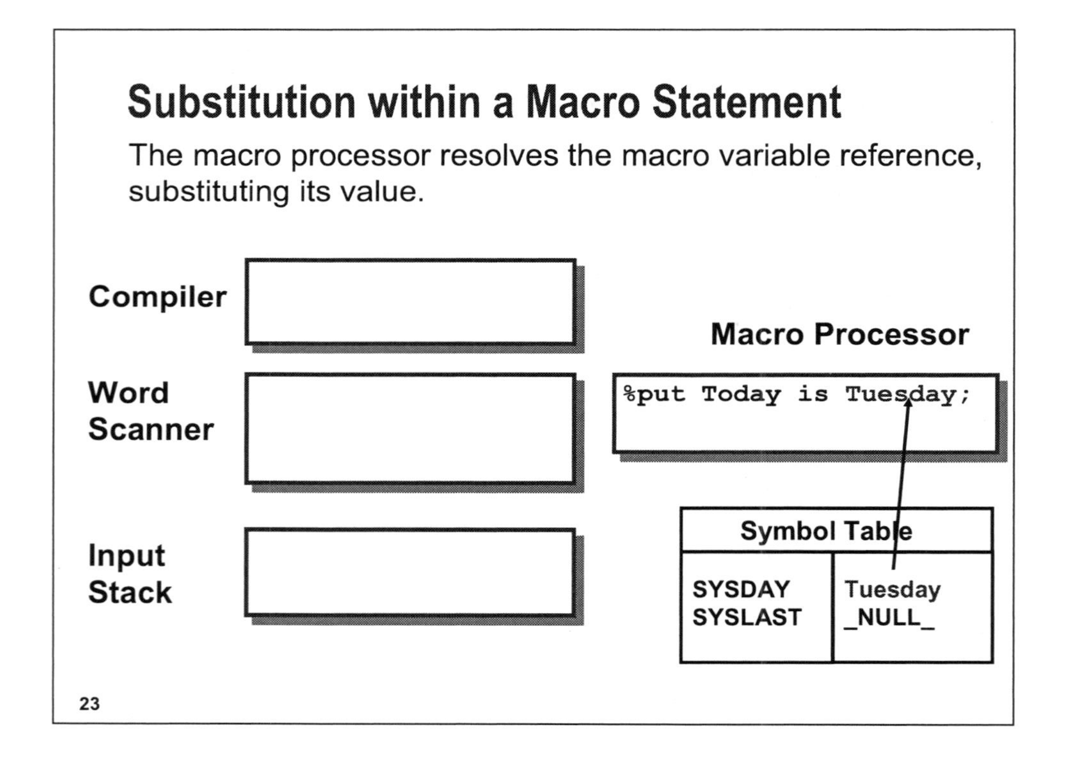

## Substitution within a Macro Statement

The macro processor executes the %PUT statement, writing the resolved text to the SAS log.

Compiler

Word Scanner

Input Stack

Macro Processor

```
%put Today is Tuesday;
```

| Symbol Table | |
|---|---|
| SYSDAY | Tuesday |
| SYSLAST | _NULL_ |

24

## Substitution within a SAS Literal

If you need to reference a macro variable within a literal, enclose the literal in double quotes.

| Global Symbol Table | |
|---|---|
| CITY | Dallas |
| DATE | 05JAN2000 |
| AMOUNT | 975 |

The word scanner continues to tokenize literals enclosed in **double** quotes, permitting macro variables to resolve.

```
where cityst CONTAINS "&city";
```

generates

```
WHERE CITYST CONTAINS "Dallas";
```

The word scanner does not tokenize literals enclosed in **single** quotes, so macro variables do not resolve.

```
where cityst contains '&city';
```

generates

```
WHERE CITYST CONTAINS '&city';
```

25

## Substitution within a SAS Literal

Example: Substitute the day of the week in a title.

**Compiler**

**Word Scanner**

**Input Stack**

```
proc print data=perm.all;
title "Today is &sysday";
run;
```

**Macro Processor**

| Symbol Table | |
|---|---|
| SYSDAY<br>SYSLAST | Tuesday<br>_NULL_ |

26

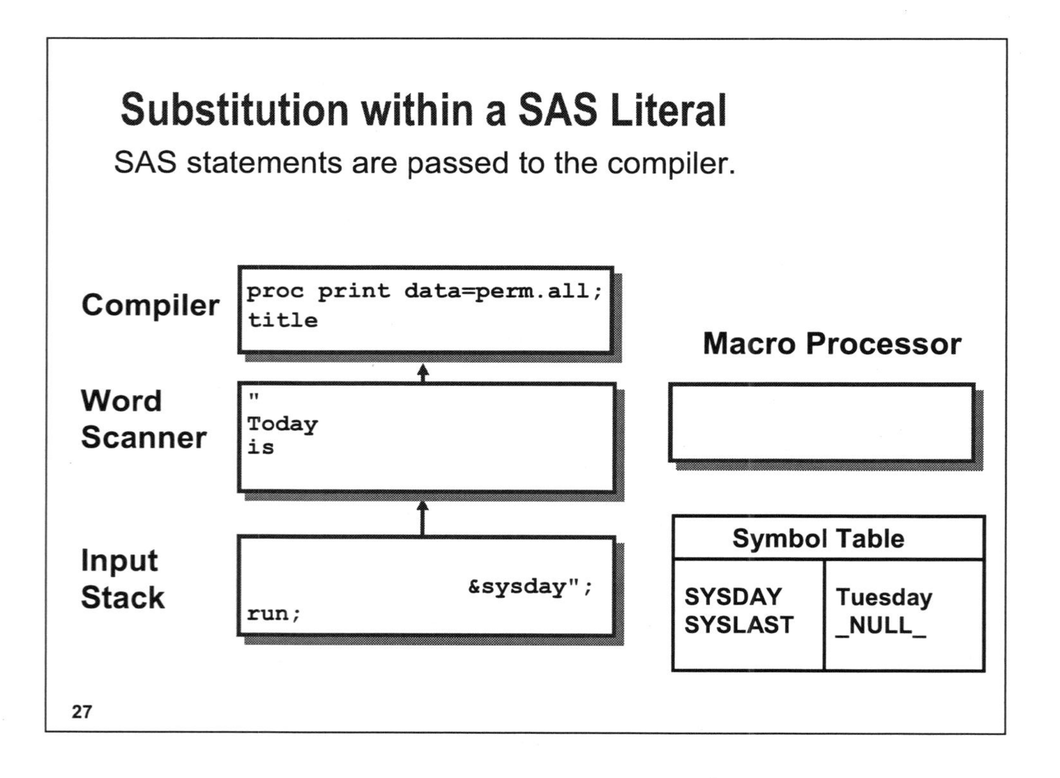

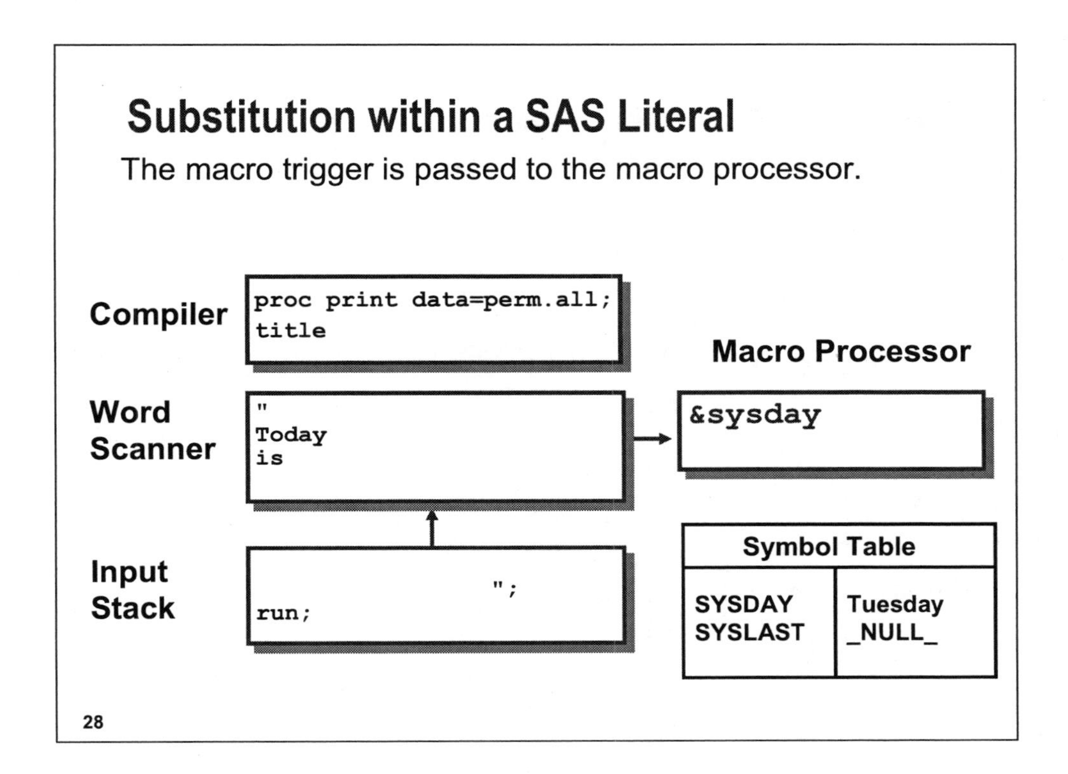
Substitution within a SAS Literal
The macro trigger is passed to the macro processor.
Compiler
proc print data=perm.all;
title
Macro Processor
Word Scanner
"
Today
is
&sysday
Input Stack
";
run;
Symbol Table
SYSDAY
SYSLAST
Tuesday
_NULL_
28

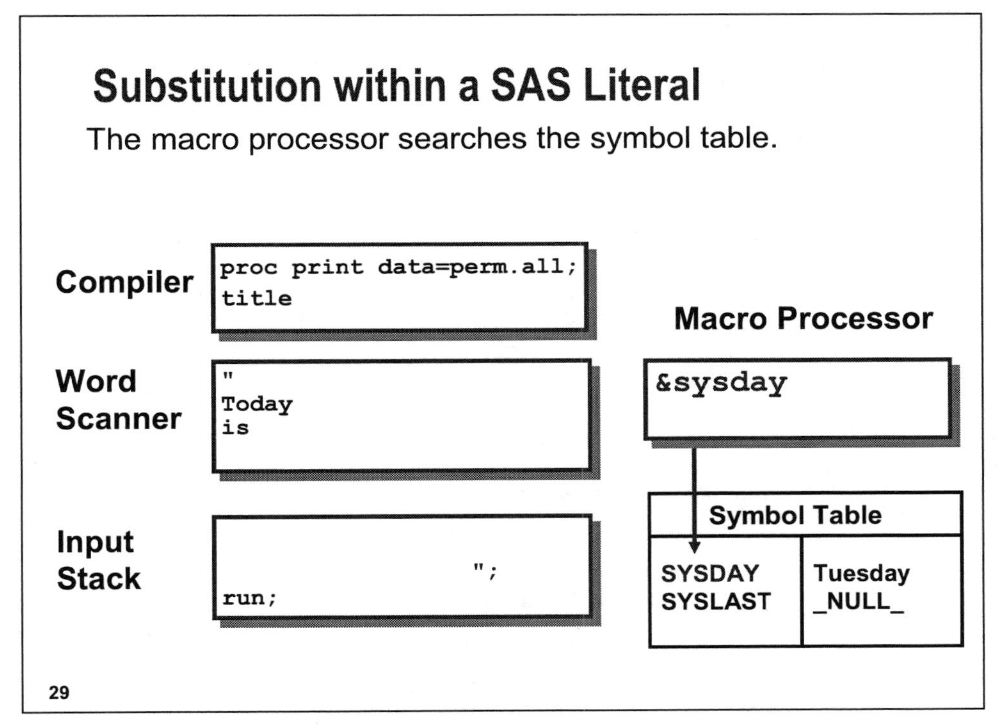
Substitution within a SAS Literal
The macro processor searches the symbol table.
Compiler
proc print data=perm.all;
title
Macro Processor
Word Scanner
"
Today
is
&sysday
Input Stack
";
run;
Symbol Table
SYSDAY
SYSLAST
Tuesday
_NULL_
29

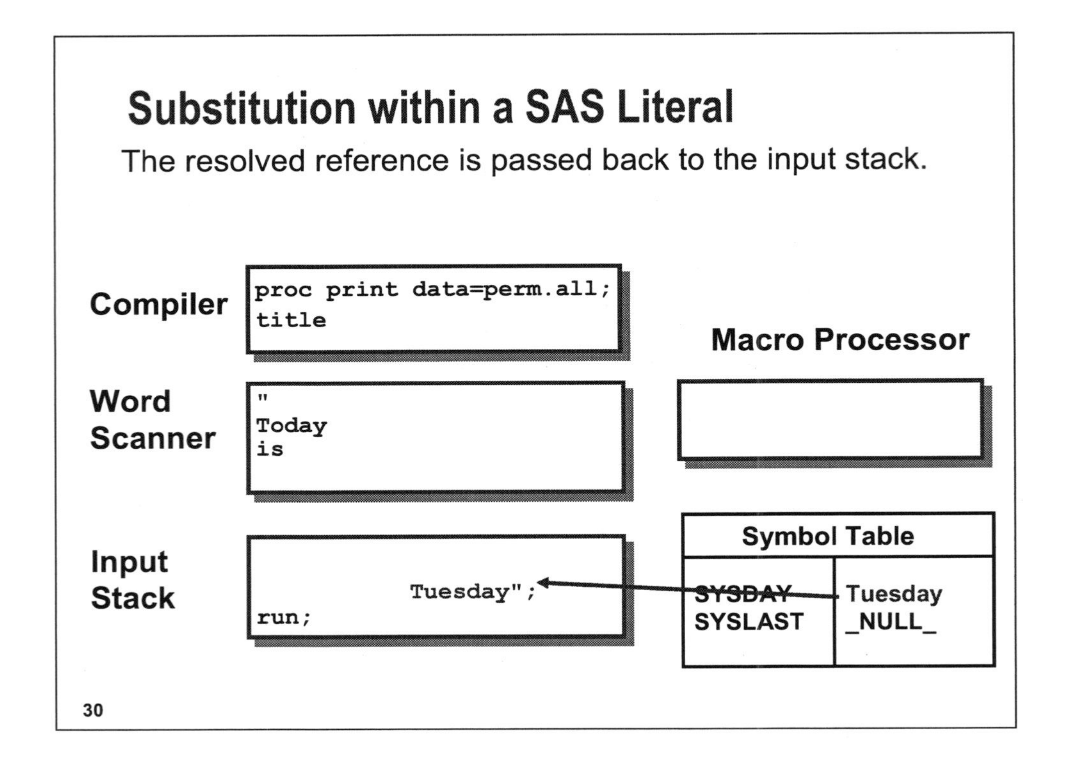
Substitution within a SAS Literal
The resolved reference is passed back to the input stack.
Compiler
proc print data=perm.all;
title
Macro Processor
Word Scanner
"
Today
is
Input Stack
Tuesday";
run;
Symbol Table
SYSDAY
SYSLAST
Tuesday
_NULL_
30

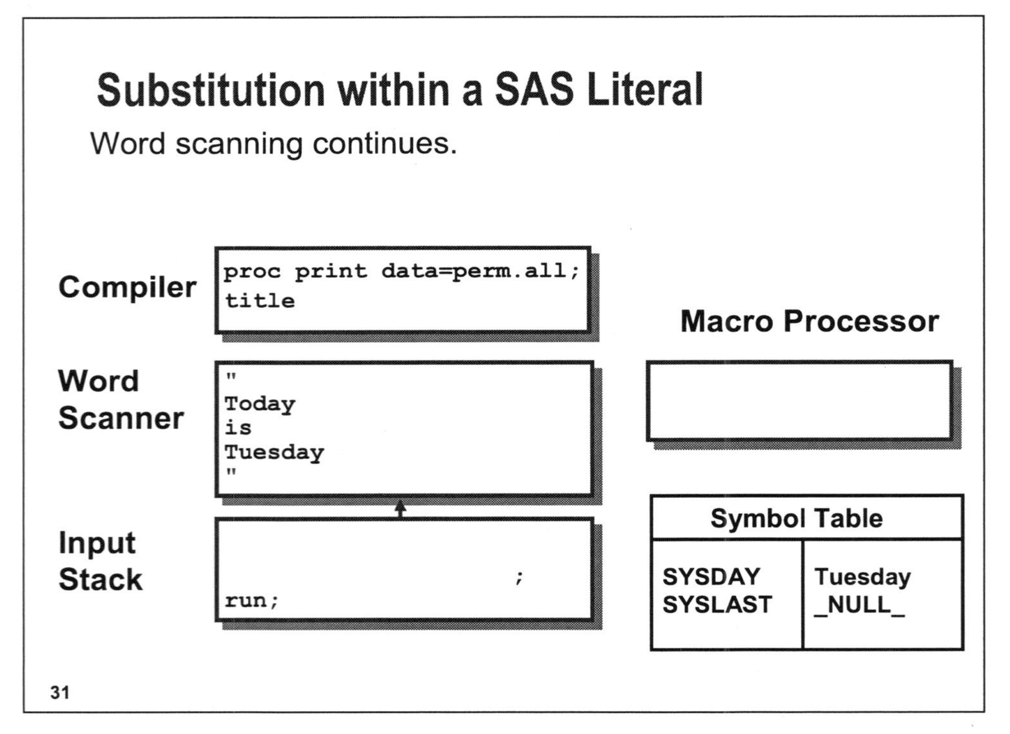
Substitution within a SAS Literal
Word scanning continues.
Compiler
proc print data=perm.all;
title
Macro Processor
Word Scanner
"
Today
is
Tuesday
"
Input Stack
;
run;
Symbol Table
SYSDAY
SYSLAST
Tuesday
_NULL_
31

## Substitution within a SAS Literal

The double-quoted string is passed to the compiler as a unit.

Compiler

```
proc print data=perm.all;
title "Today is Tuesday"
```

Word Scanner

Input Stack

```
                                 ;
run;
```

Macro Processor

| Symbol Table | |
|---|---|
| SYSDAY<br>SYSLAST | Tuesday<br>_NULL_ |

32

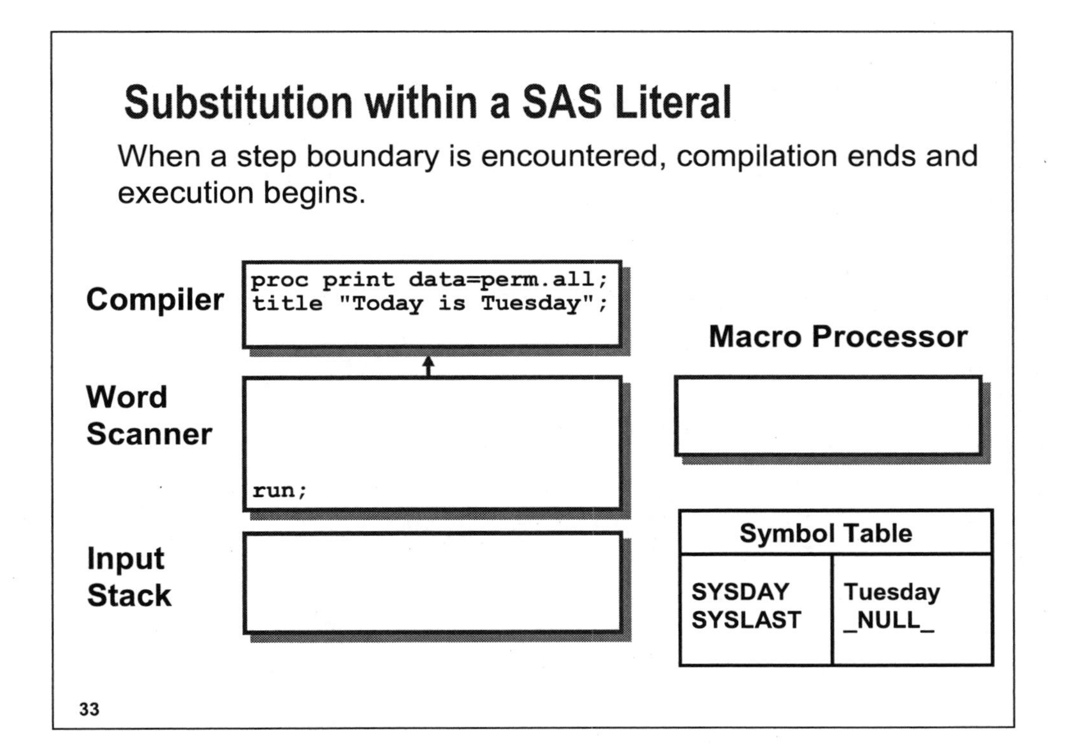

## Substitution within a SAS Literal

Example: Substitute system information in footnotes.

```
footnote1 "Created &systime &sysday, &sysdate9";
footnote2
  "on the &sysscp system using Release &sysver";
title "REVENUES FOR DALLAS TRAINING CENTER";
proc tabulate data=perm.all;
   where upcase(location)="DALLAS";
   class course_title;
   var fee;
   table course_title=" " all="TOTALS",
      fee=" "*(n*f=3. sum*f=dollar10.)
      / rts=30 box="COURSE";
run;
```

Automatic

34

## Substitution within a SAS Literal

REVENUES FOR DALLAS TRAINING CENTER

| COURSE | N | Sum |
|---|---|---|
| Artificial Intelligence | 25 | $10,000 |
| Basic Telecommunications | 18 | $14,310 |
| Computer Aided Design | 19 | $30,400 |
| Database Design | 23 | $8,625 |
| Local Area Networks | 24 | $15,600 |
| Structured Query Language | 24 | $27,600 |
| TOTALS | 133 | $106,535 |

Created 14:56 Friday, 20AUG2004
on the WIN system using Release 9.1

35

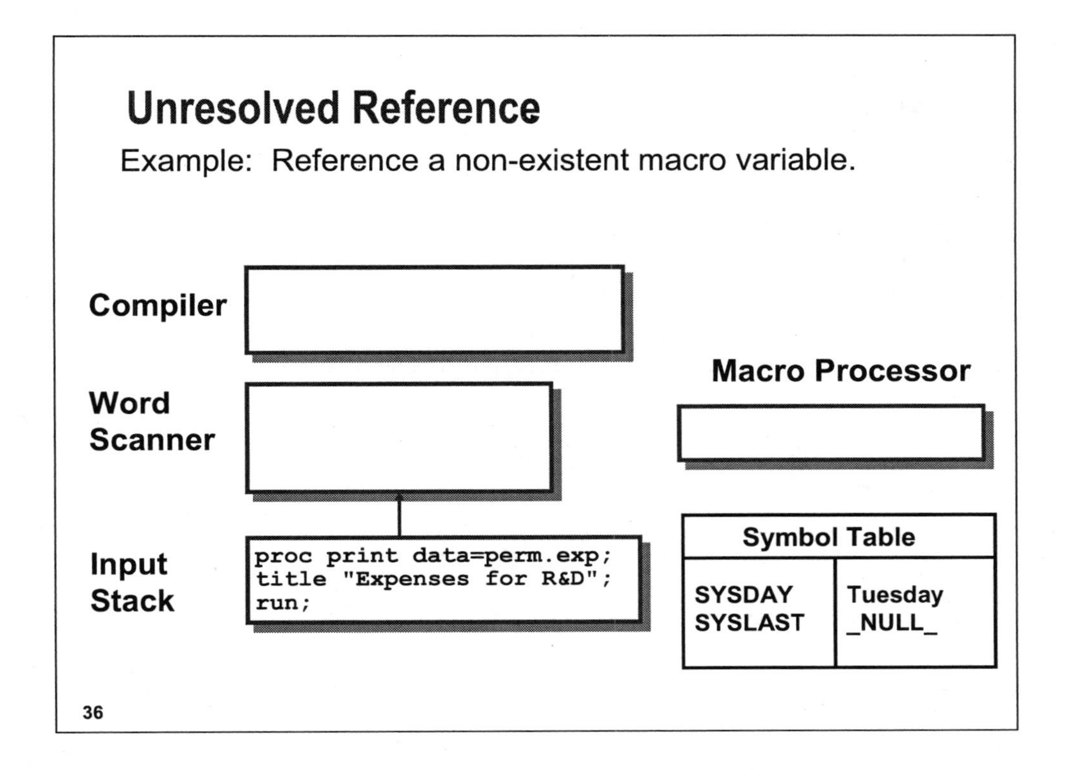
Unresolved Reference
Example: Reference a non-existent macro variable.
Compiler
Word
Scanner
Macro Processor
Input
Stack
proc print data=perm.exp;
title "Expenses for R&D";
run;
Symbol Table
SYSDAY
SYSLAST
Tuesday
_NULL_
36

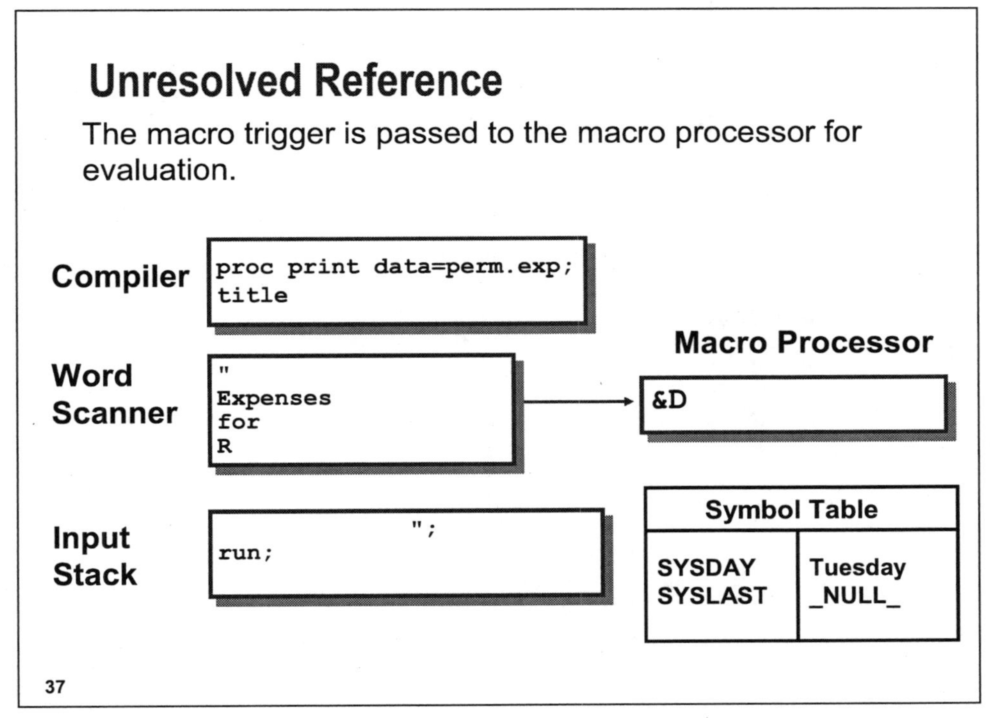
Unresolved Reference
The macro trigger is passed to the macro processor for evaluation.
Compiler
proc print data=perm.exp;
title
Word
Scanner
"
Expenses
for
R
Macro Processor
&D
Input
Stack
";
run;
Symbol Table
SYSDAY
SYSLAST
Tuesday
_NULL_
37

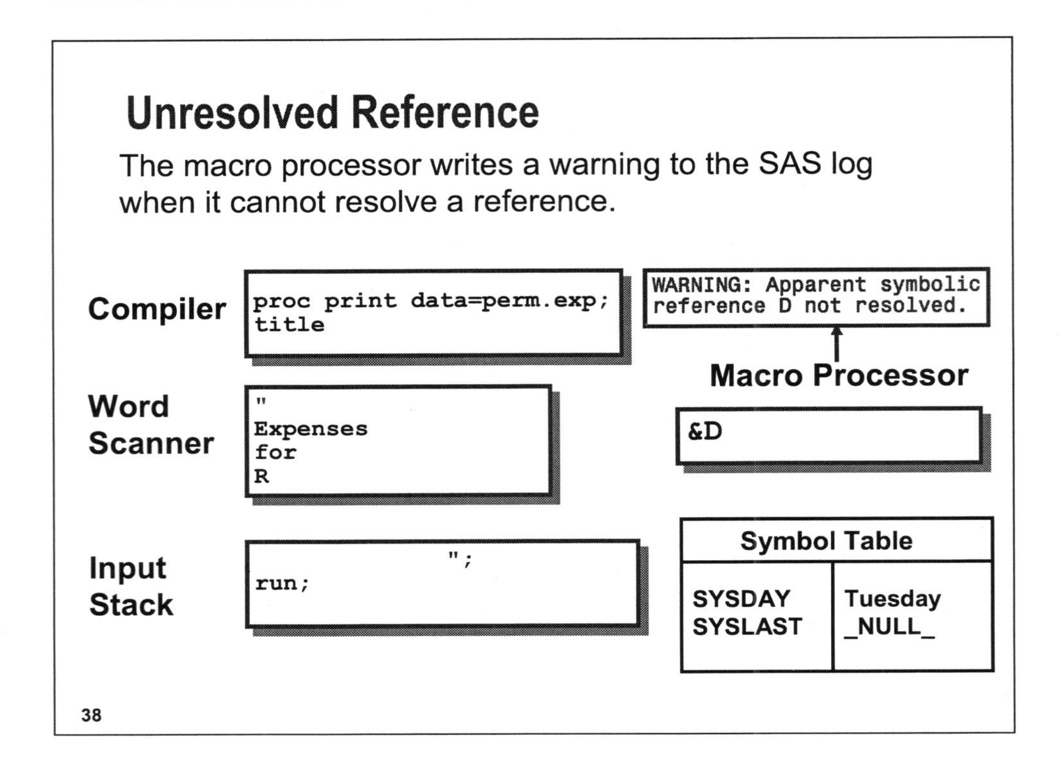
Unresolved Reference
The macro processor writes a warning to the SAS log when it cannot resolve a reference.
Compiler
proc print data=perm.exp;
title
WARNING: Apparent symbolic reference D not resolved.
Macro Processor
Word Scanner
"
Expenses
for
R
&D
Input Stack
";
run;
Symbol Table
SYSDAY
SYSLAST
Tuesday
_NULL_
38

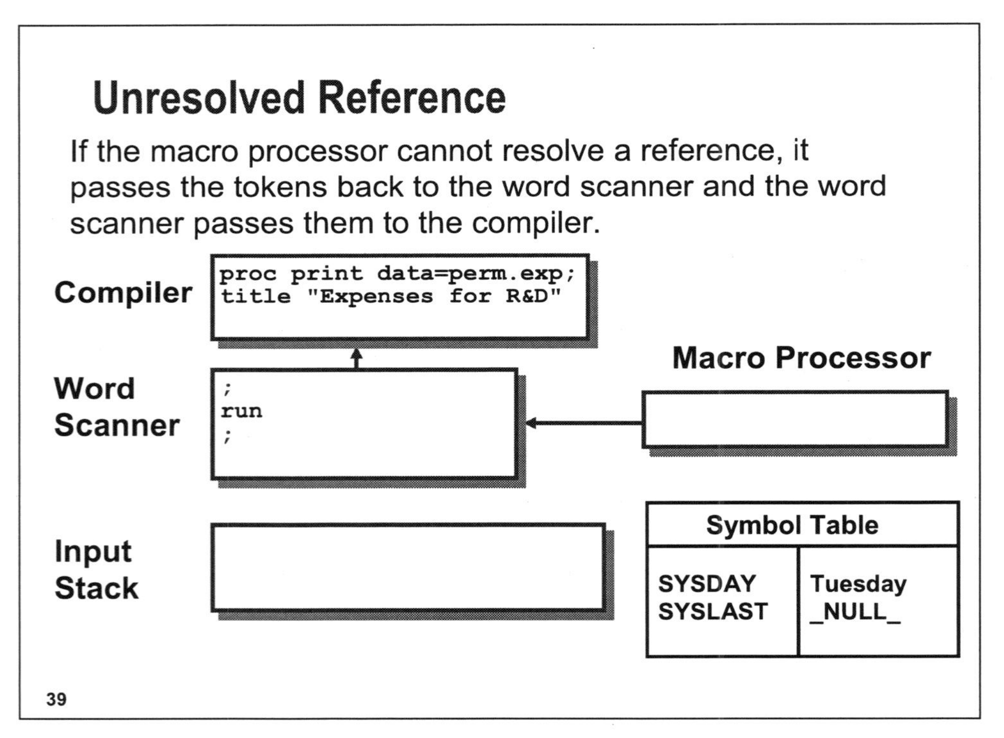
Unresolved Reference
If the macro processor cannot resolve a reference, it passes the tokens back to the word scanner and the word scanner passes them to the compiler.
Compiler
proc print data=perm.exp;
title "Expenses for R&D"
Macro Processor
Word Scanner
;
run
;
Input Stack
Symbol Table
SYSDAY
SYSLAST
Tuesday
_NULL_
39

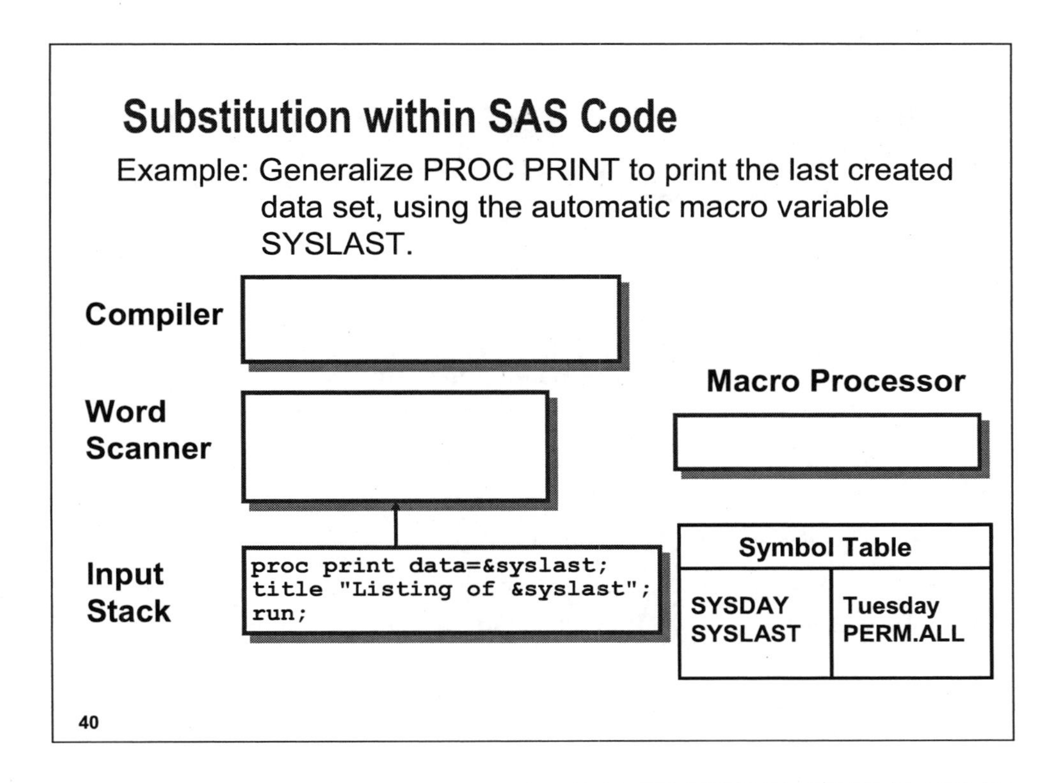
Substitution within SAS Code
Example: Generalize PROC PRINT to print the last created data set, using the automatic macro variable SYSLAST.
Compiler
Word Scanner
Macro Processor
Input Stack
proc print data=&syslast;
title "Listing of &syslast";
run;
Symbol Table
SYSDAY
SYSLAST
Tuesday
PERM.ALL
40

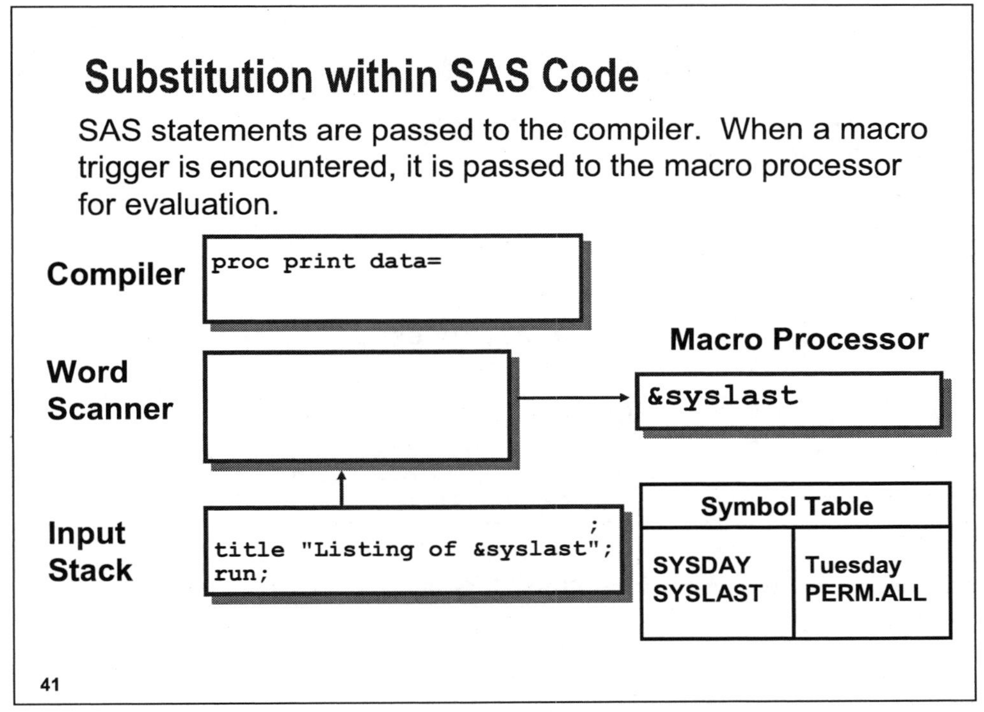
Substitution within SAS Code
SAS statements are passed to the compiler. When a macro trigger is encountered, it is passed to the macro processor for evaluation.
Compiler
proc print data=
Word Scanner
Macro Processor
&syslast
Input Stack
;
title "Listing of &syslast";
run;
Symbol Table
SYSDAY
SYSLAST
Tuesday
PERM.ALL
41

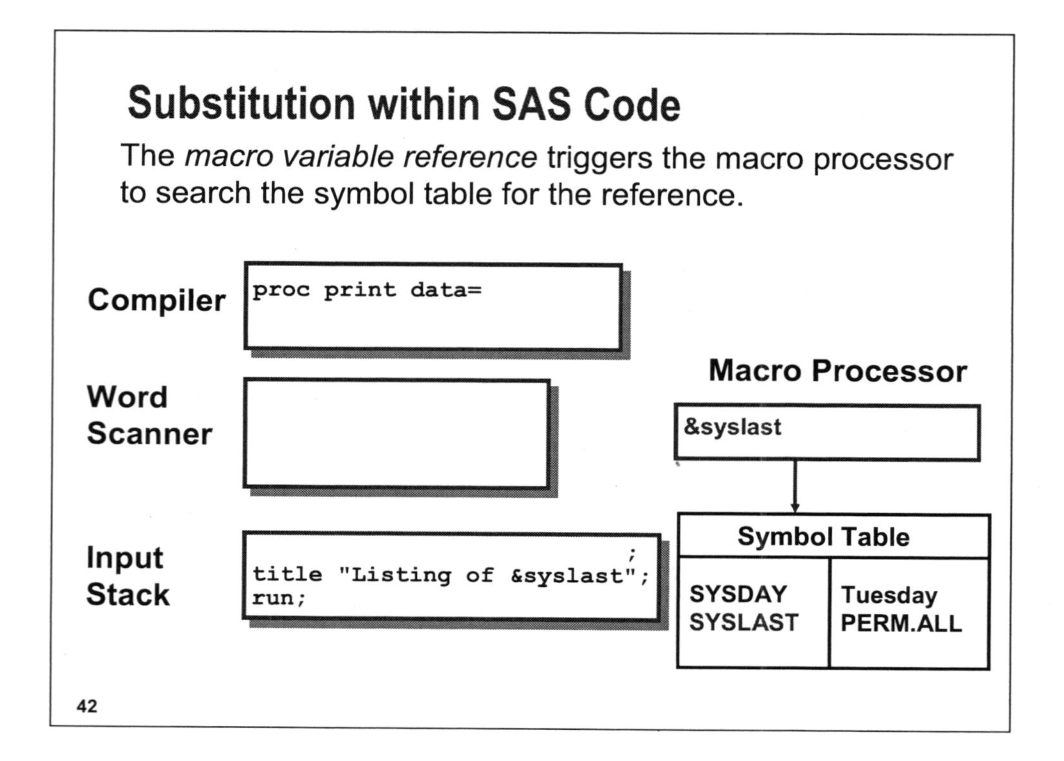
Substitution within SAS Code
The *macro variable reference* triggers the macro processor to search the symbol table for the reference.
Compiler
proc print data=
Word Scanner
Macro Processor
&syslast
Input Stack
;
title "Listing of &syslast";
run;
Symbol Table
SYSDAY
SYSLAST
Tuesday
PERM.ALL
42

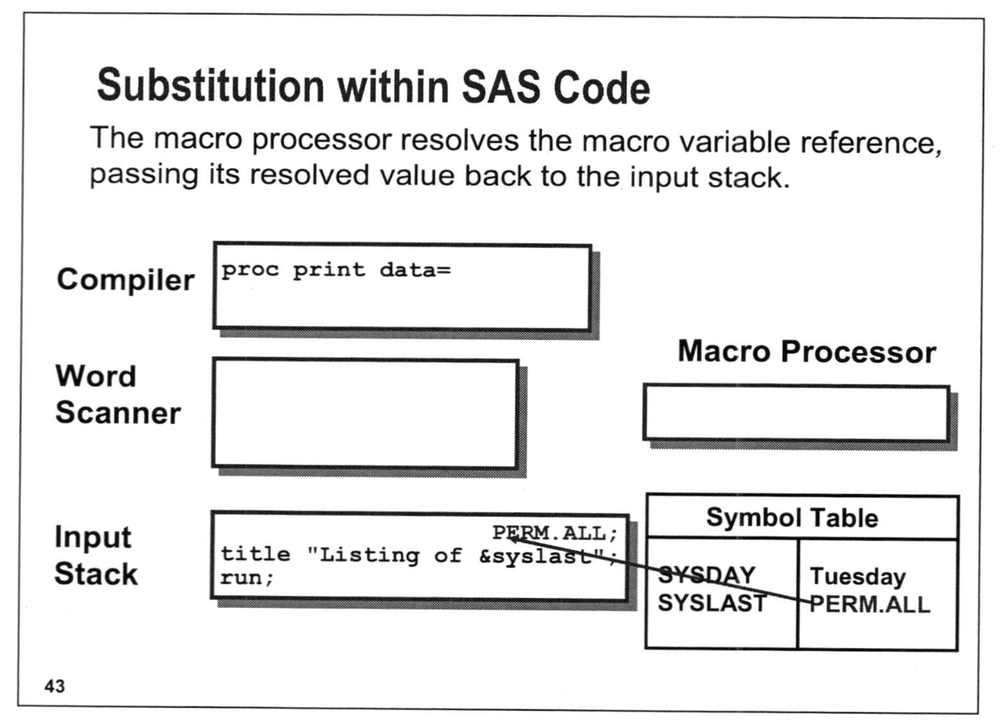
Substitution within SAS Code
The macro processor resolves the macro variable reference, passing its resolved value back to the input stack.
Compiler
proc print data=
Word Scanner
Macro Processor
Input Stack
PERM.ALL;
title "Listing of &syslast";
run;
Symbol Table
SYSDAY
SYSLAST
Tuesday
PERM.ALL
43

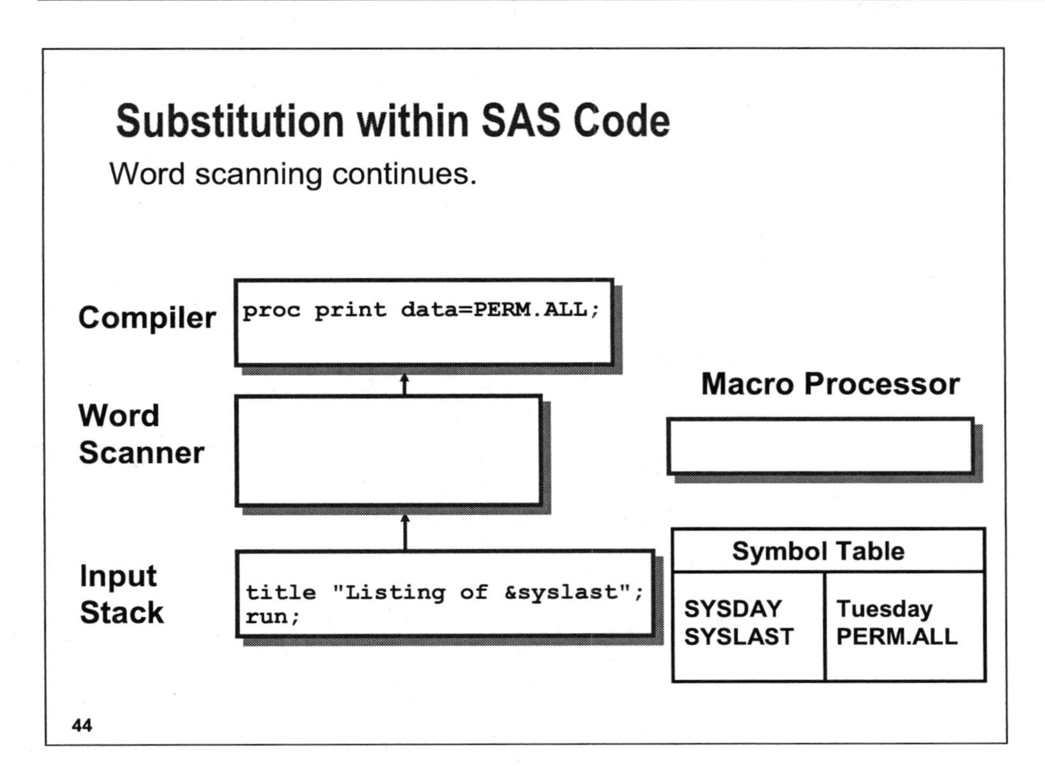
Substitution within SAS Code
Word scanning continues.
Compiler
proc print data=PERM.ALL;
Word Scanner
Input Stack
title "Listing of &syslast";
run;
Macro Processor
Symbol Table
SYSDAY Tuesday
SYSLAST PERM.ALL
44

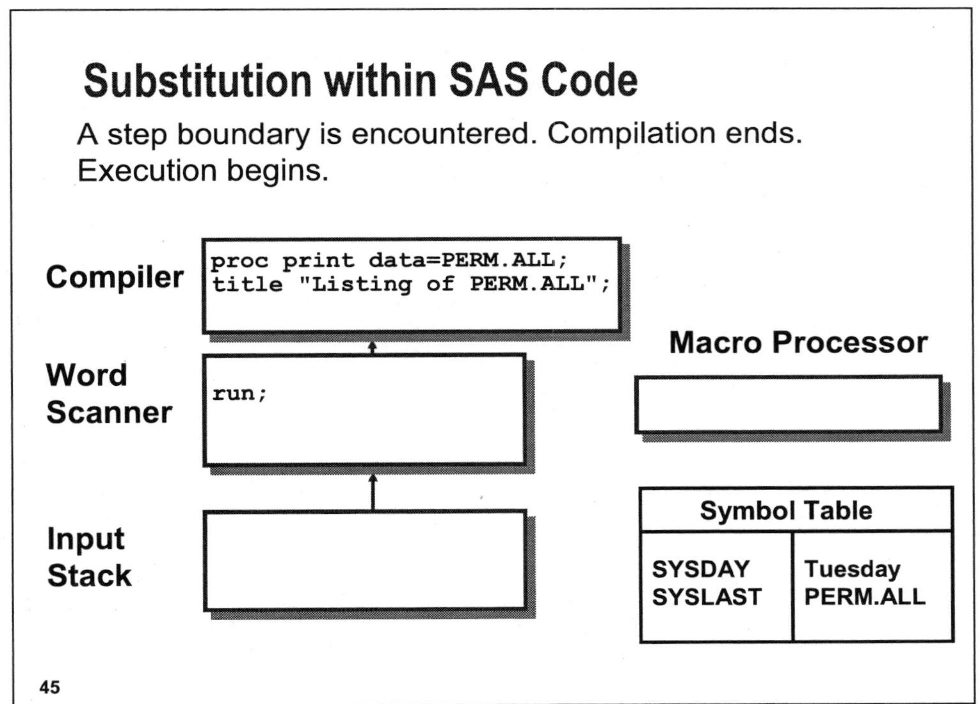
Substitution within SAS Code
A step boundary is encountered. Compilation ends.
Execution begins.
Compiler
proc print data=PERM.ALL;
title "Listing of PERM.ALL";
Word Scanner
run;
Input Stack
Macro Processor
Symbol Table
SYSDAY Tuesday
SYSLAST PERM.ALL
45

# Exercises

**1. Using Automatic Macro Variables**

Open the **babbit** program shown below into the Editor window.

```
options nocenter;
proc print data=perm.all noobs label uniform;
   where student_name contains 'Babbit';
   by student_name student_company;
   var course_title begin_date location teacher;
   title 'Courses Taken by Selected Students:';
   title2 'Those with Babbit in Their Name';
run;
```

Add a FOOTNOTE that displays today's date (use an automatic macro variable) using this text:

```
Report Created on date
```

Submit the program and examine the output it creates.

**2. Displaying Automatic Macro Variables**

**a.** Use the %PUT statement to display the values of the SYSDAY, SYSVER, and SYSLAST macro variables in the SAS log.

**b.** Use the %PUT statement to display the values of all automatic macro variables in the SAS log.

*'; *"; run;

## Solutions to Exercises

### 1. Using Automatic Macro Variables

The automatic macro variable SYSDATE9 contains the date when the current SAS session was invoked. The footnote text must be enclosed in double quotes for the macro variable reference to be resolved.

```
options nocenter;
proc print data=perm.all noobs label uniform;
   where student_name contains 'Babbit';
   by student_name student_company;
   var course_title begin_date location teacher;
   title  'Courses Taken by Selected Students';
   title2 'Those with Babbit in Their Name';
   footnote "Report Created on &sysdate9";
run;
```

```
Courses Taken by Selected Students
Those with Babbit in Their Name

Student Name=Babbitt, Mr. Bill Company=National Credit Corp.

      Description             Begin     Location        Instructor

Basic Telecommunications  24MAY2005     Dallas      Hallis, Dr. George
Artificial Intelligence   01MAR2005     Dallas      Hallis, Dr. George
Computer Aided Design     28MAR2006     Dallas      Berthan, Ms. Judy


Report Created on 05FEB2004
```

### 2. Displaying Automatic Macro Variables

a. Macro variable references are resolved before the text of the %PUT statement is displayed in the log.

```
%put Today is a &sysday;
%put This is Release &sysver of the SAS System;
%put The last data set created is &syslast;
```

Partial SAS Log

```
61   %put Today is a &sysday;
Today is a Thursday
62   %put This is Release &sysver of the SAS System;
This is Release 9.1 of the SAS System
63   %put The last data set created is &syslast;
The last data set created is _NULL_
```

b. The _AUTOMATIC_ argument in the %PUT statement displays the values of all automatic macro variables in the SAS log. Many of the values shown are dependent on the host system.

```
%put _automatic_;
```

Partial SAS Log

```
AUTOMATIC SYSBUFFR
AUTOMATIC SYSCC 3000
AUTOMATIC SYSCHARWIDTH 1
AUTOMATIC SYSCMD
AUTOMATIC SYSDATE 12FEB04
AUTOMATIC SYSDATE9 12FEB2004
AUTOMATIC SYSDAY Thursday
AUTOMATIC SYSDEVIC
AUTOMATIC SYSDMG 0
AUTOMATIC SYSDSN         _NULL_
```

# 2.4 User-Defined Macro Variables

## Objectives

- Create user-defined macro variables.
- Display values of user-defined macro variables in the SAS log.

48

## The %LET Statement

The %LET statement creates a macro variable and assigns it a value.

General form of the %LET statement:

**%LET** *variable=value*;

- *variable* follows SAS naming conventions.
- If *variable* already exists, its *value* is overwritten.
- If *variable* or *value* contain macro triggers, the triggers are evaluated before the assignment is made.

49

## The %LET Statement

*Value* can be any string:

- maximum length is 65,534 (64K) characters
- minimum length is 0 characters (*null value*)
- numeric tokens are stored as character strings
- mathematical expressions are **not** evaluated
- the case of *value* is preserved
- quotes bounding literals are stored as part of *value*
- leading and trailing blanks **are removed** from *value* before the assignment is made.

50

## %LET Statement Examples

Determine the value assigned to each macro variable by these %LET statements.

```
%let name= Ed Norton ;
%let name2=' Ed Norton ';
%let title="Joan's Report";
%let start=;
%let sum=3+4;
%let total=0;
%let total=&total+&sum;
%let x=varlist;
%let &x=name age height;
```

| Value |
|---|
| |

51

...

## %LET Statement Examples

The %LET statement truncates leading and trailing blanks.

```
%let name= Ed Norton ;
%let name2=' Ed Norton ';
%let title="Joan's Report";
%let start=;
%let sum=3+4;
%let total=0;
%let total=&total+&sum;
%let x=varlist;
%let &x=name age height;
```

| Value |
|---|
| Ed Norton |

52 ...

## %LET Statement Examples

Quotation marks are stored as part of the value.

```
%let name= Ed Norton ;
%let name2=' Ed Norton ';
%let title="Joan's Report";
%let start=;
%let sum=3+4;
%let total=0;
%let total=&total+&sum;
%let x=varlist;
%let &x=name age height;
```

| Value |
|---|
| Ed Norton |
| ' Ed Norton ' |

53 ...

## %LET Statement Examples

Quotation marks are stored as part of the value.

```
%let name= Ed Norton ;
%let name2=' Ed Norton ';
%let title="Joan's Report";
%let start=;
%let sum=3+4;
%let total=0;
%let total=&total+&sum;
%let x=varlist;
%let &x=name age height;
```

| Value |
|---|
| **Ed Norton** |
| **' Ed Norton '** |
| **"Joan's Report"** |

54 ...

## %LET Statement Examples

A null value is stored.

```
%let name= Ed Norton ;
%let name2=' Ed Norton ';
%let title="Joan's Report";
%let start=;
%let sum=3+4;
%let total=0;
%let total=&total+&sum;
%let x=varlist;
%let &x=name age height;
```

| Value |
|---|
| **Ed Norton** |
| **' Ed Norton '** |
| **"Joan's Report"** |

55 ...

## %LET Statement Examples

Mathematical expressions are not evaluated.

```
%let name= Ed Norton ;
%let name2=' Ed Norton ';
%let title="Joan's Report";
%let start=;
%let sum=3+4;
%let total=0;
%let total=&total+&sum;
%let x=varlist;
%let &x=name age height;
```

| Value |
|---|
| **Ed Norton** |
| **' Ed Norton '** |
| **"Joan's Report"** |
| |
| **3+4** |

56 ...

## %LET Statement Examples

Numeric tokens are stored as character strings.

```
%let name= Ed Norton ;
%let name2=' Ed Norton ';
%let title="Joan's Report";
%let start=;
%let sum=3+4;
%let total=0;
%let total=&total+&sum;
%let x=varlist;
%let &x=name age height;
```

| Value |
|---|
| **Ed Norton** |
| **' Ed Norton '** |
| **"Joan's Report"** |
| |
| **3+4** |
| **0** |

57 ...

## %LET Statement Examples

The macro trigger is evaluated before assignment is made. The previous value of **total** is replaced.

| Statement | Value |
|---|---|
| `%let name= Ed Norton ;` | **Ed Norton** |
| `%let name2=' Ed Norton ';` | **' Ed Norton '** |
| `%let title="Joan's Report";` | **"Joan's Report"** |
| `%let start=;` | |
| `%let sum=3+4;` | **3+4** |
| `%let total=0;` | |
| **`%let total=&total+∑`** | **0+3+4** |
| `%let x=varlist;` | |
| `%let &x=name age height;` | |

58 ...

## %LET Statement Examples

| Statement | Value |
|---|---|
| `%let name= Ed Norton ;` | **Ed Norton** |
| `%let name2=' Ed Norton ';` | **' Ed Norton '** |
| `%let title="Joan's Report";` | **"Joan's Report"** |
| `%let start=;` | |
| `%let sum=3+4;` | **3+4** |
| `%let total=0;` | |
| `%let total=&total+∑` | **0+3+4** |
| **`%let x=varlist;`** | **varlist** |
| `%let &x=name age height;` | |

59 ...

## %LET Statement Examples

The macro variable's name resolves to **varlist**.

```
%let name= Ed Norton ;
%let name2=' Ed Norton ';
%let title="Joan's Report";
%let start=;
%let sum=3+4;
%let total=0;
%let total=&total+&sum;
%let x=varlist;
%let &x=name age height;
 macro↑var name: varlist
```

| Value |
|---|
| Ed Norton |
| ' Ed Norton ' |
| "Joan's Report" |
| |
| 3+4 |
| |
| 0+3+4 |
| varlist |
| name age height |

60 ...

## %LET Statement Examples

Example: Assign the value **DALLAS** to the macro variable SITE. Reference the macro variable within the program.

```
%let site=DALLAS;
title "REVENUES FOR &site TRAINING CENTER";
proc tabulate data=perm.all;
   where upcase(location)="&site";
   class course_title;
   var fee;
   table course_title=' ' all='TOTALS',
         fee=' '*(n*f=3. sum*f=dollar10.)
         / rts=30 box='COURSE';
run;
```

LET1

61

# %LET Statement Examples

PROC TABULATE Output

REVENUES FOR DALLAS TRAINING CENTER

| COURSE | N | Sum |
|---|---|---|
| Artificial Intelligence | 25 | $10,000 |
| Basic Telecommunications | 18 | $14,310 |
| Computer Aided Design | 19 | $30,400 |
| Database Design | 23 | $8,625 |
| Local Area Networks | 24 | $15,600 |
| Structured Query Language | 24 | $27,600 |
| TOTALS | 133 | $106,535 |

62

# %LET Statement Examples

Example: Create three macro variables.

```
%let city=Dallas;
%let date=05JAN2004;
%let amount=975;
```

| Global Symbol Table | |
|---|---|
| CITY | Dallas |
| DATE | 05JAN2004 |
| AMOUNT | 975 |

Macro variables store numbers as character strings, not as numeric values.

63

## Displaying Macro Variables

Example: Display all user-defined macro variables in the SAS log.

Partial SAS Log

```
4     %put _user_;
GLOBAL DATE 05JAN2004
GLOBAL AMOUNT 975
GLOBAL CITY Dallas
```

Example: Display all user-defined and automatic macro variables in the SAS log.

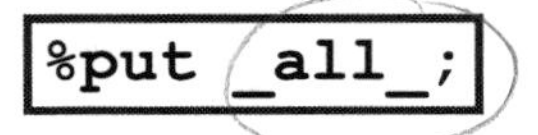


64

## Displaying Macro Variables

The SYMBOLGEN system option writes macro variable values to the SAS log as they are resolved.

General form of the SYMBOLGEN system option:

**OPTIONS** SYMBOLGEN;

The default option is NOSYMBOLGEN.

65

## Displaying Macro Variables

| Global Symbol Table | |
|---|---|
| CITY | Dallas |
| DATE | 05JAN2004 |
| AMOUNT | 975 |

Partial SAS Log

```
OPTIONS SYMBOLGEN;
where fee>&amount;
SYMBOLGEN: Macro variable AMOUNT resolves to 975
where city_state contains "&city";
SYMBOLGEN: Macro variable CITY resolves to Dallas
where city_state contains '&city';
```

Why is no message displayed for the final example?

66

## Deleting User-Defined Macro Variables

The %SYMDEL statement deletes one or more user-defined macro variables from the global symbol table.

To free up memory, delete macro variables from the global symbol table when they are no longer needed.

General form of the %SYMDEL statement:

**%SYMDEL** *macro-variables*;

Example: Delete the macro variables CITY and DATE.

```
%symdel city date;
```

67

## Developing Macro-Based Applications

If a macro-based application generates SAS code, use a four-step approach.

Step 1:

- Write and debug the desired SAS program without any macro coding.

Step 2:

- Generalize the program by removing hardcoded programming constants and substituting macro variable references.
- Initialize the macro variables with %LET statements.
- Use the SYMBOLGEN system option for debugging.

Steps 3-4 will be presented later.

68

## Exercises

**3. Defining and Using Macro Variables**

**a.** Open the **babbit** program shown below into the Editor window. Submit the program and examine the output it creates.

```
options nocenter;
proc print data=perm.all noobs label uniform;
   where student_name contains 'Babbit';
   by student_name student_company;
   var course_title begin_date location teacher;
   title 'Courses Taken by Selected Students:';
   title2 'Those with Babbit in Their Name';
run;
```

**b.** Edit the program to change the search pattern in the WHERE statement and TITLE2 statement from **Babbit** to **Ba** and resubmit. Examine the output.

**c.** Modify the program so that the two occurrences of **Ba** are replaced by references to the macro variable PATTERN. Precede the program with a %LET statement to assign the value **Ba** to PATTERN. Submit the program. It produces the same output as before.

**d.** Submit a %PUT statement to display the value of all user-defined macro variables including PATTERN.

## Solutions to Exercises

### 3. Defining and Using Macro Variables

a. Bill Babbitt is the only student whose name contains the text string **Babbit**.

```
options nocenter;
proc print data=perm.all noobs label uniform;
   where student_name contains 'Babbit';
   by student_name student_company;
   var course_title begin_date location teacher;
   title 'Courses Taken by Selected Students';
   title2 'Those with Babbit in Their Name';
run;
```

```
Courses Taken by Selected Students
Those with Babbit in Their Name

- Student Name=Babbitt, Mr. Bill Company=National Credit Corp. -

       Description            Begin Location     Instructor

 Basic Telecommunications 24MAY2005  Dallas  Hallis, Dr. George
 Artificial Intelligence  01MAR2005  Dallas  Hallis, Dr. George
 Computer Aided Design    28MAR2006  Dallas  Berthan, Ms. Judy
```

**b.** There are four students whose name contains the text string **Ba**: Bill Babbit, Vincent Baker, Ellen Bates, and Barbara Turner.

```
options nocenter;
proc print data=perm.all noobs label uniform;
   where student_name contains 'Ba';
   by student_name student_company;
   var course_title begin_date location teacher;
   title  'Courses Taken by Selected Students';
   title2 'Those with Ba in Their Name';
run;
```

Partial Output

```
Courses Taken by Selected Students
Those with Ba in Their Name

- Student Name=Babbitt, Mr. Bill Company=National Credit Corp. -

Description                      Begin Location     Instructor

Basic Telecommunications  24MAY2005 Dallas   Hallis, Dr. George
Artificial Intelligence   01MAR2005 Dallas   Hallis, Dr. George
Computer Aided Design     28MAR2006 Dallas   Berthan, Ms. Judy


-- Student Name=Baker, Mr. Vincent Company=Snowing Petroleum ---

Description                      Begin Location     Instructor

Structured Query Language 14JUN2005 Boston   Wickam, Dr. Alice


----- Student Name=Bates, Ms. Ellen Company=Reston Railway -----

Description                      Begin Location     Instructor

Basic Telecommunications  24MAY2005 Dallas   Hallis, Dr. George
Database Design           25JAN2005 Seattle  Tally, Ms. Julia
Computer Aided Design     28MAR2006 Dallas   Berthan, Ms. Judy


Student Name=Turner, Ms. Barbara Company=Gravely Finance Center

Description                      Begin Location     Instructor

Structured Query Language 06DEC2005 Seattle  Wickam, Dr. Alice
Computer Aided Design     28MAR2006 Dallas   Berthan, Ms. Judy
```

c. The macro variable PATTERN should contain the text string **Ba** without any surrounding quotes. To resolve the macro variable in the WHERE and TITLE2 statement, change the single quotes to double quotes.

```
%let pattern=Ba;
options nocenter;
proc print data=perm.all noobs label uniform;
   where student_name contains "&pattern";
   by student_name student_company;
   var course_title begin_date location teacher;
   title 'Courses Taken by Selected Students';
   title2 "Those with &pattern in Their Name";
run;
```

d. A %PUT statement can verify that the macro variable PATTERN contains the text string **Ba**. The _USER_ argument displays the values of all user-defined macro variables:

```
%put _user_;
```

Partial SAS Log

```
108  %put _user_;
GLOBAL PATTERN Ba
```

# 2.5 Delimiting Macro Variable Names

## Objectives

- Place a macro variable reference adjacent to text or another macro variable reference.

71

## Referencing Macro Variables

You can reference macro variables anywhere in your program, including these special situations:

Macro variable references adjacent to leading and/or trailing text:

**text**&*variable*
&*variable***text**
**text**&*variable***text**

Adjacent macro variable references:

&*variable*&*variable*

72

## Combining Macro Variables with Text

You can place text immediately before a macro variable reference to build a new token.

Example: Data sets are stored in a SAS data library with a naming convention of **Y***yyyymon.*

*yyyy* can be **2000 2001 2002** and so on.

*mon* can be **JAN FEB MAR** and so on.

Write an application that uses macro variables to build SAS data set names and other tokens.

73

## Combining Macro Variables with Text

```
%let month=jan;
proc chart data=perm.y2000&month;
   hbar week / sumvar=sale;
run;
proc plot data=perm.y2000&month;
   plot sale*day;
run;
```

generates

```
PROC CHART DATA=PERM.Y2000JAN;
   HBAR WEEK / SUMVAR=SALE;
RUN;
PROC PLOT DATA=PERM.Y2000JAN;
   PLOT SALE*DAY;
RUN;
```

74

## Combining Macro Variables with Text

This example illustrates adjacent macro variables references.

Example: Modify the previous program to allow both the **month** and the **year** to be substituted.

```
%let year=2000;
%let month=jan;
proc chart data=perm.y&year&month;
   hbar week / sumvar=sale;
run;
proc plot data=perm.y&year&month;
   plot sale*day;
run;
```

75

## Combining Macro Variables with Text

The generated program is identical to the program in the previous example.

```
PROC CHART DATA=PERM.Y2000JAN;
   HBAR WEEK / SUMVAR=SALE;
RUN;
PROC PLOT DATA=PERM.Y2000JAN;
   PLOT SALE*DAY;
RUN;
```

76

## Combining Macro Variables with Text

You can place text immediately after a macro variable reference if it does not change the reference.

Example: Modify the previous program to substitute the name of an analysis variable.

```
%let year=2000;
%let month=jan;
%let var=sale;
proc chart data=perm.y&year&month;
   hbar week / sumvar=&var;
run;
proc plot data=perm.y&year&month;
   plot &var*day;
run;
```

77

## Combining Macro Variables with Text

The generated program is identical to the program in the previous example.

```
PROC CHART DATA=PERM.Y2000JAN;
HBAR WEEK / SUMVAR=SALE;
RUN;
PROC PLOT DATA=PERM.Y2000JAN;
PLOT SALE*DAY;
RUN;
```

78

## Combining Macro Variables with Text

Example: Modify the previous program to allow a base SAS or SAS/GRAPH procedure.

```
/* GRAPHICS should be null or G */
%let graphics=g;
%let year=2000;
%let month=jan;
%let var=sale;
proc &graphicschart data=perm.y&year&month;
   hbar week / sumvar=&var;
run;
proc &graphicsplot data=perm.y&year&month;
   plot &var*day;
run;
```

79

## Combining Macro Variables with Text

SAS interprets the macro variable's name as GRAPHICSCHART because no delimiter separates the macro variable reference from the trailing text.

Partial Log

```
1     %let graphics=g;
2     %let year=2000;
3     %let month=jan;
4     %let var=sale;
5     proc &graphicschart data=perm.y&year&month;
           -
           10
WARNING: Apparent symbolic reference GRAPHICSCHART not resolved.

ERROR 10-205: Expecting the name of the procedure to be executed.
```

80

## Macro Variable Name Delimiter

The word scanner recognizes the end of a macro variable reference when it encounters a character that cannot be part of the reference.

A *period* (.) is a special delimiter that ends a macro variable reference and does not appear as text when the macro variable is resolved.

81

## Macro Variable Name Delimiter

Example: Correct the problem from the previous example.

```
%let graphics=g;
%let year=2000;
%let month=jan;
%let var=sale;
proc &graphics.chart data=perm.y&year&month;
   hbar week / sumvar=&var;
run;
proc &graphics.plot data=perm.y&year&month;
   plot &var*day;
run;
```

82

## Macro Variable Name Delimiter

The generated code does not include the period.

```
PROC GCHART DATA=PERM.Y2000JAN;
   HBAR WEEK / SUMVAR=SALE;
RUN;
PROC GPLOT DATA=PERM.Y2000JAN;
   PLOT SALE*DAY;
RUN;
```

83

## Macro Variable Name Delimiter

Example: Modify the previous example to include a macro variable that defines a libref.

```
%let lib=perm;
%let graphics=g;
%let year=2000;
%let month=jan;
%let var=sale;
libname &lib 'SAS-data-library';
proc &graphics.chart data=&lib.y&year&month;
   hbar week / sumvar=&var;
run;
proc &graphics.plot data=&lib.y&year&month;
   plot &var*day;
run;
```

What is the problem this time?

84

## Macro Variable Name Delimiter

The program

```
%let lib=perm;
...
libname &lib 'SAS-data-library';
proc &graphics.chart data=&lib.y&year&month;
...
```

generates

```
LIBNAME PERM 'SAS-data-library';
PROC GCHART DATA=PERMY2000JAN;
   HBAR WEEK / SUMVAR=SALE;
RUN;
PROC GPLOT DATA=PERMY2000JAN;
   PLOT SALE*DAY;
RUN;
```

The period after **&lib** is interpreted as a delimiter.

85

## Macro Variable Name Delimiter

Use another period after the delimiter period to supply the needed token.

```
%let lib=perm;
...
libname &lib 'SAS-data-library';
proc &graphics.chart data=&lib..y&year&month;
...
proc &graphics.plot data=&lib..y&year&month;
```

86

# Macro Variable Name Delimiter

delimiter — text

```
proc &graphics.chart data=&lib..y&year&month;
```

The first period is treated as a delimiter, the second as text.

The compiler receives

```
...
PROC GCHART DATA=PERM.Y2000JAN;
...
```

87

## Exercises

**4. Macro Variable References**

**a.** Open the program **countloc** shown below into the Editor window.

```
title;
proc sql;
   select location,n(location) label='Count'
      from perm.schedule,perm.register
      where schedule.course_number=
            register.course_number
      group by location;
quit;
```

Submit the program. The SELECT statement creates a listing from two SAS data sets (tables) that are merged (joined) by the common variable **course_number**. The GROUP BY clause reduces the listing to distinct values of **location**. The N function counts the number of observations that are within distinct values of the GROUP BY variable.

**b.** Modify the program so that it contains references to these macro variables:

| | |
|---|---|
| TABLE1 | second-level name of one input data set |
| TABLE2 | second-level name of the other input data set |
| JOINVAR | name of variable common to both input data sets |
| FREQVAR | name of the GROUP BY variable. |

Precede the program with %LET statements that initialize these macro variables to the values currently in the program. Submit the program and compare the listing with the one created earlier. They are identical.

**c.** Edit the program to change the values of the macro variables to create a listing from the **perm.students** and **perm.register** data sets that shows the distribution of the **city_state** variable. The two data sets share the **student_name** variable.

# Solutions to Exercises

## 4. Macro Variable References

**a.** The original program produces this output:

SAS Output

```
Location             Count
--------------------------
Boston                 150
Dallas                 133
Seattle                151
```

**b.** The references to the input data set names in the WHERE clause are followed by two periods, the first acting as the macro variable name delimiter and the second received by the compiler as part of the two-level column name.

```
%let table1=schedule;
%let table2=register;
%let joinvar=course_number;
%let freqvar=location;
title;
proc sql;
   select &freqvar,n(&freqvar) label='Count'
      from perm.&table1,perm.&table2
      where &table1..&joinvar=&table2..&joinvar
   group by &freqvar;
quit;
```

SAS Output

```
Location             Count
--------------------------
Boston                 150
Dallas                 133
Seattle                151
```

c. The only changes required are new values assigned to the macro variables in the %LET statements.

```
%let table1=register;
%let table2=students;
%let joinvar=student_name;
%let freqvar=city_state;
title;
proc sql;
   select &freqvar,n(&freqvar) label='Count'
      from perm.&table1,perm.&table2
      where &table1..&joinvar=&table2..&joinvar
   group by &freqvar;
quit;
```

Partial Output

| City,State | Count |
|---|---|
| Akron, OH | 5 |
| Albany, NY | 2 |
| Allentown, PA | 3 |
| Annapolis, MD | 7 |
| Atlanta, GA | 7 |
| Austin, TX | 3 |
| Bethesda, MD | 1 |
| Birmingham, AL | 2 |
| Bozeman, MT | 10 |
| Brea, CA | 2 |
| Buena Park, CA | 1 |
| Chicago, IL | 71 |
| Chicago, IN | 2 |
| Cincinati, OH | 1 |
| Cleveland, OH | 3 |
| Columbia, MD | 4 |
| Columbus, OH | 8 |
| Costa Mesa, CA | 9 |
| Cupertino, CA | 2 |
| Dallas, TX | 8 |

# 2.6 Macro Functions

## Objectives

Use macro functions to

- manipulate character strings
- perform arithmetic
- execute SAS functions.

90

## Macro Functions

Macro functions

- have similar syntax as corresponding DATA step character functions
- yield similar results
- manipulate macro variables and expressions
- represent macro triggers
- are executed by the macro processor.

91

## Macro Functions

Selected character string manipulation functions:

| | |
|---|---|
| %UPCASE | translates letters from lowercase to uppercase. |
| %SUBSTR | extracts a substring from a character string. |
| %SCAN | extracts a word from a character string. |
| %INDEX | searches a character string for specified text. |
| %LENGTH | returns the length of a character string or text expression. |

Other functions:

| | |
|---|---|
| %SYSFUNC | executes SAS functions. |
| %EVAL | performs arithmetic and logical operations. |
| %BQUOTE | protects blanks and other special characters. |

92

## Case Sensitivity

Character comparisons are case sensitive.

Example: Create a summary of total fees outstanding for each course.

```
%let paidval=n;
proc means data=perm.all sum maxdec=0;
   where paid="&paidval";
   var fee;
   class course_title;
title "Courses with fee status=&paidval";
run;
```

UPCASE1

93

## Case Sensitivity

Partial Log

```
539  %let paidval=n;
540  proc means data=perm.all sum maxdec=0;
541     where paid="&paidval";
542     var fee;
543     class course_title;
544  title "Courses with fee status=&paidval";
545  run;

NOTE: No observations were selected from data set PERM.ALL.
```

Because the value of the macro variable PAIDVAL was specified in **lowercase**, the WHERE expression finds no matching observations. All the values of the data set variable PAID are **uppercase**.

94

## The %UPCASE Function

The %UPCASE function translates characters to uppercase.

General form of the %UPCASE function:

**%UPCASE**(*argument*)

*argument* can be any combination of text and macro triggers.

95

## The %UPCASE Function

Example: For each course, create a summary of total fees outstanding and account for case.

```
%let paidval=n;
proc means data=perm.all sum maxdec=0;
   where paid="%upcase(&paidval)";
   var fee;
   class course_title;
title "Courses with fee status=&paidval";
run;
```

UPCASE2

96

## The %UPCASE Function

Courses with fee status=n

The MEANS Procedure

Analysis Variable : Fee Course Fee

| Description | N Obs | Sum |
|---|---|---|
| Artificial Intelligence | 24 | 9600 |
| Basic Telecommunications | 14 | 11130 |
| Computer Aided Design | 13 | 20800 |
| Database Design | 17 | 6375 |
| Local Area Networks | 19 | 12350 |
| Structured Query Language | 20 | 23000 |

97

## The %SUBSTR Function

General form of the %SUBSTR function:

**%SUBSTR**(*argument*, *position* <,*n*>)

The %SUBSTR function

- returns the portion of *argument* beginning at *position* for a length of *n* characters
- returns the portion of *argument* beginning at *position* to the end of *argument* when an *n* value is not supplied.

*continued...*

98

## The %SUBSTR Function

General form of the %SUBSTR function:

**%SUBSTR**(*argument*, *position* <,*n*>)

You can specify *argument*, *position*, and *n* values using

- constant text
- macro variable references
- macro functions
- macro calls.

It is not necessary to place *argument* in quotes because it is **always** handled as a character string by the %SUBSTR function.

99

The values of *position* and *n* can also be the result of an arithmetic expression that yields an integer. For example,

```
%substr(&var,%length(&var)-1)
```

returns the last two characters of the value of the macro variable VAR.

## The %SUBSTR Function

Example: Print courses with a BEGIN_DATE between the current date and the first day of the current month. Use the %SUBSTR function and SYSDATE9 macro variable to construct the appropriate dates.

```
proc print data=perm.schedule;
   where begin_date between
         "01%substr(&sysdate9,3)"d and
         "&sysdate9"d;
  title "All Courses Held So Far This Month";
  title2 "(as of &sysdate9)";
run;
```

SUBSTR1

100

## The %SUBSTR Function

text macro triggers text

`"01%substr(&sysdate9,3)"d`

&sysdate9 resolves: `%substr(30OCT2004,3)`

%substr executes: → `OCT2004`

final substitution: → `"01OCT2004"d`

101

# The %SUBSTR Function

All Courses Held So Far This Month
(as of 30OCT2004)

| Obs | Course_ Number | Course_ Code | Location | Begin_ Date | Teacher |
|---|---|---|---|---|---|
| 1 | 1 | C001 | Seattle | 23OCT2004 | Hallis, Dr. George |

102

## The %SCAN Function

General form of the %SCAN function:

**%SCAN**(*argument, n* < , *delimiters*>)

The %SCAN function

- returns the *n*th word of argument, where words are strings of characters separated by delimiters
- uses a default set of delimiters if none are specified
- returns a null string if there are fewer than *n* words in argument.

103

## The %SCAN Function

General form of the %SCAN function:

**%SCAN**(*argument, n* < , *delimiters*>)

You can specify values for *argument*, *n*, and *delimiters* using

- constant text
- macro variable references
- macro functions
- macro calls.

The value of *n* can also be an arithmetic expression that yields an integer.

104

Default delimiters for the %SCAN function include **blank . ( & ! $ * ) ; - / , %**

It is not necessary to place *argument* and *delimiters* in quotes because they are always handled as character strings by the %SCAN function.

## The %SCAN Function

Example: Use PROC DATASETS to investigate the structure of the last data set created.

```
data work.current;
   set perm.schedule;
   where year(begin_date) =
         year("&sysdate9"d);
run;

%let libref=%scan(&syslast,1);
%let dsname=%scan(&syslast,2,.);
proc datasets lib=&libref nolist;
title "Contents of Data Set &syslast";
   contents data=&dsname;
run;
quit;
```

SCAN1

105

## The %SCAN Function

```
%let libref=%scan(&syslast,1);
```

&syslast resolves:

```
%let libref=%scan(WORK.CURRENT,1);
```

%scan executes:

```
%let libref=WORK;
```

106

## The %SCAN Function

Partial Output

```
                       Contents of Data Set WORK.CURRENT

                            The DATASETS Procedure

 Data Set Name        WORK.CURRENT                      Observations          0
 Member Type          DATA                              Variables             5
 Engine               V9                                Indexes               0
 Created              Thu, Feb 05, 2004 02:04:21 PM     Observation Length    56
 Last Modified        Thu, Feb 05, 2004 02:04:21 PM     Deleted Observations  0
 Protection                                             Compressed            NO
 Data Set Type                                          Sorted                NO
 Label
 Data Representation  WINDOWS_32
 Encoding             wlatin1  Western (Windows)

                       Engine/Host Dependent Information

Data Set Page Size          8192
Number of Data Set Pages    1
First Data Page             1
Max Obs per Page            145
Obs in First Data Page      0
Number of Data Set Repairs  0
File Name                   C:\temp\SAS Temporary
                            Files\_TD2140\CURRENT.sas7bdat
Release Created             9.0101M0
Host Created                WIN_PRO
```

107

## The %BQUOTE Function

The %BQUOTE function removes the normal meaning of special tokens that appear as constant text.

Special tokens include: + - * / , < > =

LT EQ GT AND OR NOT LE GE NE

; ' " blank

General form of the %BQUOTE function:

**%BQUOTE**(*argument*)

*argument* can be any combination of text and macro triggers.

108

The %BQUOTE function is one of several macro quoting functions designed for specialized purposes.

## The %BQUOTE Function

The %BQUOTE function

- protects (quotes) tokens so that the macro processor does not interpret them as macro-level syntax
- enables macro triggers to work normally
- preserves leading and trailing blanks in its argument.

109

## The %BQUOTE Function

Example: Protect a special character and preserve leading blanks in macro expressions.

```
%let text=%bquote(Joan's Report);
%put %bquote(     &text is the value.);
```

Partial SAS Log

```
140  %let text=%bquote(Joan's Report);
141  %put %bquote(     &text is the value.);
     Joan's Report is the value.
```

110

## The %EVAL Function

General form of the %EVAL function:

**%EVAL**(*expression*)

The %EVAL function

- performs arithmetic and logical operations
- truncates non-integer results
- returns a character result
- returns 1 (true) or 0 (false) for logical operations
- returns a null value and issues an error message when non-integer values are used in arithmetic operations.

111

## The %EVAL Function

Example: Use the %EVAL function to compute the final year of a range.

```
%let firstyr=2004;
%let numyears=2;
%let finalyr=%eval(&firstyr+&numyears-1);
proc print data=perm.schedule;
   where year(begin_date) between
         &firstyr and &finalyr;
   title "All Courses Scheduled";
   title2 "&firstyr through &finalyr";
run;
```

EVAL1

112

# The %EVAL Function

Example: Use the %EVAL function to compute the final year of a range.

All Courses Scheduled
2004 through 2005

| Obs | Course_ Number | Course_ Code | Location | Begin_ Date | Teacher |
|---|---|---|---|---|---|
| 1 | 1 | C001 | Seattle | 26OCT2004 | Hallis, Dr. George |
| 2 | 2 | C002 | Dallas | 07DEC2004 | Wickam, Dr. Alice |
| 3 | 3 | C003 | Boston | 11JAN2005 | Forest, Mr. Peter |
| 4 | 4 | C004 | Seattle | 25JAN2005 | Tally, Ms. Julia |
| 5 | 5 | C005 | Dallas | 01MAR2005 | Hallis, Dr. George |
| 6 | 6 | C006 | Boston | 05APR2005 | Berthan, Ms. Judy |
| 7 | 7 | C001 | Dallas | 24MAY2005 | Hallis, Dr. George |
| 8 | 8 | C002 | Boston | 14JUN2005 | Wickam, Dr. Alice |
| 9 | 9 | C003 | Seattle | 19JUL2005 | Forest, Mr. Peter |
| 10 | 10 | C004 | Dallas | 16AUG2005 | Tally, Ms. Julia |
| 11 | 11 | C005 | Boston | 20SEP2005 | Tally, Ms. Julia |
| 12 | 12 | C006 | Seattle | 04OCT2005 | Berthan, Ms. Judy |
| 13 | 13 | C001 | Boston | 15NOV2005 | Hallis, Dr. George |
| 14 | 14 | C002 | Seattle | 06DEC2005 | Wickam, Dr. Alice |

113

## The %SYSFUNC Function

The %SYSFUNC macro function executes SAS functions.

General form of the %SYSFUNC function:

**%SYSFUNC**(*SAS function(argument(s)) <,format>*)

- *SAS function(argument(s))* is the name of a SAS function and its corresponding arguments.
- The second argument is an optional format for the value returned by the first argument.

114

## The %SYSFUNC Function

The automatic macro variables SYSDATE9 and SYSTIME can be used in titles:

```
title "Report Produced on &sysdate9";
title2 "at &systime";
```

generates

```
Report Produced on 11JUN2004
           at 09:21
```

SYSDATE9 and SYSTIME represent the **date** and **time** the SAS session started.

115

## The %SYSFUNC Function

Example: Generate titles containing the current date and time. Format the date and time with the WEEKDATE. and TIME8. formats, respectively.

```
title "%sysfunc(today(),weekdate.)";
title2 "%sysfunc(time(),time8.)";
```

generates

```
Tuesday, August 24, 2004
        13:06:08
```

116

## The %SYSFUNC Function

Example: Compute the first year of a range based on the current date using the TODAY function.

```
%let thisyr=%sysfunc(today(),year4.);
%let lastyr=%eval(&thisyr-1);
proc print data=perm.schedule;
  where year(begin_date) between &lastyr and &thisyr;
  title1 "Courses Scheduled &lastyr and &thisyr";
  title2 "(as of &sysdate9)";
run;
```

SYSFUNC1

117

# The %SYSFUNC Function

SAS Output

```
                Courses Scheduled 2003 and 2004
                       (as of 02AUG2004)

      Course_  Course_                    Begin_
Obs   Number    Code     Location          Date        Teacher

  1      1      C001     Seattle    26OCT2004  Hallis, Dr. George
  2      2      C002     Dallas     07DEC2004  Wickam, Dr. Alice
```

118

## The %SYSFUNC Function

Most SAS functions can be used with %SYSFUNC.
Exceptions include:

- Array processing (DIM, HBOUND, LBOUND)
- Variable information (VNAME, VLABEL, MISSING)
- Macro interface (RESOLVE, SYMGET)
- Data conversion (INPUT, PUT)
- Other functions (IORCMSG, LAG, DIF).

INPUTC and INPUTN can be used in place of INPUT.
PUTC and PUTN can be used in place of PUT.

119

Variable Information functions include functions such as VNAME and VLABEL. For a complete list, see "Functions and CALL Routines" in the *SAS® Language Reference: Dictionary.*

Because %SYSFUNC is a macro function, you do not need to enclose character values in quotation marks as you do in DATA step functions. Use commas to separate all arguments in DATA step functions within %SYSFUNC. You cannot use argument lists preceded by the word OF.

## Exercises

**5. Using Macro Functions**

**a.** Submit this program to create the **work.sorted** data set:

```
proc sort data=perm.schedule out=work.sorted;
   by course_number begin_date;
run;
```

**b.** Open the program **dictcols** shown below into the Editor window and submit it. This program uses a PROC SQL dictionary table to display the variables in a specified data set.

```
title "Variables in PERM.SCHEDULE";
proc sql;
   select name, type, length
      from dictionary.columns
      where libname="PERM" and
            memname="SCHEDULE";
quit;
```

**c.** Add a %LET statement to assign the value **perm.schedule** to a macro variable named DSN. Use the new macro variable in the TITLE statement. Use one or more macro functions to separate the value of DSN into the library reference and the data set name for substitution into the WHERE clause. Submit the modified program. You should get the same report.

**d.** Change the %LET statement to assign the value **perm.courses** to the DSN macro variable. Submit the modified program to see the new report.

**e.** Change the %LET statement to assign the value of the automatic macro variable SYSLAST to the DSN macro variable. Submit the modified program to see the new report.

# Solutions to Exercises

## 5. Using Macro Functions

a. Submit this program to create the **work.sorted** data set:

```
proc sort data=perm.schedule out=work.sorted;
   by course_number begin_date;
run;
```

b. Open the **dictcols** program shown below into the Editor window and submit it. This program uses a PROC SQL dictionary table to display the variables in a specified data set.

```
title "Variables in PERM.SCHEDULE";
proc sql;
   select name, type, length
      from dictionary.columns
      where libname="PERM" and
            memname="SCHEDULE";
quit;
```

c. The %SCAN function can divide the value of the macro variable DSN into parts. The default delimiter set will work for this example; however, the single applicable delimiter, the period (.), can be specified as the third argument to %SCAN.

The %UPCASE function may be required, because the values of **libname** and **memname** in the **dictionary.columns** table are in uppercase.

```
%let dsn=perm.schedule;
%let libref=%upcase(%scan(&dsn,1,.));
%let dsname=%upcase(%scan(&dsn,2,.));
title "Variables in %upcase(&dsn)";
proc sql;
   select name, type, length
      from dictionary.columns
      where libname="&libref" and
            memname="&dsname";
quit;
```

SAS Output

```
                    Variables in PERM.SCHEDULE

                                          Column     Column
              Column Name                 Type       Length
              ---------------------------------------------
              Course_Number               num             8
              Course_Code                 char            4
              Location                    char           15
              Begin_Date                  num             8
              Teacher                     char           20
```

Alternate Solution

```
%let dsn=perm.schedule;
title "Variables in %upcase(&dsn)";
proc sql;
   select name, type, length
   from dictionary.columns
      where libname="%upcase(%scan(&dsn,1,.))" and
            memname="%upcase(%scan(&dsn,2,.))";
quit;
```

SAS Output

```
                    Variables in PERM.SCHEDULE

                                         Column    Column
          Column Name                    Type      Length
          ------------------------------------------------
          Course_Number                  num            8
          Course_Code                    char           4
          Location                       char          15
          Begin_Date                     num            8
          Teacher                        char          20
```

**d.** Changing the value of the macro variable DSN automatically changes which data set is analyzed.

```
%let dsn=perm.courses;
%let libref=%upcase(%scan(&dsn,1,.));
%let dsname=%upcase(%scan(&dsn,2,.));
title "Variables in %upcase(&dsn)";
proc sql;
   select name, type, length
      from dictionary.columns
      where libname="&libref" and
            memname="&dsname";
quit;
```

SAS Output

```
                    Variables in PERM.COURSES

                                         Column    Column
          Column Name                    Type      Length
          ------------------------------------------------
          Course_Code                    char           4
          Course_Title                   char          25
          Days                           num            8
          Fee                            num            8
```

**e.** The value of the macro variable SYSLAST is assigned as the value of the macro variable DSN, so the **work.sorted** data set is analyzed.

```
%let dsn=&syslast;
%let libref=%upcase(%scan(&dsn,1,.));
%let dsname=%upcase(%scan(&dsn,2,.));
title "Variables in %upcase(&dsn)";
proc sql;
   select name, type, length
      from dictionary.columns
      where libname="&libref" and
            memname="&dsname";
quit;
```

SAS Output

Variables in WORK.SORTED

| Column Name | Column Type | Column Length |
|---|---|---|
| Course_Number | num | 8 |
| Course_Code | char | 4 |
| Location | char | 15 |
| Begin_Date | num | 8 |
| Teacher | char | 20 |

# Chapter 3 Macro Definitions

# 3.1 Defining and Calling a Macro

## Objectives

- Define and call a simple macro.
- Control macro storage.

3

## Defining a Macro

A *macro* or *macro definition* enables you to write *macro programs*.

General form of a macro definition:

**%MACRO** *macro-name*;
    *macro-text*
**%MEND** <*macro-name*>;

*macro-name* follows SAS naming conventions

*macro-text* can include

- any text
- SAS statements or steps
- macro variables, functions, statements, or calls
- any combination of the above.

4

## Macro Compilation

When a macro definition is submitted,

- macro language statements are
  - checked for syntax errors
  - compiled
- SAS statements and other text are **not**
  - checked for syntax errors
  - compiled
- the macro is stored as an entry in a SAS catalog, the temporary catalog **`work.sasmacr`** by default.

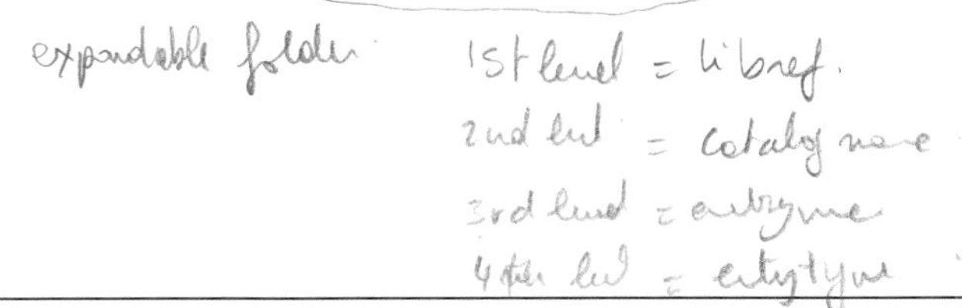


5

Do not name a macro with the name of a macro statement or function (LET or SCAN, for example). Refer to the documentation for a complete list of reserved names.

## Macro Compilation

The MCOMPILENOTE=ALL option issues a note to the SAS log after a macro definition has compiled.

General form of the MCOMPILENOTE= option:

```
OPTIONS MCOMPILENOTE=ALL | NONE;
```

The default setting is MCOMPILENOTE=NONE.

The MCOMPILENOTE= option is new in SAS®9.

6

## Macro Compilation

Example: Submit a macro definition.

```
options mcompilenote=all;
%macro time;
   %put The current time is %sysfunc
        (time(),time11.2).;
%mend time;
```

MACRO1

Partial SAS Log

```
NOTE: The macro TIME completed compilation without errors.
      3 instructions 76 bytes.
```

7

## Macro Storage

Example: Produce a list of compiled macros stored in the default temporary catalog **work.sasmacr**.

```
proc catalog cat=work.sasmacr;
   contents;
   title "My Temporary Macros";
quit;
```

PROC CATALOG Output

```
                          My Temporary Macros

                    Contents of Catalog WORK.SASMACR

# Name Type            Create Date        Modified Date Description
-------------------------------------------------------------------
1 TIME MACRO  11JUN2004:15:55:59  11JUN2004:15:55:59
```

8

## Calling a Macro

A *macro call* = execute

- causes the macro to execute
- is specified by placing a percent sign before the name of the macro
- can be made anywhere in a program (similar to a macro variable reference)
- represents a macro trigger
- is **not** a statement (no semicolon required).

General form of a macro call:

*%macro-name*

9

Placing a semicolon after a macro call may insert an inappropriate semicolon into the resulting program, leading to errors during compilation or execution.

## Calling a Macro

Example: Call the TIME macro.

```
%time
```

Partial SAS Log

```
204  %time
The current time is 15:55:59.05.
```

10

## Program Flow

When the macro processor receives *%macro-name*, it

1. searches the designated SAS catalog (WORK.SASMACR by default) for an entry named *macro-name*.MACRO
2. executes compiled macro language statements
3. sends any remaining text to the input stack for word scanning
4. pauses while the word scanner tokenizes the inserted text and SAS code executes
5. resumes execution of macro language statements after the SAS code executes.

11

## Example

A macro can generate SAS code.

Example: Write a macro that generates a PROC PRINT step. Reference macro variables within the macro.

```
%macro printdsn;
   proc print data=&dsn;
      var &vars;
   run;
%mend;
```

MACRO2

This macro contains no macro language statements.

12

## Example

Example: Call the PRINTDSN macro. Precede the call with %LET statements that populate macro variables referenced within the macro.

```
%let dsn=perm.courses;
%let vars=days fee;
%printdsn
```

13

## Program Flow

Example: Submit the %LET statements and call the PRINTDSN macro.

**Compiler**

**Symbol Table**

**Word Scanner**

**Macro Processor**

**Input Stack**

```
%let dsn=perm.courses;
%let vars=days fee;
%printdsn
```

**work.sasmacr**

| # | Name | Type |
|---|---|---|
| 1 | PRINTDSN | MACRO |
| 2 | TIME | MACRO |

14

## Program Flow

The macro processor executes the %LET statements and populates the Symbol Table.

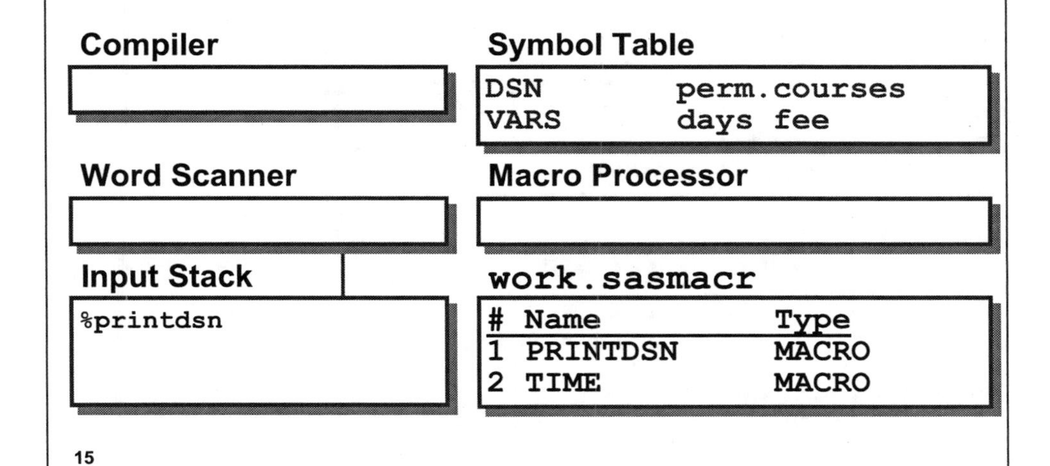


15

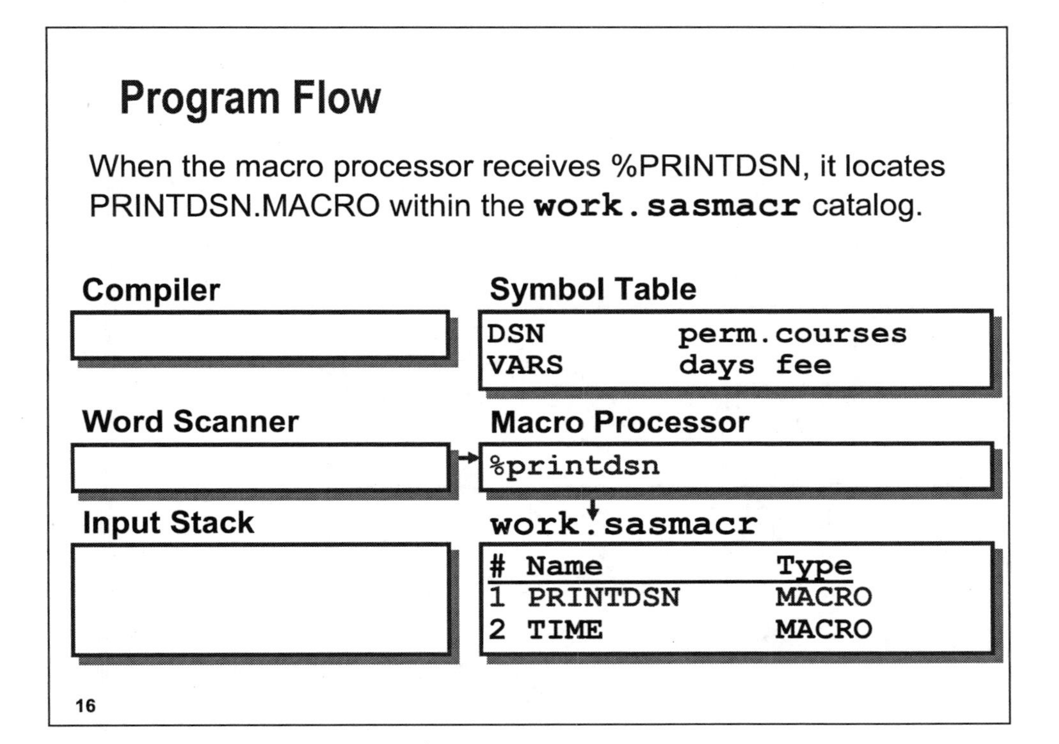

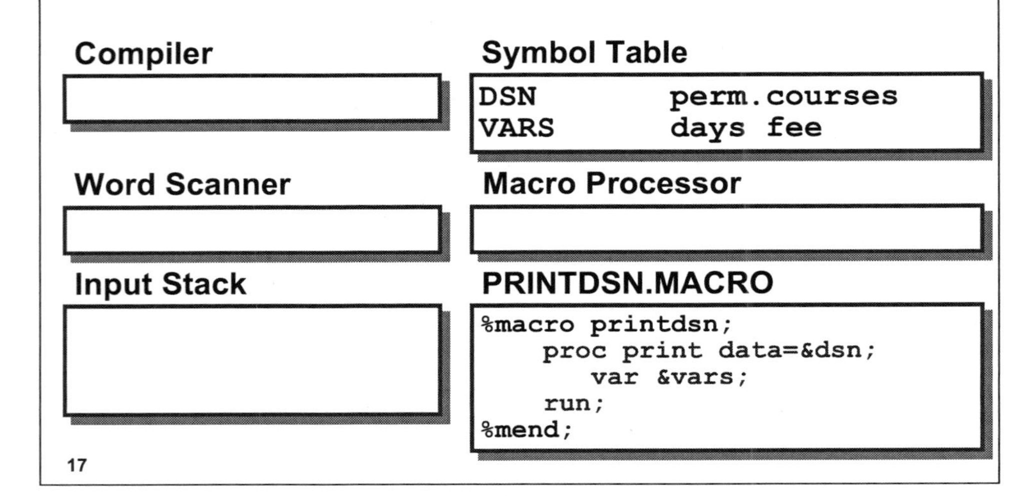
Program Flow
The macro processor opens PRINTDSN.MACRO. There are no macro language statements to execute.
Compiler
Symbol Table
DSN perm.courses
VARS days fee
Word Scanner
Macro Processor
Input Stack
PRINTDSN.MACRO
%macro printdsn;
proc print data=&dsn;
var &vars;
run;
%mend;
17

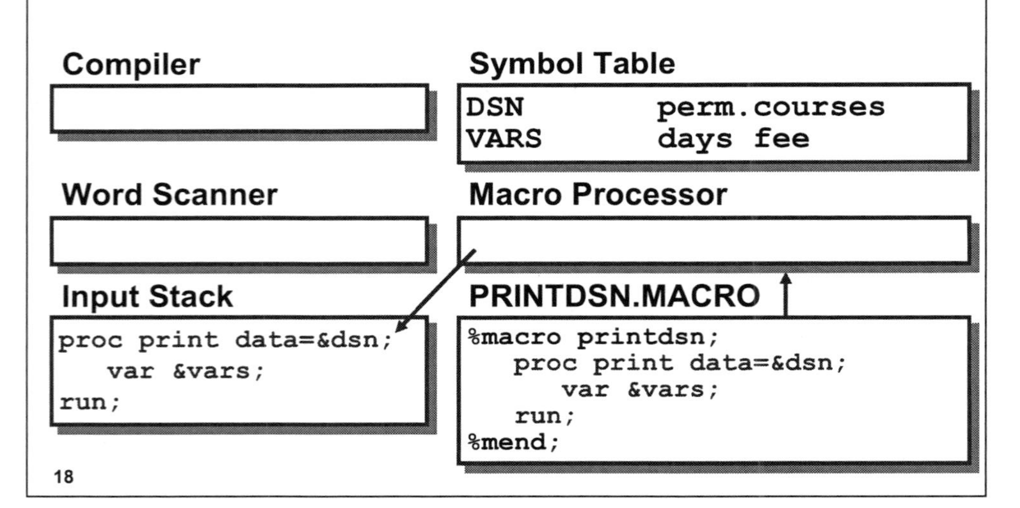
Program Flow
The macro processor places the macro text on the input stack.
Compiler
Symbol Table
DSN perm.courses
VARS days fee
Word Scanner
Macro Processor
Input Stack
proc print data=&dsn;
var &vars;
run;
PRINTDSN.MACRO
%macro printdsn;
proc print data=&dsn;
var &vars;
run;
%mend;
18

## Program Flow

Macro activity pauses while the word scanner tokenizes text placed on the input stack by the macro processor.

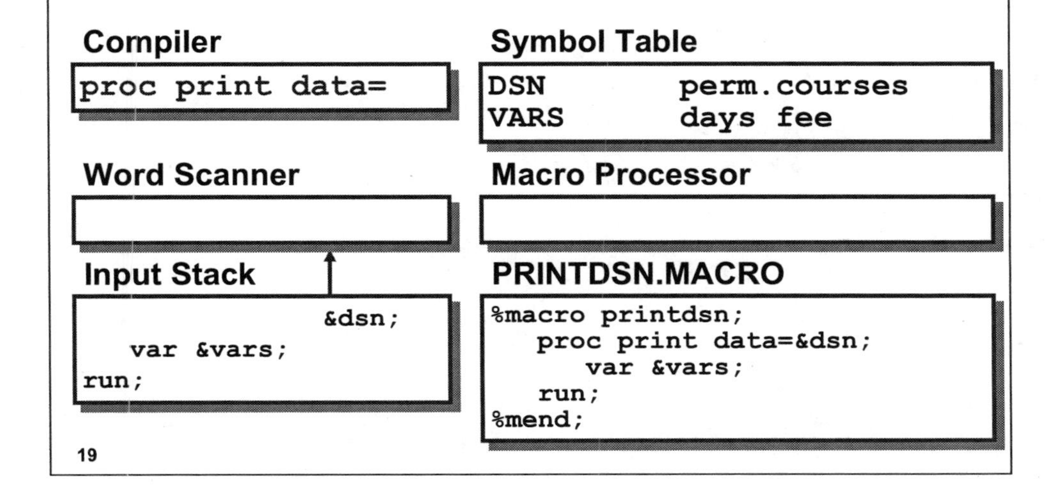


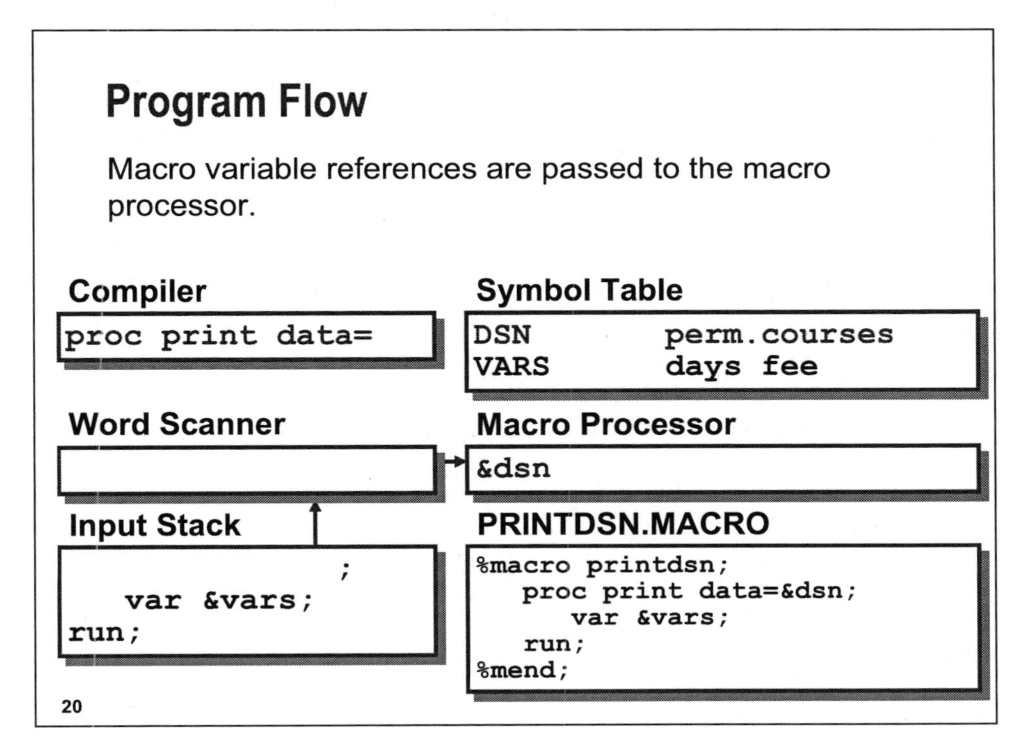

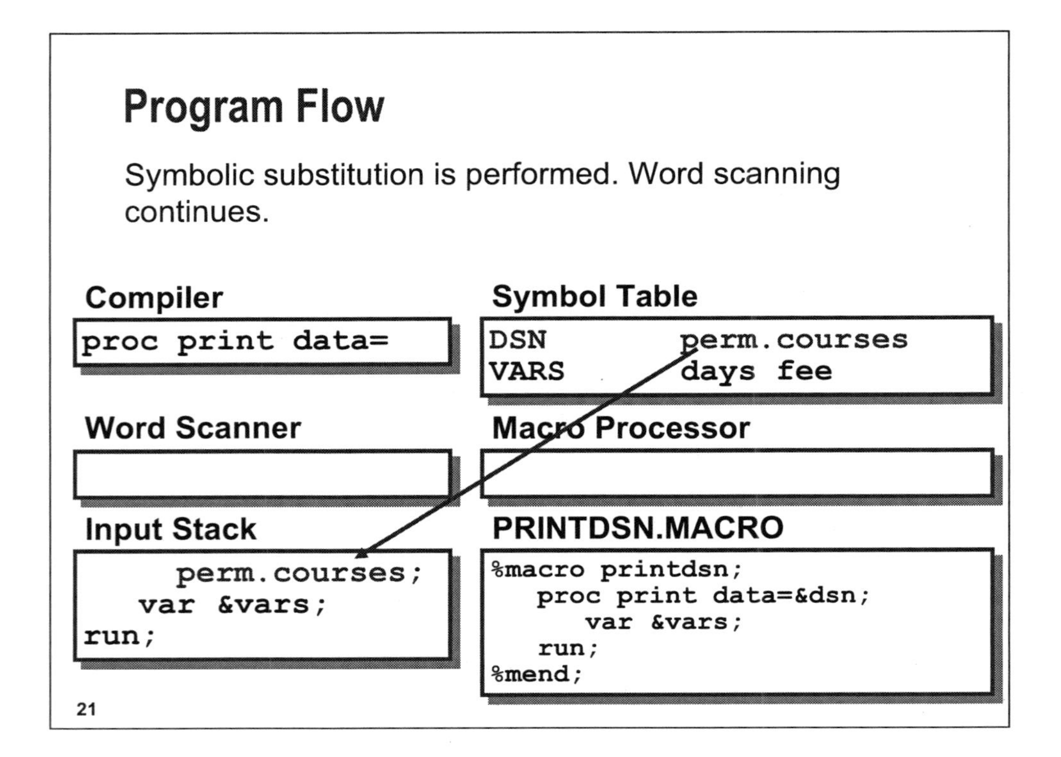


## Program Flow

When a step boundary is encountered, SAS executes the compiled step as macro activity remains paused. Macro activity stops when the %MEND statement is encountered.

**Compiler**

```
proc print data=perm.courses;
   var days fee;
```

**Symbol Table**

```
DSN          perm.courses
VARS         days fee
```

**Word Scanner**

```
run;
```

**Macro Processor**

**Input Stack**

**PRINTDSN.MACRO**

```
%macro printdsn;
   proc print data=&dsn;
      var &vars;
   run;
%mend;
```

22

## Macro Execution

The SAS log reflects that a PROC PRINT step executed.

Partial SAS Log

```
243  %let dsn=perm.courses;
244  %let vars=days fee;
245  %printdsn

NOTE: There were 6 observations read from the data set PERM.COURSES.
NOTE: PROCEDURE PRINT used (Total process time):
      real time           0.00 seconds
      cpu time            0.00 seconds
```

Why does PROC PRINT source code not appear in the SAS log?

23

## Macro Execution

The MPRINT option writes to the SAS log the text sent to the SAS compiler as a result of macro execution.

General form of the MPRINT|NOMPRINT option:

**OPTIONS** MPRINT;
**OPTIONS** NOMPRINT;

The default setting is NOMPRINT.

24

## Macro Execution

Example: Set the MPRINT option before calling the macro.

Partial SAS Log

```
267  options mprint;
268  %printdsn
MPRINT(PRINTDSN):   proc print data=perm.courses;
MPRINT(PRINTDSN):   var days fee;
MPRINT(PRINTDSN):   run;

NOTE: There were 6 observations read from the data set PERM.COURSES.
NOTE: PROCEDURE PRINT used (Total process time):
      real time           0.00 seconds
      cpu time            0.01 seconds
```

25

Macro generated code is treated as a series of tokens. The MPRINT option shows each statement on a new line without indentation.

## Macro Storage

Example: Produce a list of compiled macros stored in the default temporary catalog **work.sasmacr**.

```
proc catalog cat=work.sasmacr;
   contents;
   title "My Temporary Macros";
quit;
```

PROC CATALOG Output

```
                           My Temporary Macros

                     Contents of Catalog WORK.SASMACR

# Name      Type           Create Date        Modified Date Description
-----------------------------------------------------------------------
1 PRINTDSN MACRO  15JUN2004:15:58:21  15JUN2004:15:58:21
2 TIME      MACRO  15JUN2004:15:55:59  15JUN2004:15:55:59
```

26

## Macro Storage

Macros are stored in the **`work`** library by default.

The MSTORED system option enables storage of compiled macros in a permanent SAS library.

The SASMSTORE= system option designates a permanent library to store compiled macros.

```
OPTIONS MSTORED SASMSTORE=libref;
```

*libref* points to an allocated SAS data library.

27

## Macro Storage

General form of a macro definition for permanent macro storage:

```
%MACRO macro-name / STORE <SOURCE>;
      macro-text
%MEND macro-name;
```

The STORE option stores the compiled macro in the library indicated by the SASMSTORE= system option.

The SOURCE option stores the macro source code along with the compiled code.

✎ The SOURCE option is new in SAS®9. In earlier releases, be sure to save your source code externally.

28

## Macro Storage

Example: Store the PRINTDSN macro, along with its source code, in a permanent library.

```
libname perm '.';
options mstored sasmstore=perm;
%macro printdsn / store source;
   proc print data=&dsn;
      var &vars;
   run;
%mend printdsn;
```

Call the PRINTDSN macro in a new SAS session.

```
libname perm '.';
options mstored sasmstore=perm;
%let dsn=perm.courses;
%let vars=days fee;
%printdsn
```

MACRO3

29

## Macro Storage

Use a %COPY statement to access stored macro source code.

> **%COPY** *macro-name* / **SOURCE**
> <***OUT=***'*external file*'>;

If the OUT= option is omitted, source code is written to the SAS log.

✎ The %COPY statement is new in SAS®9.

30

## Macro Storage

Example: Copy the source code from the stored PRINTDSN macro to the SAS log.

```
%copy printdsn / source;
```

Partial SAS Log

```
265  %copy printdsn / source;
%macro printdsn / store source;
   proc print data=&dsn;
      var &vars;
   run;
%mend printdsn;
```

31

## Exercises

### 1. Defining and Calling a Macro

Open the **printnum** program into the Editor window. The **printnum** program contains this PROC PRINT step:

```
proc print data=perm.all label noobs n;
   where course_number=3;
   var student_name student_company;
   title "Enrollment for Course 3";
run;
```

**a.** Change the hardcoded **3** in WHERE and TITLE statements to reference the macro variable NUM. Convert this program into a macro. Submit the macro definition to compile the macro.

**b.** Submit a %LET statement to assign the value 8 to the macro variable NUM. Call the macro defined in the previous step.

**c.** Activate the appropriate system options to display the source code received by the SAS compiler and to track macro variable resolution during macro execution. Call the macro again.

# Solutions to Exercises

## 1. Defining and Calling a Macro

a. %MACRO and %MEND statements surround the PROC PRINT step to create a macro program.

```
%macro printnum;
   proc print data=perm.all label noobs n;
      where course_number=&num;
      var student_name student_company;
      title "Enrollment for Course &num";
   run;
%mend printnum;
```

b. To execute the macro, use a percent sign followed by the name of the macro. The value of the macro variable NUM will be resolved during word scanning, after the text of the program is copied to the input stack.

```
%let num=8;
%printnum
```

Partial SAS Log

```
173  %macro printnum;
174    proc print data=perm.all label noobs n;
175       where course_number=&num;
176       var student_name student_company;
177       title "Enrollment for Course &num";
178    run;
179  %mend printnum;
180  %let num=8;
181  %printnum

NOTE: There were 20 observations read from the dataset PERM.ALL.
      WHERE course_number=8;
NOTE: PROCEDURE PRINT used:
      real time           11.18 seconds
      cpu time            0.12 seconds
```

Partial Output

```
                          Enrollment for Course 8
     Student Name                     Company

     Baker, Mr. Vincent               Snowing Petroleum
     Blayney, Ms. Vivian              Southern Gas Co.
     Boyd, Ms. Leah                   United Shoes Co.
     Chevarley, Ms. Arlene            Motor Communications
     Coley, Mr. John                  California Dept. of Insurance
     Crace, Mr. Ron                   Von Crump Seafood
     Garza, Ms. Cheryl                Admiral Research & Development Co.
     Hamilton, Mr. Paul               Imperial Steel
     Huels, Ms. Mary Frances          Basic Home Services
     Kendig, Ms. Linda                Crossbow of California
     Knight, Ms. Susan                K&P Products
     Koleff, Mr. Jim                  Emulate Research
     Leon, Mr. Quinton                Dept. of Defense
     Lochbihler Mr. Mark              K&P Products
     Nicholson, Ms. Elizabeth         Silver, Sachs & Co.
     Purvis, Mr. Michael              Roam Publishers
     Ramsey, Ms. Kathleen             Pacific Solid State Corp.
     Shipman, Ms. Jan                 Southern Edison Co.
     Sulzbach, Mr. Bill               Sailbest Ships
     Woods, Mr. Joseph                Federal Landmarks

                                      N = 20
```

**c.** To display the code received by the SAS compiler, including all resolved macro variable references, use the MPRINT system option. To track the resolution of macro variables, use the SYMBOLGEN system option.

```
options mprint symbolgen;
%printnum
```

Partial SAS Log

```
182  options mprint symbolgen;
183  %printnum
MPRINT(PRINTNUM):   proc print data=perm.all label noobs n;
SYMBOLGEN:  Macro variable NUM resolves to 8
MPRINT(PRINTNUM):   where course_number=8;
MPRINT(PRINTNUM):   var student_name student_company;
SYMBOLGEN:  Macro variable NUM resolves to 8
MPRINT(PRINTNUM):   title "Enrollment for Course 8";
MPRINT(PRINTNUM):   run;
NOTE: There were 20 observations read from the dataset PERM.ALL.
      WHERE course_number=8;
NOTE: PROCEDURE PRINT used:
      real time           11.64 seconds
      cpu time            0.14 seconds
```

# 3.2 Macro Parameters

## Objectives

- Define and call macros with parameters.
- Describe the difference between positional and keyword parameters.

34

## Introduction

Example: Note macro variable references within the PRINTDSN macro.

```
%macro printdsn;
   proc print data=&dsn;
      var &vars;
   run;
%mend;
```

35

## Introduction

Example: Call the macro twice, each time substituting different values of the macro variables DSN and VARS.

```
%let dsn=perm.courses;
%let vars=days fee;
%printdsn

%let dsn=perm.schedule;
%let vars=location teacher;
%printdsn
```

The user must submit three lines per macro call. How can this be simplified?

36

## Macro Parameters

Macros can be defined with a *parameter list* of macro variables referenced within the macro.

```
%macro printdsn(dsn,vars);
   proc print data=&dsn;
      var &vars;
   run;
%mend;
```

37

## Macro Parameters

Example: Call the PRINTDSN macro and provide parameter values.

```
%macro printdsn(dsn,vars);
   proc print data=&dsn;
      var &vars;
   run;
%mend;

%printdsn(perm.courses,days fee)
```

38

## Macro Parameters

General form of a macro definition with a parameter list:

**%MACRO** *macro-name*(*parameter-1, ... parameter-n*);
*macro text*
**%MEND**;

Parameter names are

- parenthesized
- comma delimited.

39

## Macro Parameters

General form of a macro call with parameters:

%*macro-name*(*value-1*, ... *value-n*)

Parameter values are

- parenthesized
- comma delimited.

Parameter values can be any text, null values, macro variable references, or macro calls.

40

To assign a null value to one or more positional parameters, use commas as placeholders for the omitted values.

## Local Symbol Tables

When a macro with a parameter list is called, the parameters are created in a separate symbol table called a *local table*.

The macro call

```
%printdsn(perm.courses, days fee)
```

initializes a local table:

Local Table

| | |
|---|---|
| DSN | perm.courses |
| VARS | days fee |

Global Table

| | |
|---|---|
| SYSDAY | Tuesday |
| SYSLAST | _NULL_ |
| CITY | Dallas |
| AMOUNT | 975 |

41

## Local Symbol Tables

A local symbol table is

- created when a macro with a parameter list is called
- deleted when the macro finishes execution.

Macro variables in the local table are available only during macro execution and therefore can be referenced only within the macro.

42

## Positional Parameters

*Positional parameters* use a one-to-one correspondence between

- parameter names supplied on the macro definition
- parameter values supplied on the macro call.

```
%macro printdsn(dsn,vars);
   proc print data=&dsn;
      var &vars;
   run;
%mend;

%printdsn(perm.courses,days fee)
```



## Positional Parameters

Example: Define and call a macro with positional parameters.

```
%macro attend(opts, start, stop);
   %let start=%upcase(&start);
   %let stop=%upcase(&stop);
   proc freq data=perm.all;
      where begin_date between
            "&start"d and "&stop"d;
      table location / &opts;
      title1 "Enrollment from &start to &stop";
   run;
%mend;

options mprint;
%attend(nocum,01jan2005,31dec2005)
%attend(,01oct2005,31dec2005)
```

PARAM1

## Macros with Positional Parameters

PARAM1

Define a macro that creates reports showing enrollment for individual training centers. Use positional parameters to specify a range of dates and options for the TABLES statement in the FREQ procedure.

```
%macro attend(opts, start, stop);
   %let start=%upcase(&start);
   %let stop=%upcase(&stop);
   proc freq data=perm.all;
      where begin_date between "&start"d and "&stop"d;
      table location / &opts;
      title1 "Enrollment from &start to &stop";
   run;
%mend;

options mprint;
%attend(nocum,01jan2005,31dec2005)
%attend(,01oct2005,31dec2005)
```

A null value is passed for OPTS in the second call.

Partial SAS Log for **%attend(nocum,01jan2005,31dec2005)**

```
MPRINT(ATTEND):   proc freq data=perm.all;
MPRINT(ATTEND):   where begin_date between "01JAN2005"d and
"31DEC2005"d;
MPRINT(ATTEND):   table location / nocum;
MPRINT(ATTEND):   title1 "Enrollment from 01JAN2005 to 31DEC2005";
MPRINT(ATTEND):   run;
NOTE: There were 299 observations read from the dataset PERM.ALL.
      WHERE ((begin_date>='01JAN2005'D and begin_date<='31DEC2005'D));
NOTE: PROCEDURE FREQ used:
      real time           28.40 seconds
      cpu time            0.36 seconds
```

Partial SAS Log for **%attend(,01oct2005,31dec2005)**

```
MPRINT(ATTEND):   proc freq data=perm.all;
MPRINT(ATTEND):   where begin_date between "01OCT2005"d and "31DEC2005"d;
MPRINT(ATTEND):   table location / ;
MPRINT(ATTEND):   title1 "Enrollment from 01OCT2005 to 31DEC2005";
MPRINT(ATTEND):   run;
NOTE: There were 81 observations read from the dataset PERM.ALL.
      WHERE ((begin_date>='01OCT2005'D and begin_date<='31DEC2005'D));
NOTE: PROCEDURE FREQ used:
      real time           0.10 seconds
      cpu time            0.10 seconds
```

## Keyword Parameters

A parameter list can include *keyword parameters*.

General form of a macro definition with keyword parameters:

**%MACRO** *macro-name*(*keyword*=*value*, ..., *keyword*=*value*);
*macro text*
**%MEND**;

Keyword parameters are assigned a default or null value after an equal (=) sign.

46

## Keyword Parameters

General form of a macro call with keyword parameters:

%*macro-name*(*keyword*=*value*, ..., *keyword*=*value*)

*keyword*=*value* combinations can be

- specified in any order
- omitted from the call without placeholders.

If omitted from the call, a keyword parameter receives its default value. To omit every keyword parameter from a macro call, specify *%macro-name*(). Specifying *%macro-name* without the parentheses may not immediately execute the macro.

47

## Keyword Parameters

Example: Assign default parameter values by defining the macro with keyword parameters.

```
%macro attend(opts=,start=01jan05,stop=31dec05);
   %let start=%upcase(&start);
   %let stop=%upcase(&stop);
   proc freq data=perm.all;
      where begin_date between
            "&start"d and "&stop"d;
      table location / &opts;
      title1 "Enrollment from &start to &stop";
   run;
%mend;
options mprint;
%attend(opts=nocum)
%attend(stop=30jun05,opts=nocum nopercent)
%attend()
```

48 PARAM2

## Macros with Keyword Parameters

PARAM2

Alter the previous macro by using keyword parameters. Issue various calls to the macro.

```
%macro attend(opts=,start=01jan05,stop=31dec05);
   %let start=%upcase(&start);
   %let stop=%upcase(&stop);
   proc freq data=perm.all;
      where begin_date between "&start"d and "&stop"d;
      table location / &opts;
      title1 "Enrollment from &start to &stop";
   run;
%mend;

options mprint;
%attend(opts=nocum)
%attend(stop=30jun05,opts=nocum nopercent)
%attend()
```

What are the values of the omitted parameters in each call?

Partial SAS Log for **%attend(opts=nocum)**

```
MPRINT(ATTEND):   proc freq data=perm.all;
MPRINT(ATTEND):   where begin_date between "01JAN05"d and "31DEC05"d;
MPRINT(ATTEND):   table location / nocum;
MPRINT(ATTEND):   title1 "Enrollment from 01JAN05 to 31DEC05";
NOTE: There were 299 observations read from the dataset PERM.ALL.
      WHERE ((begin_date>='01JAN2005'D and begin_date<='31DEC2005'D));
NOTE: PROCEDURE FREQ used:
      real time           0.12 seconds
      cpu time            0.10 seconds
```

Partial SAS Log for **%attend(stop=30jun05,opts=nocum nopercent)**

```
MPRINT(ATTEND):   proc freq data=perm.all;
MPRINT(ATTEND):   where begin_date between "01JAN05"d and "30JUN05"d;
MPRINT(ATTEND):   table location / nocum nopercent;
MPRINT(ATTEND):   title1 "Enrollment from 01JAN05 to 30JUN05";
MPRINT(ATTEND):   run;
NOTE: There were 137 observations read from the dataset PERM.ALL.
      WHERE ((begin_date>='01JAN2005'D and begin_date<='30JUN2005'D));
NOTE: PROCEDURE FREQ used:
      real time           0.11 seconds
      cpu time            0.09 seconds
```

Partial SAS Log for **%attend()**

```
MPRINT(ATTEND):   proc freq data=perm.all;
MPRINT(ATTEND):   where begin_date between "01JAN05"d and "31DEC05"d;
MPRINT(ATTEND):   table location / ;
MPRINT(ATTEND):   title1 "Enrollment from 01JAN05 to 31DEC05";
MPRINT(ATTEND):   run;
NOTE: There were 299 observations read from the dataset PERM.ALL.
      WHERE ((begin_date>='01JAN2005'D and begin_date<='31DEC2005'D));
NOTE: PROCEDURE FREQ used:
      real time           0.09 seconds
      cpu time            0.09 seconds
```

## Mixed Parameter Lists

You can use a combination of positional and keyword parameters. In a *mixed parameter list*, positional parameters must be listed before keyword parameters on both the macro definition and the macro call.

1st

50

## Mixed Parameter Lists

Example: Use a combination of positional and keyword parameters.

```
%macro attend(opts,start=01jan05,stop=31dec05);
   %let start=%upcase(&start);
   %let stop=%upcase(&stop);
   proc freq data=perm.all;
      where begin_date between
            "&start"d and "&stop"d;
      table location / &opts;
      title1 "Enrollment from &start to &stop";
   run;
%mend;
options mprint;
%attend(nocum)
%attend(stop=30jun05,start=01apr05)
%attend(nocum nopercent,stop=30jun05)
%attend()
```

PARAM3

51

# Macros with Mixed Parameter Lists

PARAM3

Alter the previous macro by using a mixed parameter list. Issue various calls to the macro.

```
82   %macro attend(opts,start=01jan05,stop=31dec05);
83      %let start=%upcase(&start);
84      %let stop=%upcase(&stop);
85      proc freq data=perm.all;
86         where begin_date between
87             "&start"d and "&stop"d;
88         table location / &opts;
89         title1 "Enrollment from &start to &stop";
90      run;
91   %mend;
92   options mprint;
93   %attend(nocum)
MPRINT(ATTEND):   proc freq data=perm.all;
MPRINT(ATTEND):   where begin_date between "01JAN05"d and "31DEC05"d;
MPRINT(ATTEND):   table location / nocum;
MPRINT(ATTEND):   title1 "Enrollment from 01JAN05 to 31DEC05";
MPRINT(ATTEND):   run;

NOTE: There were 299 observations read from the data set PERM.ALL.
      WHERE (begin_date>='01JAN2005'D and begin_date<='31DEC2005'D);

94   %attend(stop=30jun05,start=01apr05)
MPRINT(ATTEND):   proc freq data=perm.all;
MPRINT(ATTEND):   where begin_date between "01APR05"d and "30JUN05"d;
MPRINT(ATTEND):   table location / ;
MPRINT(ATTEND):   title1 "Enrollment from 01APR05 to 30JUN05";
MPRINT(ATTEND):   run;

NOTE: There were 65 observations read from the data set PERM.ALL.
      WHERE (begin_date>='01APR2005'D and begin_date<='30JUN2005'D);

95   %attend(nocum nopercent,stop=30jun05)
MPRINT(ATTEND):   proc freq data=perm.all;
MPRINT(ATTEND):   where begin_date between "01JAN05"d and "30JUN05"d;
MPRINT(ATTEND):   table location / nocum nopercent;
MPRINT(ATTEND):   title1 "Enrollment from 01JAN05 to 30JUN05";
MPRINT(ATTEND):   run;

NOTE: There were 137 observations read from the data set PERM.ALL.
      WHERE (begin_date>='01JAN2005'D and begin_date<='30JUN2005'D);
```

```
96   %attend()
MPRINT(ATTEND):   proc freq data=perm.all;
MPRINT(ATTEND):   where begin_date between "01JAN05"d and "31DEC05"d;
MPRINT(ATTEND):   table location / ;
MPRINT(ATTEND):   title1 "Enrollment from 01JAN05 to 31DEC05";
MPRINT(ATTEND):   run;

NOTE: There were 299 observations read from the data set PERM.ALL.
      WHERE (begin_date>='01JAN2005'D and begin_date<='31DEC2005'D);
```

## Developing Macro-Based Applications

If a macro-based application generates SAS code, use a four-step approach.

1. Write and debug the SAS program without any macro coding.
2. Generalize the program by replacing hardcoded constants with macro variable references and initialize the macro variables with %LET statements.
3. Create a macro definition by placing %MACRO and %MEND statements around your program. Convert %LET statements to macro parameters as appropriate.

Step 4 is presented later.

53

These steps permit rapid development and debugging because they isolate syntax and logic at the SAS code level from the syntax and logic at the macro level.

# Exercises

**2. Defining and Using Macro Parameters**

Open the **printnum** program into the Editor window.

```
proc print data=perm.all label noobs n;
   where course_number=3;
   var student_name student_company;
   title "Enrollment for Course 3";
run;
```

**a.** Change the hardcoded **3** in WHERE and TITLE statements to reference the macro variable NUM. Convert this program into a macro with a positional parameter. Select a name for the parameter based on the macro variable references in the program. Submit the macro definition to compile the macro.

**b.** Activate the appropriate system option to display the source code received by the SAS compiler. Call the macro defined in the previous step with a value of 8 for the parameter.

**c.** Call the macro again, but with a parameter value of 10.

**d.** Change the positional parameter to a keyword parameter with a default value of 1. Submit the revised macro definition to compile the macro.

**e.** Call the macro defined in the previous step with a value of 8 for the keyword parameter.

**f.** Call the macro again, but allow the macro to use its default parameter value.

# Solutions to Exercises

## 2. Defining and Using Macro Parameters

a. The macro parameter name should be NUM because the program contains the macro references **&num**. When you define positional parameters, enclose the names of the parameter in parentheses following the macro name.

```
%macro prtrost(num);
   proc print data=perm.all label noobs n;
      where course_number=&num;
      var student_name student_company;
      title "Enrollment for Course &num";
   run;
%mend prtrost;
```

b. To display the code received by the SAS compiler, including all resolved macro variable references, use the MPRINT system option. To execute the macro, use a percent sign followed by the name of the macro. To assign a value to a positional parameter, supply the desired value within parentheses following the macro name.

```
options mprint;
%prtrost(8)
```

Partial SAS Log

```
200  %prtrost(8)
MPRINT(PRTROST):   proc print data=perm.all label noobs n;
MPRINT(PRTROST):   where course_number=8;
MPRINT(PRTROST):   var student_name student_company;
MPRINT(PRTROST):   title "Enrollment for Course 8";
MPRINT(PRTROST):   run;
NOTE: There were 20 observations read from the dataset PERM.ALL.
      WHERE course_number=8;
NOTE: PROCEDURE PRINT used:
      real time           11.05 seconds
      cpu time            0.16 seconds
```

Partial Output

```
                         Enrollment for Course 8

    Student Name                 Company

    Baker, Mr. Vincent           Snowing Petroleum
    Blayney, Ms. Vivian          Southern Gas Co.
    Boyd, Ms. Leah               United Shoes Co.
    Chevarley, Ms. Arlene        Motor Communications
    Coley, Mr. John              California Dept. of Insurance
    Crace, Mr. Ron               Von Crump Seafood
    Garza, Ms. Cheryl            Admiral Research & Development Co.
    Hamilton, Mr. Paul           Imperial Steel
    Huels, Ms. Mary Frances      Basic Home Services
    Kendig, Ms. Linda            Crossbow of California
    Knight, Ms. Susan            K&P Products
    Koleff, Mr. Jim              Emulate Research
    Leon, Mr. Quinton            Dept. of Defense
    Lochbihler Mr. Mark          K&P Products
    Nicholson, Ms. Elizabeth     Silver, Sachs & Co.
    Purvis, Mr. Michael          Roam Publishers
    Ramsey, Ms. Kathleen         Pacific Solid State Corp.
    Shipman, Ms. Jan             Southern Edison Co.
    Sulzbach, Mr. Bill           Sailbest Ships
    Woods, Mr. Joseph            Federal Landmarks

                                 N = 20
```

**c.** The macro definition does not need to be resubmitted with each macro call. The macro call does not end with a semicolon.

```
%prtrost(10)
```

Partial SAS Log

```
MPRINT(PRTROST):   proc print data=perm.all label noobs n;
MPRINT(PRTROST):   where course_number=10;
MPRINT(PRTROST):   var student_name student_company;
MPRINT(PRTROST):   title "Enrollment for Course 10";
MPRINT(PRTROST):   run;
NOTE: There were 23 observations read from the dataset PERM.ALL.
      WHERE course_number=10;
NOTE: PROCEDURE PRINT used:
      real time           11.44 seconds
      cpu time            0.17 seconds
```

**d.** When you define keyword parameters, an equal sign (=) must follow the name of each parameter. A default value for each parameter can be specified following the equal sign.

```
%macro prtrost(num=1);
   proc print data=perm.all label noobs n;
      where course_number=&num;
      var student_name student_company;
      title "Enrollment for Course &num";
   run;
%mend prtrost;
```

**e.** To assign a value to a keyword parameter, specify the name of the parameter followed by an equal sign (=), followed by the desired value.

```
%prtrost(num=8)
```

Partial SAS Log

```
18    %prtrost(num=8)
MPRINT(PRTROST):   proc print data=perm.all label noobs n;
MPRINT(PRTROST):   where course_number=8;
MPRINT(PRTROST):   var student_name student_company;
MPRINT(PRTROST):   title "Enrollment for Course 8";
MPRINT(PRTROST):   run;
NOTE: There were 20 observations read from the dataset PERM.ALL.
      WHERE course_number=8;
NOTE: PROCEDURE PRINT used:
      real time           10.51 seconds
      cpu time            0.12 seconds
```

**f.** To request that all default parameter values be used, follow the macro call with an empty set of parentheses.

```
%prtrost()
```

Partial SAS Log

```
19    %prtrost()
MPRINT(PRTROST):   proc print data=perm.all label noobs n;
MPRINT(PRTROST):   where course_number=1;
MPRINT(PRTROST):   var student_name student_company;
MPRINT(PRTROST):   title "Enrollment for Course 1";
MPRINT(PRTROST):   run;
NOTE: There were 23 observations read from the dataset PERM.ALL.
      WHERE course_number=1;
NOTE: PROCEDURE PRINT used:
      real time           13.20 seconds
      cpu time            0.15 seconds
```

# Chapter 4 DATA Step and SQL Interfaces

# 4.1 Creating Macro Variables in the DATA Step

## Objectives

- Create macro variables during DATA step execution.
- Describe the difference between the SYMPUT routine and the %LET statement.

3

## The DATA Step Interface

Example: Automate production of the report below, with an appropriate footnote.

Paid Status for Course 3

| Obs | Student_Name | Student_Company | Paid |
|---|---|---|---|
| 1 | Bills, Ms. Paulette | Reston Railway | Y |
| 2 | Chevarley, Ms. Arlene | Motor Communications | N |
| 3 | Clough, Ms. Patti | Reston Railway | N |
| 4 | Crace, Mr. Ron | Von Crump Seafood | Y |
| 5 | Davis, Mr. Bruce | Semi;Conductor | Y |
| 6 | Elsins, Ms. Marisa F. | SSS Inc. | N |
| 7 | Gandy, Dr. David | Paralegal Assoc. | Y |
| 8 | Gash, Ms. Hedy | QA Information Systems Center | Y |
| 9 | Haubold, Ms. Ann | Reston Railway | Y |
| 10 | Hudock, Ms. Cathy | So. Cal. Medical Center | Y |
| 11 | Kimble, Mr. John | Alforone Chemical | N |
| 12 | Kochen, Mr. Dennis | Reston Railway | Y |
| 13 | Larocque, Mr. Bret | Physicians IPA | Y |
| 14 | Licht, Mr. Bryan | SII | Y |
| 15 | McKnight, Ms. Maureen E. | Federated Bank | Y |
| 16 | Scannell, Ms. Robin | Amberly Corp. | N |
| 17 | Seitz, Mr. Adam | Lomax Services | Y |
| 18 | Smith, Ms. Jan | Reston Railway | N |
| 19 | Sulzbach, Mr. Bill | Sailbest Ships | Y |
| 20 | Williams, Mr. Gene | Snowing Petroleum | Y |

Some Fees Due

4

Many applications require macro variables to have values based on data values, programming logic, or expressions.

# The DATA Step Interface

```
%let crsnum=3;
data revenue;
  set perm.all end=final;
  where course_number=&crsnum;
  total+1;
  if paid='Y' then paidup+1;
  if final then do;
    put total= paidup=;
    if paidup<total then do;
      %let foot=Some Fees Due;
    end;
    else do;
      %let foot=All Students Paid;
    end;
  end;
run;
proc print data=revenue;
   var student_name student_company paid;
   title "Paid Status for Course &crsnum";
   footnote "&foot";
run;
```

SYMPUT1

5

# The DATA Step Interface

Why is the footnote incorrect?

Paid Status for Course 3

| Obs | Student_Name | Student_Company | Paid |
|---|---|---|---|
| 1 | Bills, Ms. Paulette | Reston Railway | Y |
| 2 | Chevarley, Ms. Arlene | Motor Communications | N |
| 3 | Clough, Ms. Patti | Reston Railway | N |
| 4 | Crace, Mr. Ron | Von Crump Seafood | Y |
| 5 | Davis, Mr. Bruce | Semi;Conductor | Y |
| 6 | Elsins, Ms. Marisa F. | SSS Inc. | N |
| 7 | Gandy, Dr. David | Paralegal Assoc. | Y |
| 8 | Gash, Ms. Hedy | QA Information Systems Center | Y |
| 9 | Haubold, Ms. Ann | Reston Railway | Y |
| 10 | Hudock, Ms. Cathy | So. Cal. Medical Center | Y |
| 11 | Kimble, Mr. John | Alforone Chemical | N |
| 12 | Kochen, Mr. Dennis | Reston Railway | Y |
| 13 | Larocque, Mr. Bret | Physicians IPA | Y |
| 14 | Licht, Mr. Bryan | SII | Y |
| 15 | McKnight, Ms. Maureen E. | Federated Bank | Y |
| 16 | Scannell, Ms. Robin | Amberly Corp. | N |
| 17 | Seitz, Mr. Adam | Lomax Services | Y |
| 18 | Smith, Ms. Jan | Reston Railway | N |
| 19 | Sulzbach, Mr. Bill | Sailbest Ships | Y |
| 20 | Williams, Mr. Gene | Snowing Petroleum | Y |

All Students Paid

6

## The DATA Step Interface

Word scanning begins. Macro trigger encountered.

```
%let crsnum=3;
data revenue;
  set perm.all end=final;
  where course_number=&crsnum;
  total+1;
  if paid='Y' then paidup+1;
  if final then do;
    put total= paidup=;
    if paidup<total then do;
      %let foot=Some Fees Due;
    end;
    else do;
      %let foot=All Students Paid;
    end;
  end;
run;
```

Symbol Table

crsnum 3

7

## The DATA Step Interface

Compiling begins. Macro variable reference resolved.

```
data revenue;
  set perm.all end=final;
  where course_number=3;
  total+1;
  if paid='Y' then paidup+1;
  if final then do;
    put total= paidup=;
    if paidup<total then do;
      %let foot=Some Fees Due;
    end;
    else do;
      %let foot=All Students Paid;
    end;
  end;
run;
```

Symbol Table

crsnum 3

8

## The DATA Step Interface

Macro trigger passed to macro processor.

```
data revenue;
  set perm.all end=final;
  where course_number=3;
  total+1;
  if paid='Y' then paidup+1;
  if final then do;
    put total= paidup=;
    if paidup<total then do;
      %let foot=Some Fees Due;
    end;
    else do;
      %let foot=All Students Paid;
    end;
  end;
run;
```

Symbol Table

| | |
|---|---|
| crsnum | 3 |
| foot | Some Fees Due |

9

## The DATA Step Interface

Macro trigger overwrites previous value.

```
data revenue;
  set perm.all end=final;
  where course_number=3;
  total+1;
  if paid='Y' then paidup+1;
  if final then do;
    put total= paidup=;
    if paidup<total then do;

    end;
    else do;
      %let foot=All Students Paid;
    end;
  end;
run;
```

Symbol Table

| | |
|---|---|
| crsnum | 3 |
| foot | All Students Paid |

10

%LET statements execute at word scanning time, while non-macro SAS statements are sent to the compiler.

## The DATA Step Interface

Compile phase complete. Ready for execution.

```
data revenue;
  set perm.all end=final;
  where course_number=3;
  total+1;
  if paid='Y' then paidup+1;
  if final then do;
    put total= paidup=;
    if paidup<total then do;

    end;
    else do;

    end;
  end;
run;
```

Symbol Table

| | |
|---|---|
| crsnum | 3 |
| foot | All Students Paid |

Nothing in this DATA step affects the value of FOOT.

It remains `All Students Paid.`

11

## The SYMPUT Routine

The SYMPUT routine

- is an **executable** DATA step statement
- assigns to a macro variable any value available to the DATA step during execution time
- can create macro variables with
  - static values
  - dynamic (data dependent) values
  - dynamic (data dependent) names.

**DATA step variables**
**DATA step expressions**
**character literals**

SYMPUT →

Symbol Table

12

## The SYMPUT Routine

The SYMPUT routine creates a macro variable and assigns it a value.

General form of the SYMPUT routine:

**CALL SYMPUT**(*macro-variable, text*);

*macro-variable* is assigned the character value of *text*.

If *macro-variable* already exists, its value is replaced.

If either argument represents a literal value, it must be quoted.

13

## The SYMPUT Routine

Example: The SYMPUT routine can be controlled with DATA step execution time logic.

```
%let crsnum=3;
data revenue;
   set perm.all end=final;
   where course_number=&crsnum;
   total+1;
   if paid='Y' then paidup+1;
   if final then do;
      put total= paidup=;
      if paidup<total then do;
         call symput('foot','Some Fees Due');
      end;
      else do;
         call symput('foot','All Students Paid');
      end;
   end;
run;
```

No macro triggers within DO groups

Fixed Macro Variable Name

Fixed Macro Variable Value

SYMPUT2

14

## The SYMPUT Routine

Note corrected footnote.

```
                          Paid Status for Course 3

Obs   Student_Name               Student_Company                    Paid

  1   Bills, Ms. Paulette        Reston Railway                       Y
  2   Chevarley, Ms. Arlene      Motor Communications                 N
  3   Clough, Ms. Patti          Reston Railway                       N
  4   Crace, Mr. Ron             Von Crump Seafood                    Y
  5   Davis, Mr. Bruce           Semi;Conductor                       Y
  6   Elsins, Ms. Marisa F.      SSS Inc.                             N
  7   Gandy, Dr. David           Paralegal Assoc.                     Y
  8   Gash, Ms. Hedy             QA Information Systems Center        Y
  9   Haubold, Ms. Ann           Reston Railway                       Y
 10   Hudock, Ms. Cathy          So. Cal. Medical Center              Y
 11   Kimble, Mr. John           Alforone Chemical                    N
 12   Kochen, Mr. Dennis         Reston Railway                       Y
 13   Larocque, Mr. Bret         Physicians IPA                       Y
 14   Licht, Mr. Bryan           SII                                  Y
 15   McKnight, Ms. Maureen E.   Federated Bank                       Y
 16   Scannell, Ms. Robin        Amberly Corp.                        N
 17   Seitz, Mr. Adam            Lomax Services                       Y
 18   Smith, Ms. Jan             Reston Railway                       N
 19   Sulzbach, Mr. Bill         Sailbest Ships                       Y
 20   Williams, Mr. Gene         Snowing Petroleum                    Y

                               Some Fees Due
```

15

## The SYMPUT Routine

SYMPUT2

Conditionally assign a text value to a macro variable FOOT based on DATA step values. Reference this macro variable later in the program.

```
options symbolgen;
%let crsnum=3;
data revenue;
   set perm.all end=final;
   where course_number=&crsnum;
   total+1;
   if paid='Y' then paidup+1;
   if final then do;
      if paidup<total then do;
         call symput('foot','Some Fees Due');
      end;
      else do;
         call symput('foot','All Students Paid');
      end;
   end;
run;

proc print data=revenue;
   var student_name student_company paid;
   title "Paid Status for Course &crsnum";
   footnote "&foot";
run;
```

The value assigned to the macro variable FOOT is set dynamically to either `Some Fees Due` or `All Students Paid`, based on DATA step execution time logic.

SAS Output

```
                      Paid Status for Course 3

Obs   Student_Name             Student_Company                  Paid

  1   Bills, Ms. Paulette      Reston Railway                    Y
  2   Chevarley, Ms. Arlene    Motor Communications              N
  3   Clough, Ms. Patti        Reston Railway                    N
  4   Crace, Mr. Ron           Von Crump Seafood                 Y
  5   Davis, Mr. Bruce         Semi;Conductor                    Y
  6   Elsins, Ms. Marisa F.    SSS Inc.                          N
  7   Gandy, Dr. David         Paralegal Assoc.                  Y
  8   Gash, Ms. Hedy           QA Information Systems Center     Y
  9   Haubold, Ms. Ann         Reston Railway                    Y
 10   Hudock, Ms. Cathy        So. Cal. Medical Center           Y
 11   Kimble, Mr. John         Alforone Chemical                 N
 12   Kochen, Mr. Dennis       Reston Railway                    Y
 13   Larocque, Mr. Bret       Physicians IPA                    Y
 14   Licht, Mr. Bryan         SII                               Y
 15   McKnight, Ms. Maureen E. Federated Bank                    Y
 16   Scannell, Ms. Robin      Amberly Corp.                     N
 17   Seitz, Mr. Adam          Lomax Services                    Y
 18   Smith, Ms. Jan           Reston Railway                    N
 19   Sulzbach, Mr. Bill       Sailbest Ships                    Y
 20   Williams, Mr. Gene       Snowing Petroleum                 Y

                            Some Fees Due
```

## The SYMPUT Routine

Example: Enhance the title and footnote as below.

Fee Status for Local Area Networks (#3)

| Student_Name | Student_Company | Paid |
|---|---|---|
| Bills, Ms. Paulette | Reston Railway | Y |
| Chevarley, Ms. Arlene | Motor Communications | N |
| Clough, Ms. Patti | Reston Railway | N |
| Crace, Mr. Ron | Von Crump Seafood | Y |
| Davis, Mr. Bruce | Semi;Conductor | Y |
| Elsins, Ms. Marisa F. | SSS Inc. | N |
| Gandy, Dr. David | Paralegal Assoc. | Y |
| Gash, Ms. Hedy | QA Information Systems Center | Y |
| Haubold, Ms. Ann | Reston Railway | Y |
| Hudock, Ms. Cathy | So. Cal. Medical Center | Y |
| Kimble, Mr. John | Alforone Chemical | N |
| Kochen, Mr. Dennis | Reston Railway | Y |
| Larocque, Mr. Bret | Physicians IPA | Y |
| Licht, Mr. Bryan | SII | Y |
| McKnight, Ms. Maureen E. | Federated Bank | Y |
| Scannell, Ms. Robin | Amberly Corp. | N |
| Seitz, Mr. Adam | Lomax Services | Y |
| Smith, Ms. Jan | Reston Railway | N |
| Sulzbach, Mr. Bill | Sailbest Ships | Y |
| Williams, Mr. Gene | Snowing Petroleum | Y |

Note: 14 out of 20 paid

17

## The SYMPUT Routine

You can copy the current value of a DATA step variable into a macro variable by using the name of a DATA step variable as the second argument to the SYMPUT routine.

**CALL SYMPUT**('*macro-variable*', *DATA-step-variable*);

- A maximum of 32,767 characters can be assigned to the receiving macro variable.
- Any leading or trailing blanks within the DATA step variable's value **are stored** in the macro variable.
- Values of numeric variables are converted automatically to character using the BEST12. format.

18

## The SYMPUT Routine

```
%let crsnum=3;
data revenue;
   set perm.all end=final;
   where course_number=&crsnum;
   total+1;
   if paid='Y' then paidup+1;
   if final then do;
      call symput('numpaid',paidup); copying # data value.
      call symput('numstu',total);
      call symput('crsname',course_title);
   end;
run;
proc print data=revenue noobs;
   var student_name student_company paid;
   title "Fee Status for &crsname (#&crsnum)";
   footnote "Note: &numpaid out of &numstu paid";
run;
```

SYMPUT3

19

## The SYMPUT Routine

SYMPUT3

Create a report for any of the courses held showing the students' name, their company, and paid status. The title should contain course title and course number. Include the following footnote to summarize how many students have paid their fees: "Note: *xx* out of *yy* paid" where *xx* represents paid students and *yy* represents total students in the course.

```
%let crsnum=3;
data revenue;
   set perm.all end=final;
   where course_number=&crsnum;
   total+1;
   if paid='Y' then paidup+1;
   if final then do;
      call symput('numpaid',paidup);
      call symput('numstu',total);
      call symput('crsname',course_title);
   end;
run;
proc print data=revenue noobs;
   var student_name student_company paid;
   title "Fee Status for &crsname (#&crsnum)";
   footnote "Note: &numpaid out of &numstu paid";
run;
```

Program Output

```
             Fee Status for Local Area Networks          (#3)

    Student_Name                Student_Company                 Paid

    Bills, Ms. Paulette         Reston Railway                    Y
    Chevarley, Ms. Arlene       Motor Communications              N
    Clough, Ms. Patti           Reston Railway                    N
    Crace, Mr. Ron              Von Crump Seafood                 Y
    Davis, Mr. Bruce            Semi;Conductor                    Y
    Elsins, Ms. Marisa F.       SSS Inc.                          N
    Gandy, Dr. David            Paralegal Assoc.                  Y
    Gash, Ms. Hedy              QA Information Systems Center     Y
    Haubold, Ms. Ann            Reston Railway                    Y
    Hudock, Ms. Cathy           So. Cal. Medical Center           Y
    Kimble, Mr. John            Alforone Chemical                 N
    Kochen, Mr. Dennis          Reston Railway                    Y
    Larocque, Mr. Bret          Physicians IPA                    Y
    Licht, Mr. Bryan            SII                               Y
    McKnight, Ms. Maureen E.    Federated Bank                    Y
    Scannell, Ms. Robin         Amberly Corp.                     N
    Seitz, Mr. Adam             Lomax Services                    Y
    Smith, Ms. Jan              Reston Railway                    N
    Sulzbach, Mr. Bill          Sailbest Ships                    Y
    Williams, Mr. Gene          Snowing Petroleum                 Y

             Note:       14 out of          20 paid
```

Note the extra blanks between the course title and course number, as well as extra blanks before `14` and `20` in the footnote.

## The SYMPUT Routine

You can use DATA step functions and expressions in the SYMPUT routine's second argument to

- left-align character strings created by numeric-to-character conversion
- remove trailing blanks
- format data values
- perform arithmetic operations on numeric data values.

**CALL SYMPUT**('*macro-variable*',*expression*);

21

## The SYMPUT Routine

```
%let crsnum=3;
data revenue;
   set perm.all end=final;
   where course_number=&crsnum;
   total+1;
   if paid='Y' then paidup+1;
   if final then do;
      call symput('numpaid',trim(left(paidup)));
      call symput('numstu',trim(left(total)));
      call symput('crsname',trim(course_title));
   end;
run;
proc print data=revenue noobs;
   var student_name student_company paid;
   title "Fee Status for &crsname (#&crsnum)";
   footnote "Note: &numpaid out of &numstu paid";
run;
```

SYMPUT4

22

## The SYMPUT Routine

SYMPUT4

Remove leading blanks from the macro variables NUMSTU and NUMPAID. Remove trailing blanks from CRSNAME.

```
%let crsnum=3;
data revenue;
   set perm.all end=final;
   where course_number=&crsnum;
   total+1;
   if paid='Y' then paidup+1;
   if final then do;
      call symput('numpaid',trim(left(paidup)));
      call symput('numstu',trim(left(total)));
      call symput('crsname',trim(course_title));
   end;
run;

proc print data=revenue noobs;
   var student_name student_company paid;
   title "Fee Status for &crsname (#&crsnum)";
   footnote "Note: &numpaid out of &numstu paid";
run;
```

The LEFT function left-justifies the value. The TRIM function removes trailing blanks. Both functions expect character arguments. Numeric arguments cause automatic numeric-to-character conversion, with notes written to the SAS log.

12 digits => we will have leading blank

## Program Output

```
                   Fee Status for Local Area Networks (#3)

NAME                        COMPANY                          PAID

Bills, Ms. Paulette         Reston Railway                    Y
Chevarley, Ms. Arlene       Motor Communications              N
Clough, Ms. Patti           Reston Railway                    N
Crace, Mr. Ron              Von Crump Seafood                 Y
Davis, Mr. Bruce            Semi;Conductor                    Y
Elsins, Ms. Marisa F.       SSS Inc.                          N
Gandy, Dr. David            Paralegal Assoc.                  Y
Gash, Ms. Hedy              QA Information Systems Center     Y
Haubold, Ms. Ann            Reston Railway                    Y
Hudock, Ms. Cathy           So. Cal. Medical Center           Y
Kimble, Mr. John            Alforone Chemical                 N
Kochen, Mr. Dennis          Reston Railway                    Y
Larocque, Mr. Bret          Physicians IPA                    Y
Licht, Mr. Bryan            SII                               Y
McKnight, Ms. Maureen E.    Federated Bank                    Y
Scannell, Ms. Robin         Amberly Corp.                     N
Seitz, Mr. Adam             Lomax Services                    Y
Smith, Ms. Jan              Reston Railway                    N
Sulzbach, Mr. Bill          Sailbest Ships                    Y
Williams, Mr. Gene          Snowing Petroleum                 Y

                          Note: 14 out of 20 paid
```

## The SYMPUTX Routine

The SYMPUTX routine automatically removes leading and trailing blanks from both arguments.

General form of the SYMPUTX routine:

**CALL SYMPUTX**(*macro-variable*, *expression*);

The SYMPUTX routine is new in SAS®9.

24

## The SYMPUTX Routine

```
%let crsnum=3;
data revenue;
   set perm.all end=final;
   where course_number=&crsnum;
   total+1;
   if paid='Y' then paidup+1;
   if final then do;
      call symputx('numpaid',paidup);
      call symputx('numstu',total);
      call symputx('crsname',course_title);
   end;
run;
proc print data=revenue noobs;
   var student_name student_company paid;
   title "Fee Status for &crsname (#&crsnum)";
   footnote "Note: &numpaid out of &numstu paid";
run;
```

25 SYMPUT5

# The SYMPUTX Routine

Example: Further enhance the report as below.

```
          Fee Status for Local Area Networks (#3) Held 01/11/2005

Obs    Student_Name               Student_Company                  Paid

  1    Bills, Ms. Paulette        Reston Railway                    Y
  2    Chevarley, Ms. Arlene      Motor Communications              N
  3    Clough, Ms. Patti          Reston Railway                    N
  4    Crace, Mr. Ron             Von Crump Seafood                 Y
  5    Davis, Mr. Bruce           Semi;Conductor                    Y
  6    Elsins, Ms. Marisa F.      SSS Inc.                          N
  7    Gandy, Dr. David           Paralegal Assoc.                  Y
  8    Gash, Ms. Hedy             QA Information Systems Center     Y
  9    Haubold, Ms. Ann           Reston Railway                    Y
 10    Hudock, Ms. Cathy          So. Cal. Medical Center           Y
 11    Kimble, Mr. John           Alforone Chemical                 N
 12    Kochen, Mr. Dennis         Reston Railway                    Y
 13    Larocque, Mr. Bret         Physicians IPA                    Y
 14    Licht, Mr. Bryan           SII                               Y
 15    McKnight, Ms. Maureen E.   Federated Bank                    Y
 16    Scannell, Ms. Robin        Amberly Corp.                     N
 17    Seitz, Mr. Adam            Lomax Services                    Y
 18    Smith, Ms. Jan             Reston Railway                    N
 19    Sulzbach, Mr. Bill         Sailbest Ships                    Y
 20    Williams, Mr. Gene         Snowing Petroleum                 Y

                    Note: $3,900 in Unpaid Fees
```

26

# The SYMPUTX Routine

```
%let crsnum=3;
data revenue;
   set perm.all end=final;
   where course_number=&crsnum;
   total+1;
   if paid='Y' then paidup+1;
   if final then do;
      call symputx('crsname',course_title);
      call symputx('date',put(begin_date,mmddyy10.));
      call symputx('due',put(fee*(total-paidup),dollar8.));
   end;
run;
proc print data=revenue;
   var student_name student_company paid;
   title "Fee Status for &crsname (#&crsnum) Held &date";
   footnote "Note: &due in Unpaid Fees";
run;
```

SYMPUT6

27

## The SYMPUTX Routine

SYMPUT6

Format the value of the numeric variable **begin_date** with the MMDDYY. format and assign it to the macro variable DATE. Format the result of an expression involving **FEE**, **TOTAL**, and **PAIDUP** as a dollar amount and assign it to the macro variable DUE.

```
%let crsnum=3;
data revenue;
   set perm.all end=final;
   where course_number=&crsnum;
   total+1;
   if paid='Y' then paidup+1;
   if final then do;
      call symputx('crsname',course_title);
      call symputx('date',put(begin_date,mmddyy10.));
      call symputx('due',put(fee*(total-paidup),dollar8.));
   end;
run;
proc print data=revenue;
   var student_name student_company paid;
   title "Fee Status for &crsname (#&crsnum) Held &date";
   footnote "Note: &due in Unpaid Fees";
run;
```

The PUT function returns the character string formed by writing a value with a specified format.

You can use the PUT function to

- format the result of a numeric expression
- perform explicit numeric-to-character conversion.

General form of the PUT function

| **PUT**(*source*, *format*) |
|---|

*source* is a constant, variable, or expression (numeric or character)

*format* is any SAS or user-defined format.

*format* determines

the width of the resulting string

whether the string is right- or left-aligned.

## Program Output

```
     Fee Status for Local Area Networks (#3) Held 01/11/2005

Obs    Student_Name                Student_Company                  Paid

  1    Bills, Ms. Paulette         Reston Railway                    Y
  2    Chevarley, Ms. Arlene       Motor Communications              N
  3    Clough, Ms. Patti           Reston Railway                    N
  4    Crace, Mr. Ron              Von Crump Seafood                 Y
  5    Davis, Mr. Bruce            Semi;Conductor                    Y
  6    Elsins, Ms. Marisa F.       SSS Inc.                          N
  7    Gandy, Dr. David            Paralegal Assoc.                  Y
  8    Gash, Ms. Hedy              QA Information Systems Center     Y
  9    Haubold, Ms. Ann            Reston Railway                    Y
 10    Hudock, Ms. Cathy           So. Cal. Medical Center           Y
 11    Kimble, Mr. John            Alforone Chemical                 N
 12    Kochen, Mr. Dennis          Reston Railway                    Y
 13    Larocque, Mr. Bret          Physicians IPA                    Y
 14    Licht, Mr. Bryan            SII                               Y
 15    McKnight, Ms. Maureen E.    Federated Bank                    Y
 16    Scannell, Ms. Robin         Amberly Corp.                     N
 17    Seitz, Mr. Adam             Lomax Services                    Y
 18    Smith, Ms. Jan              Reston Railway                    N
 19    Sulzbach, Mr. Bill          Sailbest Ships                    Y
 20    Williams, Mr. Gene          Snowing Petroleum                 Y


                      Note: $3,900 in Unpaid Fees
```

## Passing Values Between Steps

Example: Based on user-selected time periods, dynamically compute statistics for automatic inclusion within titles, footnotes, and a graphic reference line.

Report from 01Jan2005 to 31Dec2005

Students this period: 299

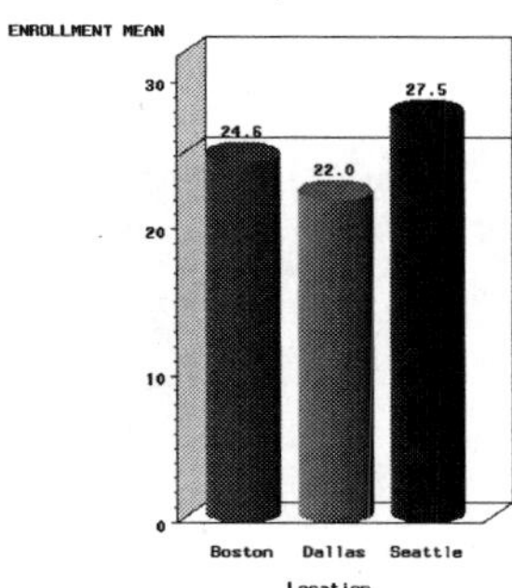


Enrollment average: 24.9

29

## Passing Values Between Steps

```
%let start=01Jan2005;
%let stop=31Dec2005;
proc freq data = perm.all;
  where begin_date between "&start"d and "&stop"d;
  table course_code*location / noprint
         out=stats (rename=(count=ENROLLMENT));
run;
data _null_;
  set stats end=last;
  classes+1;
  students+enrollment;
  if last;
  call symputx('students',students);
  call symputx('average',put(students/classes,4.1));
run;
options nolabel;
proc gchart data=stats;
  vbar3d location / patternid=midpoint cframe=w shape=c
          sumvar=enrollment type=mean mean ref=&average;
  title1 "Report from &start to &stop";
  title2 h=2 f=swiss "Students this period: " c=b "&students";
  footnote1 h=2 f=swiss "Enrollment average: " c=b "&average";
run;
```

30 SYMPUT7

## Passing Values Between Steps

SYMPUT7

Generate a horizontal bar chart for a specified period, with dynamically assigned title, footnote, and reference line position.

```
%let start=01Jan2005;
%let stop=31Dec2005;
proc freq data = perm.all;
   where begin_date between "&start"d and "&stop"d;
   table course_code*location / noprint
         out=stats (rename=(count=ENROLLMENT));
run;
```

Listing of STATS data set

| Obs | Course_ Code | Location | ENROLLMENT | PERCENT |
|---|---|---|---|---|
| 1 | C001 | Boston | 28 | 9.3645 |
| 2 | C001 | Dallas | 18 | 6.0201 |
| 3 | C002 | Boston | 20 | 6.6890 |
| 4 | C002 | Seattle | 33 | 11.0368 |
| 5 | C003 | Boston | 20 | 6.6890 |
| 6 | C003 | Seattle | 30 | 10.0334 |
| 7 | C004 | Dallas | 23 | 7.6923 |
| 8 | C004 | Seattle | 27 | 9.0301 |
| 9 | C005 | Boston | 28 | 9.3645 |
| 10 | C005 | Dallas | 25 | 8.3612 |
| 11 | C006 | Boston | 27 | 9.0301 |
| 12 | C006 | Seattle | 20 | 6.6890 |

```
data _null_;
   set stats end=last;
   classes+1;
   students+enrollment;
   if last;
   call symput('students',trim(left(students)));
   call symput('average',put(students/classes,4.1));
run;
%put _user_;
```

```
42   %put _user_;
GLOBAL STUDENTS 299
GLOBAL START 01Jan2005
GLOBAL STOP 31Dec2005
GLOBAL AVERAGE 24.9
```

```
options nolabel;
proc gchart data=stats;
   vbar3d location / patternid=midpoint cframe=w shape=c
                     sumvar=enrollment type=mean mean ref=&average;
   title1 "Report from &start to &stop";
   title2 h=2 f=swiss "Students this period: " c=b "&students";
   footnote1 h=2 f=swiss "Enrollment average: " c=b "&average";
run;
quit;
```

Output from PROC GCHART

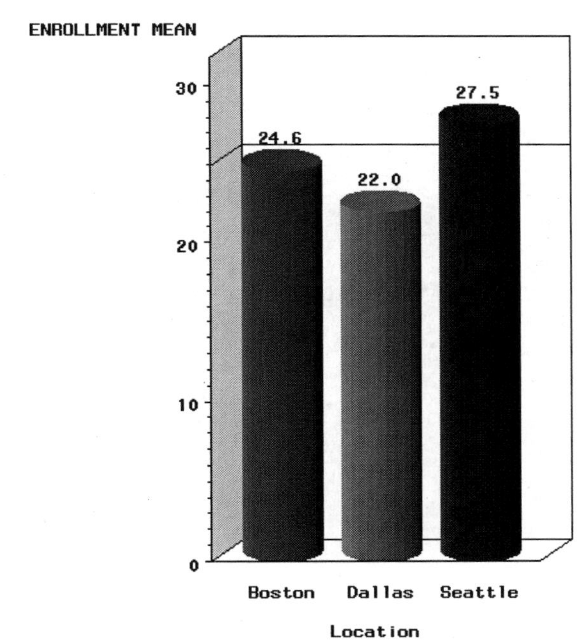


Enrollment average: 24.9

## Exercises

**1. Creating Macro Variables with the SYMPUT Routine**

**a.** Reset the system option DATE|NODATE to NODATE using the OPTIONS statement:

```
options nodate;
```

You may want to activate the SYMBOLGEN option also.

**b.** Write a DATA step that creates a macro variable named DATE. This macro variable's value should be today's date in the MMDDYY10. format.

The TODAY function returns today's date as a SAS date value.

**c.** Insert the value of the macro variable DATE into a TITLE statement:

```
title "Courses Offered as of &date";
```

**d.** Verify that the text of the title resolved correctly by printing the **`perm.courses`** data set or by opening the TITLES window.

**e.** Modify the DATA step so that the macro variable DATE has a value that reflects the WORDDATE20. format (*month dd, year*).

Verify the text of the title again. Make sure there are no extra blanks in the title.

## Solutions to Exercises

**1. Creating Macro Variables with the SYMPUT Routine**

**a.** Reset the system option DATE|NODATE to NODATE using the OPTIONS statement:

```
options nodate;
```

You may want to activate the SYMBOLGEN option also.

**b.** The PUT function converts the numeric SAS date value returned by the TODAY function into a character string representing today's date in *mm/dd/yyyy* form.

```
data _null_;
   call symput('date',put(today(),mmddyy10.));
run;
```

**c.** Insert the value of the macro variable DATE into a TITLE statement:

```
title "Courses Offered as of &date";
```

**d.** This PROC PRINT step should display the desired title:

```
proc print data=perm.courses;
run;
```

```
                  Courses offered as of 07/19/2004


               Course_
         Obs    Code       Course_Title                  Days       Fee

          1     C001       Basic Telecommunications        3        $795
          2     C002       Structured Query Language       4       $1150
          3     C003       Local Area Networks             3        $650
          4     C004       Database Design                 2        $375
          5     C005       Artificial Intelligence         2        $400
          6     C006       Computer Aided Design           5       $1600
```

**e.** The WORDDATE20. format typically generates leading blanks. Use the TRIM and LEFT functions to remove them.

```
options nodate symbolgen;
data _null_;
   call symput('date',trim(left(put(today(),
               worddate20.))));
run;

title "Courses offered as of &date";

proc print data=perm.courses;
run;
```

```
                  Courses offered as of July 19, 2004

             Course_
     Obs      Code       Course_Title                  Days      Fee

      1       C001       Basic Telecommunications        3       $795
      2       C002       Structured Query Language       4      $1150
      3       C003       Local Area Networks             3       $650
      4       C004       Database Design                 2       $375
      5       C005       Artificial Intelligence         2       $400
      6       C006       Computer Aided Design           5      $1600
```

# 4.2 Indirect References to Macro Variables

## Objectives

- Reference macro variables indirectly.
- Create a series of macro variables using the SYMPUT routine.

macro don't want result immediately or result delayed var.

34

## Table Lookup Application

Example: Use the **`perm.register`** data set to create a roster for a given course. The report title should display the instructor for the course.

```
            Roster for Course 3
        Taught by Forest, Mr. Peter

          Student_Name          Paid

        Scannell, Ms. Robin      N
        Seitz, Mr. Adam          Y
        Smith, Ms. Jan           N
        Sulzbach, Mr. Bill       Y
        Williams, Mr. Gene       Y
```

35

## Table Lookup Application

Step 1: Hardcode the entire program, including the course number and instructor's name.

```
proc print data=perm.register noobs;
   where course_number=3;
   var student_name paid;
   title1 "Roster for Course 3";
   title2 "Taught by Forest, Mr. Peter";
run;
```

teacher.

36

## Table Lookup Application

Step 2: Use a macro variable to control the subset and display the course number in the report title.

```
%let crs=3;
proc print data=perm.register noobs;
   where course_number=&crs;
   var student_name paid;
   title1 "Roster for Course &crs";
run;
```

How can we add the instructor's name in TITLE2 without hardcoding it?

37

## Table Lookup Application

The **perm.schedule** data set contains **Course_Number** and **Teacher** variables.

Partial Listing of PERM.SCHEDULE Data Set

| Obs | Course_ Number | Course_ Code | Location | Begin_ Date | Teacher |
|---|---|---|---|---|---|
| 1 | 1 | C001 | Seattle | 26OCT2004 | Hallis, Dr. George |
| 2 | 2 | C002 | Dallas | 07DEC2004 | Wickam, Dr. Alice |
| 3 | 3 | C003 | Boston | 11JAN2005 | Forest, Mr. Peter |
| 4 | 4 | C004 | Seattle | 25JAN2005 | Tally, Ms. Julia |
| 5 | 5 | C005 | Dallas | 01MAR2005 | Hallis, Dr. George |
| 6 | 6 | C006 | Boston | 05APR2005 | Berthan, Ms. Judy |
| 7 | 7 | C001 | Dallas | 24MAY2005 | Hallis, Dr. George |
| 8 | 8 | C002 | Boston | 14JUN2005 | Wickam, Dr. Alice |
| 9 | 9 | C003 | Seattle | 19JUL2005 | Forest, Mr. Peter |
| 10 | 10 | C004 | Dallas | 16AUG2005 | Tally, Ms. Julia |

38

## Table Lookup Application

Step 3: Add a DATA step to create a macro variable with the instructor's name from **perm.schedule** and resolve the name in TITLE2.

```
%let crs=3;
data _null_;
   set perm.schedule;
   where course_number=&crs;
   call symput('teacher',trim(teacher));
run;
proc print data=perm.register noobs;
   where course_number=&crs;
   var student_name paid;
   title1 "Roster for Course &crs";
   title2 "Taught by &teacher";
run;
```

39

## Table Lookup Application

Each time you select a course number to generate a different report, you must re-run the DATA step. This is inefficient.

```
%let crs=4;  ← Change
data _null_;
   set perm.schedule;
   where course_number=&crs;
   call symput('teacher',trim(teacher));
run;
proc print data=perm.register noobs;
   where course_number=&crs;
   var student_name paid;
   title1 "Roster for Course &crs";
   title2 "Taught by &teacher";
run;
```

INDIRECT1

40

## Creating a Series of Macro Variables

Solution: Execute the DATA step one time only, creating a numbered series of macro variables to store instructor names. Derive unique macro variable names by appending the **Course_Number** variable, unique on every observation (1-18), to the prefix (root) TEACH.

**Symbol Table**

| Variable | Value |
|---|---|
| TEACH1 | Hallis, Dr. George |
| TEACH2 | Wickam, Dr. Alice |
| TEACH3 | Forest, Mr. Peter |
| ... | ... |

41

## Creating a Series of Macro Variables

To create a series of macro variables, use the SYMPUT or SYMPUTX routine with a DATA step variable or expression in *argument1*.

**CALL SYMPUT**(*expression1*,*expression2*);

**CALL SYMPUTX**(*expression1*,*expression2*);

*expression1* evaluates to a character value that is a valid macro variable name, unique to each execution of the routine.

*expression2* value to assign to each macro variable.

42

## Creating a Series of Macro Variables

Step 4: Create a series of macro variables containing the name of the instructor assigned to a specific course.

```
data _null_;
   set perm.schedule;
   call symput('teach'||left(course_number),
               trim(teacher));
run;
%put _user_;
```

INDIRECT2

macro variable name is unique

43

## Creating a Series of Macro Variables

SAS Log

```
137  %put _user_;
GLOBAL TEACH1 Hallis, Dr. George
GLOBAL TEACH13 Hallis, Dr. George
GLOBAL TEACH12 Berthan, Ms. Judy
GLOBAL TEACH3 Forest, Mr. Peter
GLOBAL TEACH15 Forest, Mr. Peter
GLOBAL TEACH2 Wickam, Dr. Alice
GLOBAL TEACH14 Wickam, Dr. Alice
GLOBAL TEACH17 Hallis, Dr. George
GLOBAL TEACH16 Tally, Ms. Julia
GLOBAL TEACH18 Berthan, Ms. Judy
GLOBAL TEACH9 Forest, Mr. Peter
GLOBAL TEACH8 Wickam, Dr. Alice
GLOBAL TEACH5 Hallis, Dr. George
GLOBAL TEACH4 Tally, Ms. Julia
GLOBAL TEACH7 Hallis, Dr. George
GLOBAL TEACH11 Tally, Ms. Julia
GLOBAL TEACH6 Berthan, Ms. Judy
GLOBAL TEACH10 Tally, Ms. Julia
```

44

Because there are no macro triggers, the entire DATA step is passed to the compiler. The compiled DATA step executes after the RUN statement is encountered.

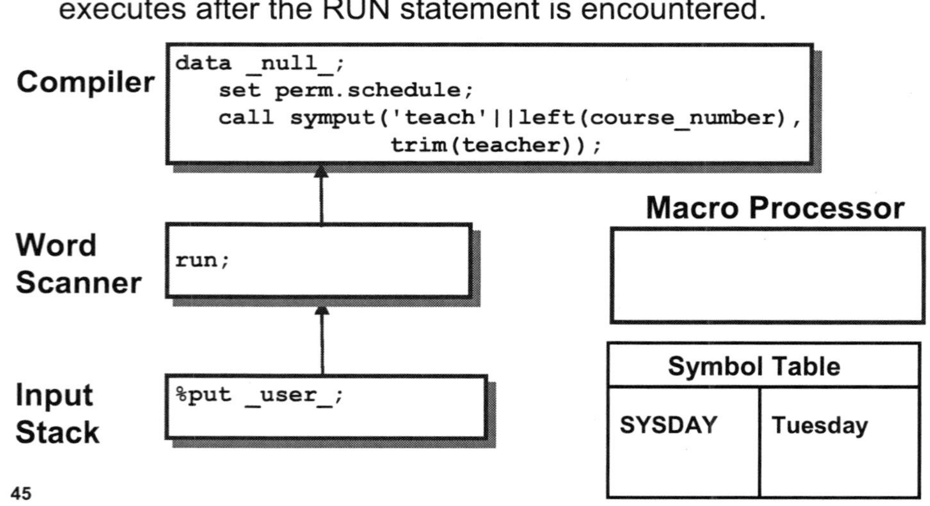


45

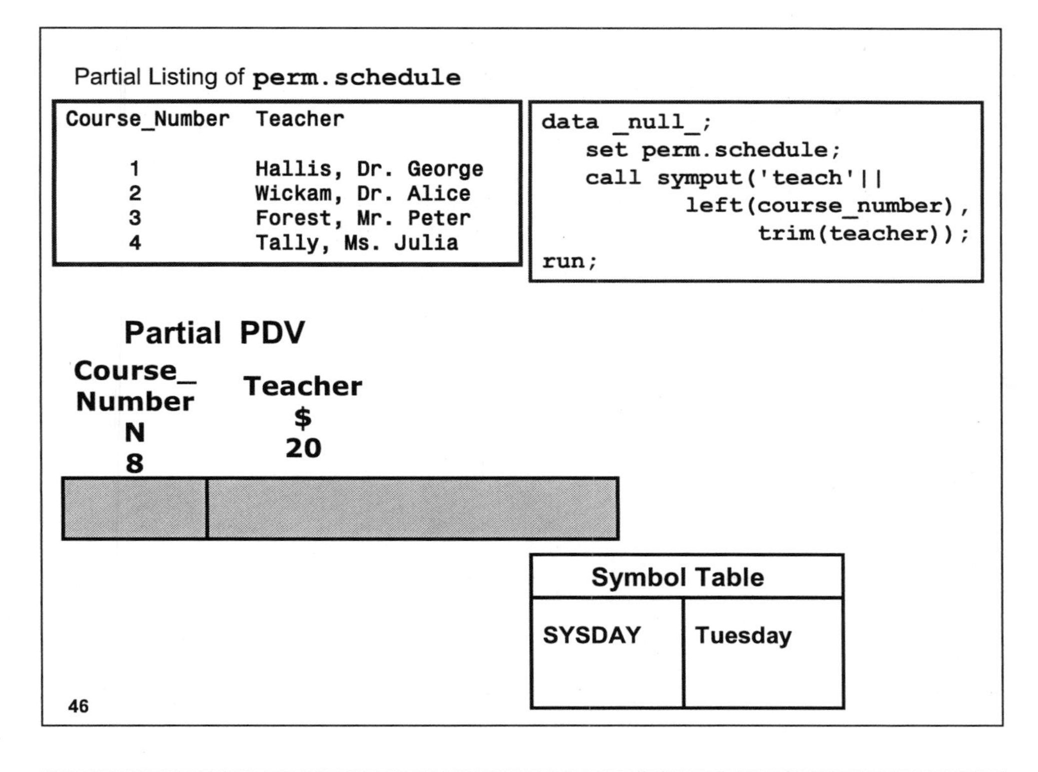
Partial Listing of perm.schedule
Course_Number Teacher
1 Hallis, Dr. George
2 Wickam, Dr. Alice
3 Forest, Mr. Peter
4 Tally, Ms. Julia
data _null_;
set perm.schedule;
call symput('teach'||
left(course_number),
trim(teacher));
run;
Partial PDV
Course_ Number
N
8
Teacher
$
20
Symbol Table
SYSDAY
Tuesday
46

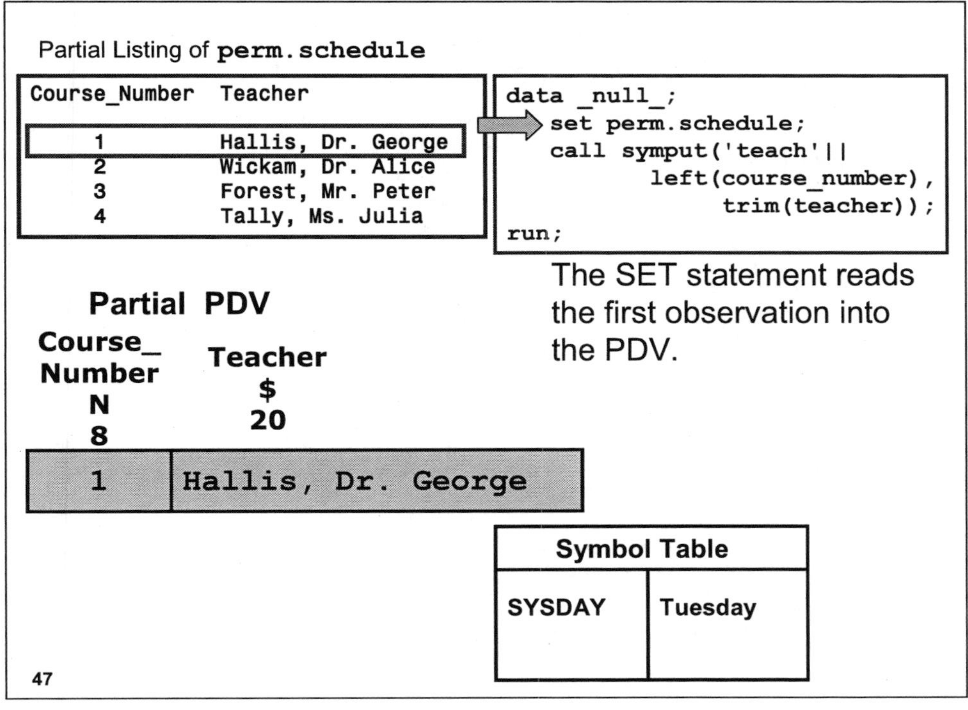
Partial Listing of perm.schedule
Course_Number Teacher
1 Hallis, Dr. George
2 Wickam, Dr. Alice
3 Forest, Mr. Peter
4 Tally, Ms. Julia
data _null_;
set perm.schedule;
call symput('teach'||
left(course_number),
trim(teacher));
run;
The SET statement reads the first observation into the PDV.
Partial PDV
Course_ Number
N
8
Teacher
$
20
1
Hallis, Dr. George
Symbol Table
SYSDAY
Tuesday
47

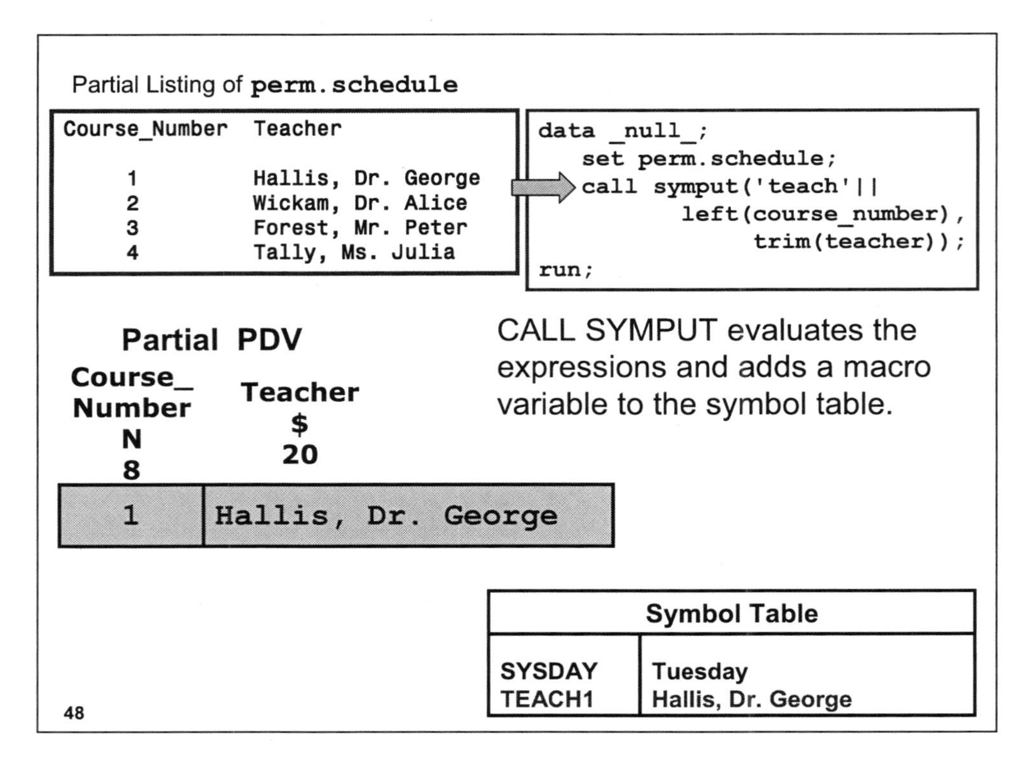
Partial Listing of perm.schedule
Course_Number Teacher
1 Hallis, Dr. George
2 Wickam, Dr. Alice
3 Forest, Mr. Peter
4 Tally, Ms. Julia
data _null_;
set perm.schedule;
call symput('teach'||
left(course_number),
trim(teacher));
run;
Partial PDV
Course_ Number N 8
Teacher $ 20
1
Hallis, Dr. George
CALL SYMPUT evaluates the expressions and adds a macro variable to the symbol table.
Symbol Table
SYSDAY Tuesday
TEACH1 Hallis, Dr. George
48

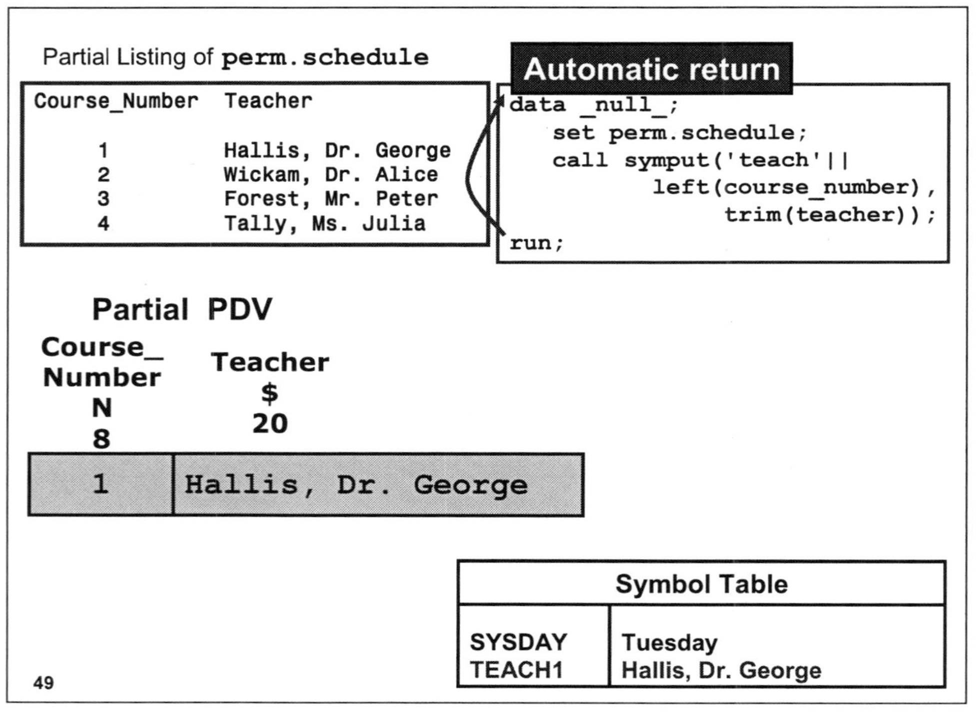
Partial Listing of perm.schedule
Course_Number Teacher
1 Hallis, Dr. George
2 Wickam, Dr. Alice
3 Forest, Mr. Peter
4 Tally, Ms. Julia
Automatic return
data _null_;
set perm.schedule;
call symput('teach'||
left(course_number),
trim(teacher));
run;
Partial PDV
Course_ Number N 8
Teacher $ 20
1
Hallis, Dr. George
Symbol Table
SYSDAY Tuesday
TEACH1 Hallis, Dr. George
49

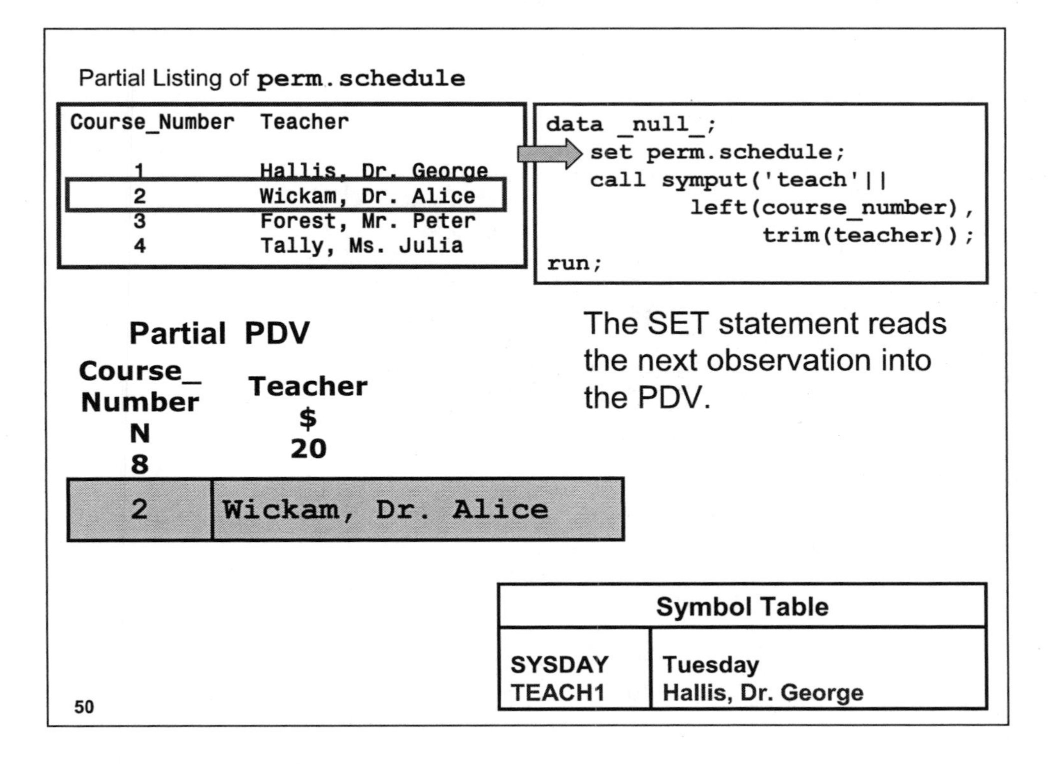
Partial Listing of perm.schedule
Course_Number Teacher
1 Hallis, Dr. George
2 Wickam, Dr. Alice
3 Forest, Mr. Peter
4 Tally, Ms. Julia
data _null_;
set perm.schedule;
call symput('teach'||
left(course_number),
trim(teacher));
run;
Partial PDV
Course_ Number N 8
Teacher $ 20
2
Wickam, Dr. Alice
The SET statement reads the next observation into the PDV.
Symbol Table
SYSDAY Tuesday
TEACH1 Hallis, Dr. George
50

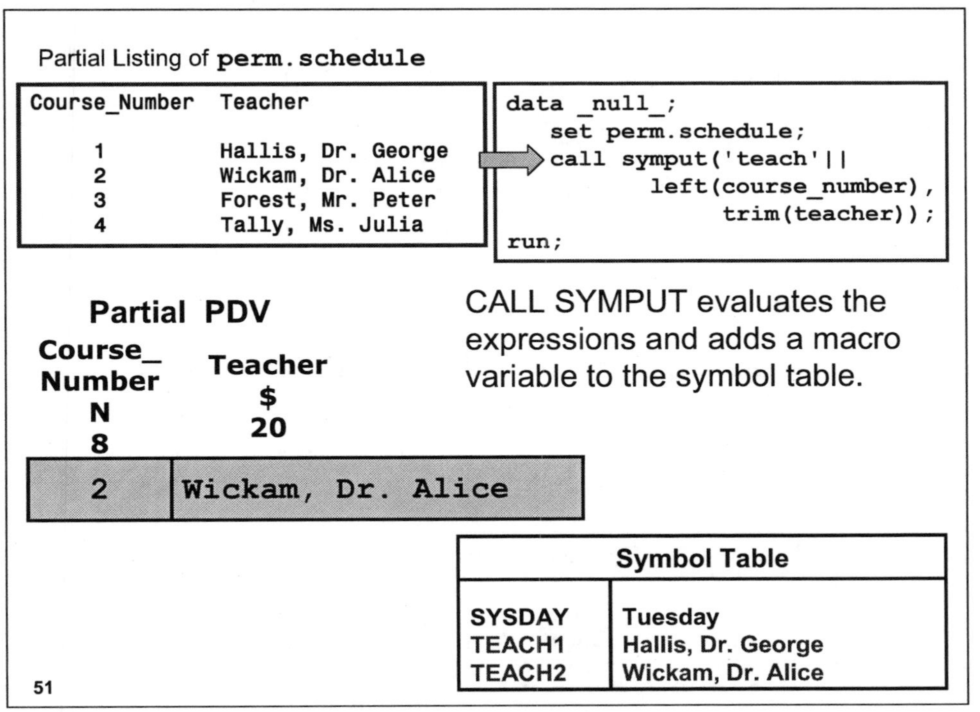
Partial Listing of perm.schedule
Course_Number Teacher
1 Hallis, Dr. George
2 Wickam, Dr. Alice
3 Forest, Mr. Peter
4 Tally, Ms. Julia
data _null_;
set perm.schedule;
call symput('teach'||
left(course_number),
trim(teacher));
run;
Partial PDV
Course_ Number N 8
Teacher $ 20
2
Wickam, Dr. Alice
CALL SYMPUT evaluates the expressions and adds a macro variable to the symbol table.
Symbol Table
SYSDAY Tuesday
TEACH1 Hallis, Dr. George
TEACH2 Wickam, Dr. Alice
51

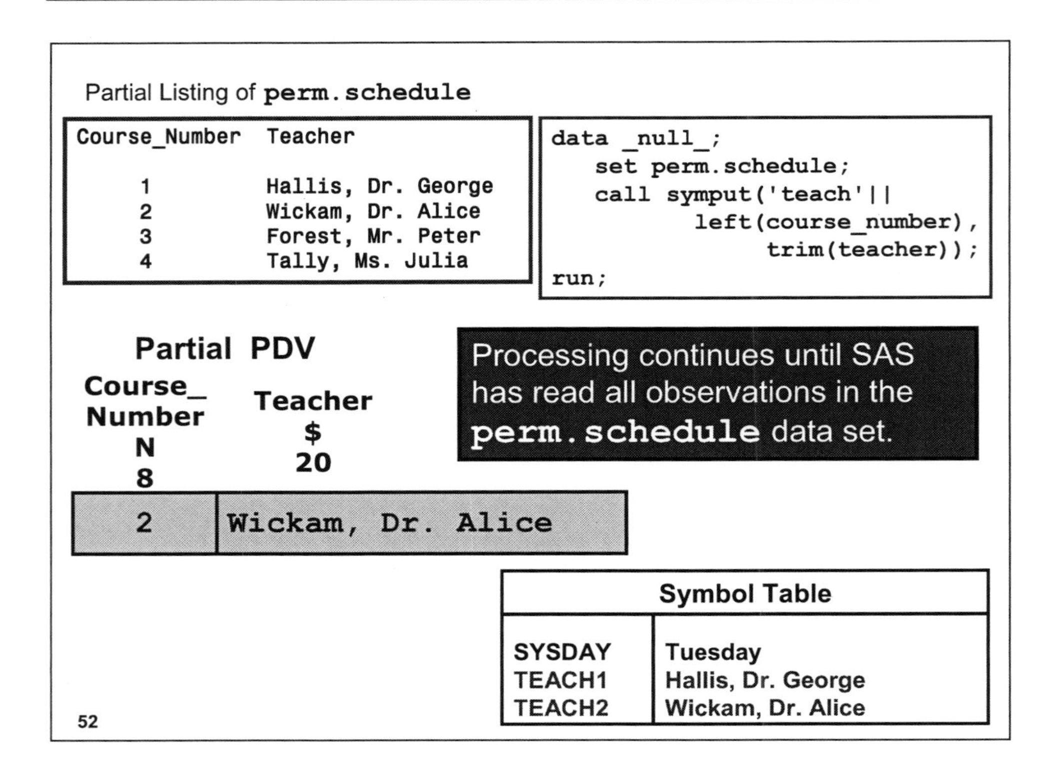
Partial Listing of perm.schedule
Course_Number Teacher
1 Hallis, Dr. George
2 Wickam, Dr. Alice
3 Forest, Mr. Peter
4 Tally, Ms. Julia
data _null_;
set perm.schedule;
call symput('teach'||
left(course_number),
trim(teacher));
run;
Partial PDV
Course_ Number N 8
Teacher $ 20
2
Wickam, Dr. Alice
Processing continues until SAS has read all observations in the perm.schedule data set.
Symbol Table
SYSDAY Tuesday
TEACH1 Hallis, Dr. George
TEACH2 Wickam, Dr. Alice
52

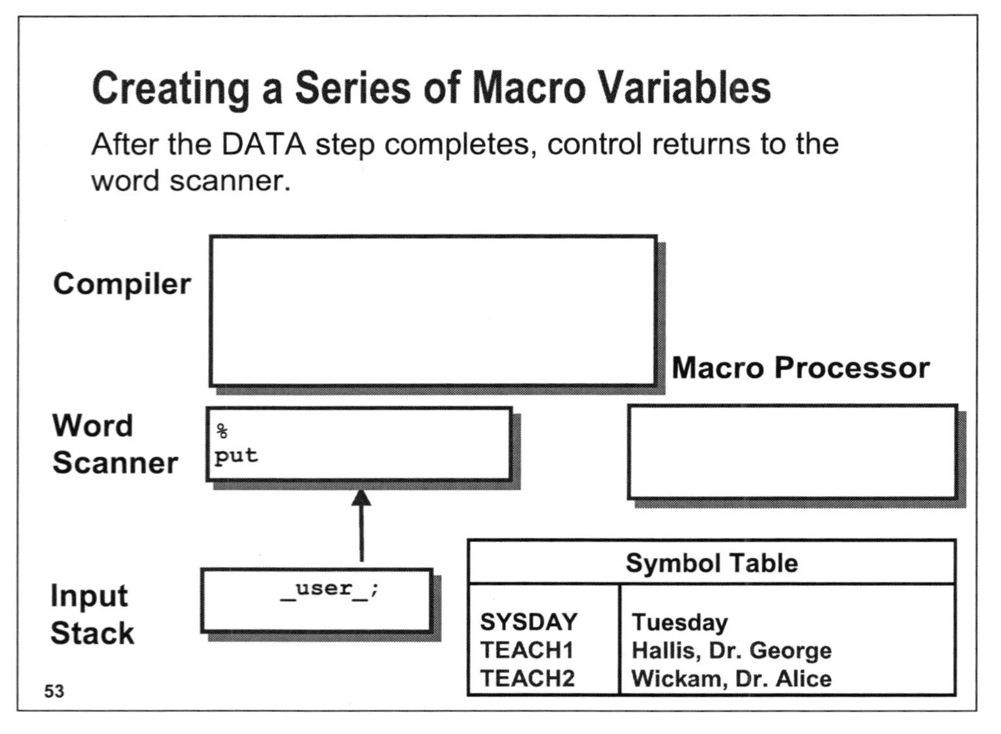
Creating a Series of Macro Variables
After the DATA step completes, control returns to the word scanner.
Compiler
Macro Processor
Word Scanner
%
put
Input Stack
_user_;
Symbol Table
SYSDAY Tuesday
TEACH1 Hallis, Dr. George
TEACH2 Wickam, Dr. Alice
53

## Creating a Series of Macro Variables

The %PUT statement is passed to the macro processor for execution.

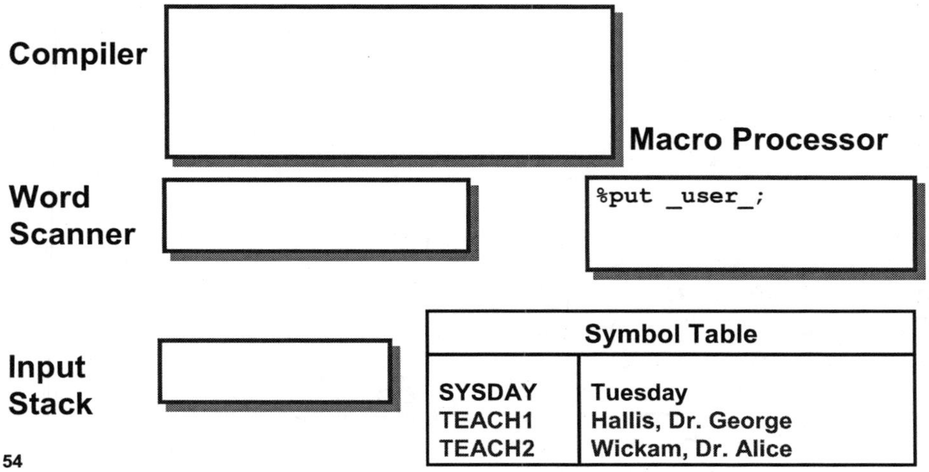

**Compiler**

**Word Scanner**

**Input Stack**

**Macro Processor**

```
%put _user_;
```

| Symbol Table | |
|---|---|
| SYSDAY | Tuesday |
| TEACH1 | Hallis, Dr. George |
| TEACH2 | Wickam, Dr. Alice |

54

## Creating a Series of Macro Variables

SAS Log

```
137  %put _user_;
GLOBAL TEACH1 Hallis, Dr. George
GLOBAL TEACH13 Hallis, Dr. George
GLOBAL TEACH12 Berthan, Ms. Judy
GLOBAL TEACH3 Forest, Mr. Peter
GLOBAL TEACH15 Forest, Mr. Peter
GLOBAL TEACH2 Wickam, Dr. Alice
GLOBAL TEACH14 Wickam, Dr. Alice
GLOBAL TEACH17 Hallis, Dr. George
GLOBAL TEACH16 Tally, Ms. Julia
GLOBAL TEACH18 Berthan, Ms. Judy
GLOBAL TEACH9 Forest, Mr. Peter
GLOBAL TEACH8 Wickam, Dr. Alice
GLOBAL TEACH5 Hallis, Dr. George
GLOBAL TEACH4 Tally, Ms. Julia
GLOBAL TEACH7 Hallis, Dr. George
GLOBAL TEACH11 Tally, Ms. Julia
GLOBAL TEACH6 Berthan, Ms. Judy
GLOBAL TEACH10 Tally, Ms. Julia
```

55

## Creating a Series of Macro Variables

You can now reference the correct name without rerunning the DATA step.

**Symbol Table**

| Variable | Value |
|---|---|
| CRS | 2 |
| TEACH1 | Hallis, Dr. George |
| TEACH2 | Wickam, Dr. Alice |
| TEACH3 | Forest, Mr. Peter |
| ... | ... |

```
%let crs=2;
proc print data=perm.register noobs;
   where course_number=&crs;
   var student_name paid;
   title1 "Roster for Course &crs";
   title2 "Taught by &teach2";
run;
```

INDIRECT3

56

## Creating a Series of Macro Variables

But now you must change two lines of code for every new report. How can this be improved?

**Symbol Table**

| Variable | Value |
|---|---|
| CRS | 3 |
| TEACH1 | Hallis, Dr. George |
| TEACH2 | Wickam, Dr. Alice |
| TEACH3 | Forest, Mr. Peter |
| ... | ... |

```
%let crs=3;                                    <- Change
proc print data=perm.register noobs;
   where course_number=&crs;
   var student_name paid;
   title1 "Roster for Course &crs";
   title2 "Taught by &teach3";                 <- Change
run;
```

57

## Indirect References to Macro Variables

Because the CRS macro variable matches **part of** the name of a TEACH macro variable, the CRS macro variable can **indirectly reference** a TEACH macro variable.

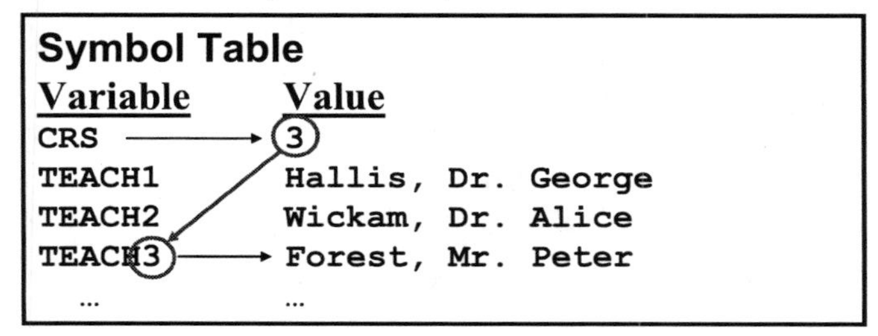


58

## Indirect References to Macro Variables

The Forward Rescan Rule:

- Multiple ampersands preceding a name token denote an indirect reference that ends when a token is encountered that cannot be part of a macro variable reference, that is, a token other than a name, an ampersand, or a period delimiter.
- The macro processor will re-scan an indirect reference, left to right, from the point where the multiple ampersands begin.
- Two ampersands (&&) resolve to one ampersand (&).
- Scanning continues until no more triggers can be resolved.

59

## Indirect References to Macro Variables

Step 5: Use an indirect reference.

```
%let crs=3;
proc print data=perm.register noobs;
     where course_number=&crs;
     var student_name paid;
     title1 "Roster for Course &crs";
     title2 "Taught by &&teach&crs";
run;
```

INDIRECT4

```
                Roster for Course 3
             Taught by Forest, Mr. Peter

                 Student_Name        Paid

              Scannell, Ms. Robin     N
              Seitz, Mr. Adam         Y
              Smith, Ms. Jan          N
              Sulzbach, Mr. Bill      Y
              Williams, Mr. Gene      Y
```

60

## Indirect References to Macro Variables

Placing two ampersands at the start of the original token sequence alters the processing of the tokens and macro triggers.

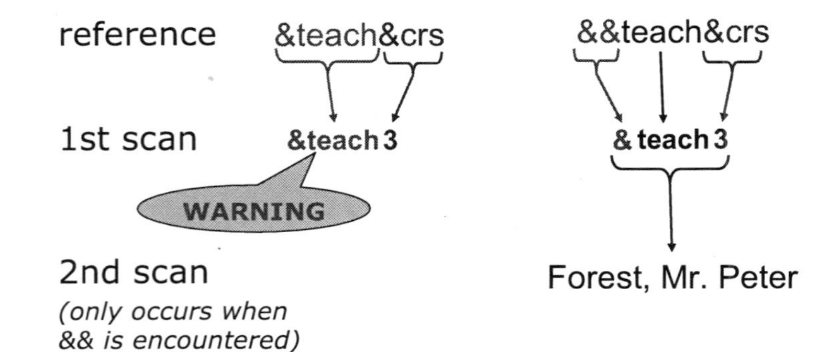


61

...

## Indirect References to Macro Variables

The CRS macro variable is an **indirect reference** to a TEACH macro variable.

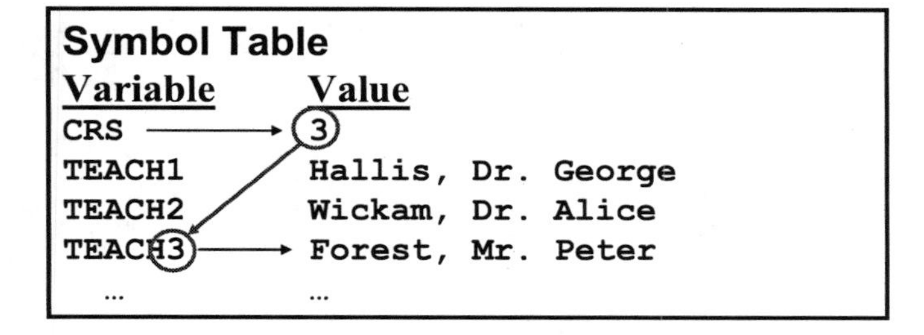


**Scan sequence:**

```
&&teach&crs ——→ &teach3 ——→ Forest, Mr. Peter
```

62

## Indirect References to Macro Variables

INDIRECT4

Create a series of macro variables TEACH1 to TEACH*n*, each containing the name of the instructor assigned to a specific course. Reference one of these variables when a course number is designated.

```
options symbolgen;
data _null_;
   set perm.schedule;
   call symput('teach'||left(course_number),trim(teacher));
run;

%let crs=3;
proc print data=perm.register noobs;
   where course_number=&crs;
   var student_name paid;
   title1 "Roster for Course &crs";
   title2 "Taught by &&teach&crs";
run;
```

Partial SAS Log

```
65  %let crs=3;
66  proc print data=perm.register noobs;
67     where course_number=&crs;
SYMBOLGEN:  Macro variable CRS resolves to 3
68     var student_name paid;
SYMBOLGEN:  Macro variable CRS resolves to 3
69     title1 "Roster for Course &crs";
SYMBOLGEN:  && resolves to &.
SYMBOLGEN:  Macro variable CRS resolves to 3
SYMBOLGEN:  Macro variable TEACH3 resolves to Forest, Mr. Peter
70     title2 "Taught by &&teach&crs";
71  run;

NOTE: There were 20 observations read from the dataset PERM.REGISTER.
      WHERE course_number=3;
NOTE: PROCEDURE PRINT used:
      real time           2.03 seconds
      cpu time            0.03 seconds
```

SAS Output

```
                  Roster for Course 3
                Taught by Forest, Mr. Peter

              Student_Name                Paid

              Bills, Ms. Paulette          Y
              Chevarley, Ms. Arlene        N
              Clough, Ms. Patti            N
              Crace, Mr. Ron               Y
              Davis, Mr. Bruce             Y
              Elsins, Ms. Marisa F.        N
              Gandy, Dr. David             Y
              Gash, Ms. Hedy               Y
              Haubold, Ms. Ann             Y
              Hudock, Ms. Cathy            Y
              Kimble, Mr. John             N
              Kochen, Mr. Dennis           Y
              Larocque, Mr. Bret           Y
              Licht, Mr. Bryan             Y
              McKnight, Ms. Maureen E.     Y
              Scannell, Ms. Robin          N
              Seitz, Mr. Adam              Y
              Smith, Ms. Jan               N
              Sulzbach, Mr. Bill           Y
              Williams, Mr. Gene           Y
```

## Table Lookup Application (Self-Study)

Example: Use the **perm.schedule** data set to create a list of offerings of a given course. The report title should display the name of the course.

Schedule for Structured Query Language

| Location | Begin | Instructor |
|---|---|---|
| Dallas | 07DEC2004 | Wickam, Dr. Alice |
| Boston | 14JUN2005 | Wickam, Dr. Alice |
| Seattle | 06DEC2005 | Wickam, Dr. Alice |

64

## Table Lookup Application (Self-Study)

The **perm.courses** data set contains course names that can be transferred into macro variables as in the previous example.

The values of **Course_Code** are unique and can be used as macro variable names without alteration.

Listing of PERM.COURSES Data Set

| Obs | Course_ Code | Course_Title | Days | Fee |
|---|---|---|---|---|
| 1 | C001 | Basic Telecommunications | 3 | $795 |
| 2 | C002 | Structured Query Language | 4 | $1150 |
| 3 | C003 | Local Area Networks | 3 | $650 |
| 4 | C004 | Database Design | 2 | $375 |
| 5 | C005 | Artificial Intelligence | 2 | $400 |
| 6 | C006 | Computer Aided Design | 5 | $1600 |

65

## Table Lookup Application (Self-Study)

Example: Create a series of macro variables, one for each course code. Assign the corresponding value of the variable **course_title** to each macro variable.

```
data _null_;
   set perm.courses;
   call symputx(course_code, course_title);
run;
```

INDIRECT5

Because the values of **Course_Code** represent valid macro variable names, there is no need to precede the value of **Course_Code** with a separate prefix (root).

66

## Table Lookup Application (Self-Study)

Because the value of one macro variable exactly matches the name of another macro variable, three ampersands appear together in this indirect macro variable reference.

```
%let crsid=C002;
proc print data=perm.schedule noobs label;
   where course_code="&crsid";
   var location begin_date teacher;
   title1 "Schedule for &&&crsid";
run;
```

INDIRECT6

67

## Table Lookup Application (Self-Study)

Use **three ampersands** when the value of one macro variable matches **the entire** name of a second macro variable.

**Symbol Table**

| Variable | Value |
|---|---|
| CRSID | C002 |
| C001 | Basic Telecommunications |
| C002 | Structured Query Language |
| C003 | Local Area Networks |
| C004 | Database Design |
| C005 | Artificial Intelligence |
| C006 | Computer Aided Design |

**Scan sequence:**

`&&&crsid` → `&c002` → `Structured Query Language`

68

## Table Lookup Application (Self-Study)

Placing three ampersands at the start of the original token sequence alters the processing of the tokens and macro triggers.

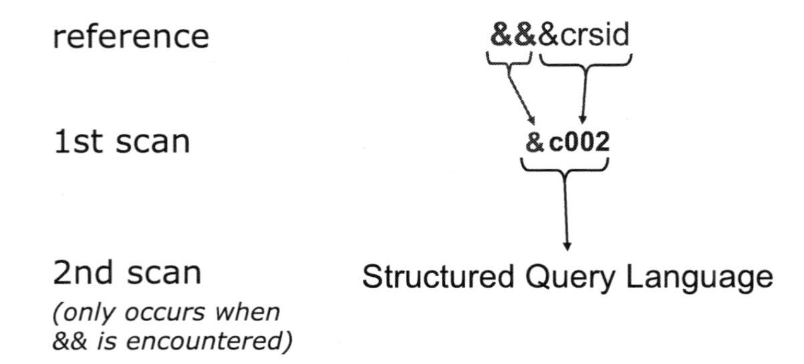


69

## Exercises

**2. Creating Multiple Macro Variables with the SYMPUT Routine**

**a.** The **perm.schedule** data set contains the variable **begin_date**, which contains the starting date of each course. Use a DATA step to create a series of macro variables named START1 through START*n*, one for each course offered. The value of each START macro variable should be the starting date of the corresponding class in the MMDDYY10. format.

**b.** Open the **prtrost** program shown below into the Editor window. Modify the TITLE statement so the series of Xs is replaced with an indirect macro variable reference to one of the START variables based on the current value of CRS. Submit the modified program.

```
%let crs=4;
proc print data=perm.all noobs n;
   where course_number=&crs;
   var student_name student_company;
   title1 "Roster for Course &crs";
   title2 "Beginning on XXXXX";
run;
```

# Solutions to Exercises

## 2. Creating Multiple Macro Variables with the SYMPUT Routine

a. Concatenating the text **start** with the value of the **course_number** variable specifies the name of each macro variable. Because the **course_number** variable is numeric, the LEFT function is required to remove the leading blanks introduced by the automatic numeric-to-character conversion. The %PUT statement displays the names and values of all user-created macro variables.

```
data _null_;
   set perm.schedule;
   call symput('start'||trim(left(course_number)),
               put(begin_date,mmddyy10.));
run;

%put _user_;
```

**b.** Because each macro variable that contains a course date has a common root at the start of its name (START) and a suffix that corresponds to the value of the CRS macro variable, two ampersands are used in front of the complete reference.

```
options symbolgen;
%let crs=4;
proc print data=perm.all noobs n;
   where course_number=&crs;
   var student_name student_company;
   title1 "Roster for Course &crs";
   title2 "Beginning on &&start&crs";
run;
```

Partial SAS Log

```
161  options symbolgen;
162  %let crs=4;
163  proc print data=perm.all noobs n;
164     where course_number=&crs;
SYMBOLGEN:  Macro variable CRS resolves to 4
165     var student_name student_company;
SYMBOLGEN:  Macro variable CRS resolves to 4
166     title1 "Roster for Course &crs";
SYMBOLGEN:  && resolves to &.
SYMBOLGEN:  Macro variable CRS resolves to 4
SYMBOLGEN:  Macro variable START4 resolves to 01/25/2005
167     title2 "Beginning on &&start&crs";
168  run;
```

Partial Output

```
                          Roster for Course 4
                         Beginning on 1/25/2005

     Student_Name                Student_Company

     Bates, Ms. Ellen            Reston Railway
     Boyd, Ms. Leah              United Shoes Co.
     Chan, Mr. John              California Lawyers Assn.
     Chevarley, Ms. Arlene       Motor Communications
     Chow, Ms. Sylvia            Bostic Amplifier Inc.
     Crace, Mr. Ron              Von Crump Seafood
     Edwards, Mr. Charles        Gorman Tire Corp.
     Garza, Ms. Cheryl           Admiral Research & Development Co.
     Geatz, Mr. Patrick D.       San Juan Gas and Electric
     Keever, Ms. Linda           Crossbow of California
     Kelley, Ms. Gail            Crossbow of California
     Kendig, Mr. James           Rocks International
     Kimble, Mr. John            Alforone Chemical
     Koleff, Mr. Jim             Emulate Research
     Montgomery, Mr. Jeff        Bonstell Electronics
     Moore, Mr. John             California Dept. of Insurance
     Page, Mr. Scott             Applied Technologies
     Parker, Mr. Robert          SMASH Hardware Inc.
```

## 4.3 Retrieving Macro Variables in the DATA Step (Self-Study)

### Objectives

- Obtain the value of a macro variable during DATA step execution.
- Describe the difference between the SYMGET function and macro variable references.

72

### The SYMGET Function

| | create macro variables | retrieve macro variables |
|---|---|---|
| word scanning time | %LET | &macvar |
| execution time | CALL SYMPUT | SYMGET(macvar) |

77

## The SYMGET Function

Retrieve a macro variable's value during DATA step execution with the SYMGET function.



78

## The SYMGET Function

General form of the SYMGET function:

**SYMGET(*macro-variable*)**

*macro-variable* can be specified as a

- character literal
- DATA step character expression.

A DATA step variable created by the SYMGET function is a character variable with a length of 200 bytes **unless it has been previously defined**.

79

# The SYMGET Function

The SYMGET function can be used in table lookup applications.

Example: Use the SYMPUT routine to create a series of macro variables.

```
data _null_;
   set perm.schedule;
   call symput('teach'||left(course_number),
                    trim(teacher));
run;
```

SYMGET1

| Symbol Table | |
|---|---|
| teach1 | Hallis, Dr. George |
| teach2 | Wickam, Dr. Alice |
| teach3 | Forest, Mr. Peter |

80

# The SYMGET Function

Example: Look up the teacher's name from the symbol table by deriving the corresponding macro variable's name from the data set variable **course_number**.

```
data teachers;
   set perm.register;
   length teacher $ 20;
   teacher=symget('teach'||left(course_number));
run;
```

SYMGET1

81

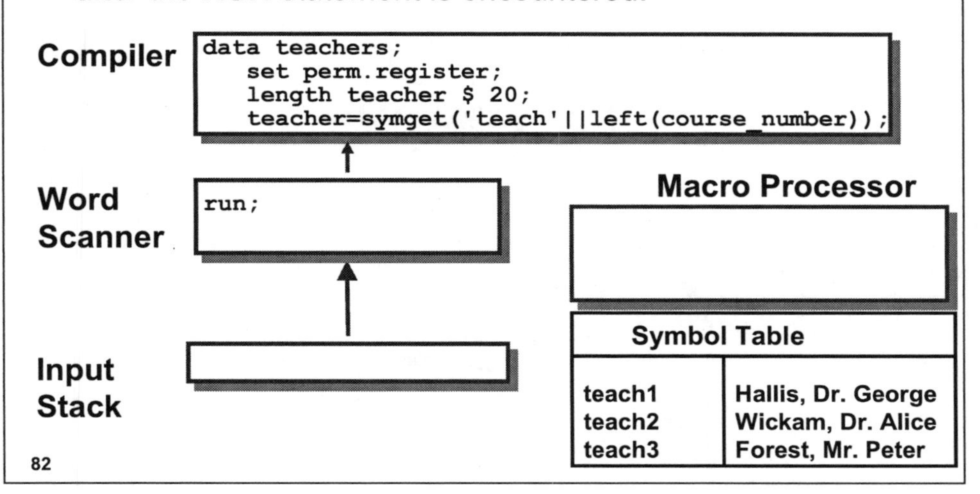
The SYMGET Function
Because there are no macro triggers, the entire DATA step is passed to the compiler. The DATA step executes after the RUN statement is encountered.
Compiler
data teachers;
set perm.register;
length teacher $ 20;
teacher=symget('teach'||left(course_number));
Word Scanner
run;
Macro Processor
Input Stack
Symbol Table
teach1
teach2
teach3
Hallis, Dr. George
Wickam, Dr. Alice
Forest, Mr. Peter
82

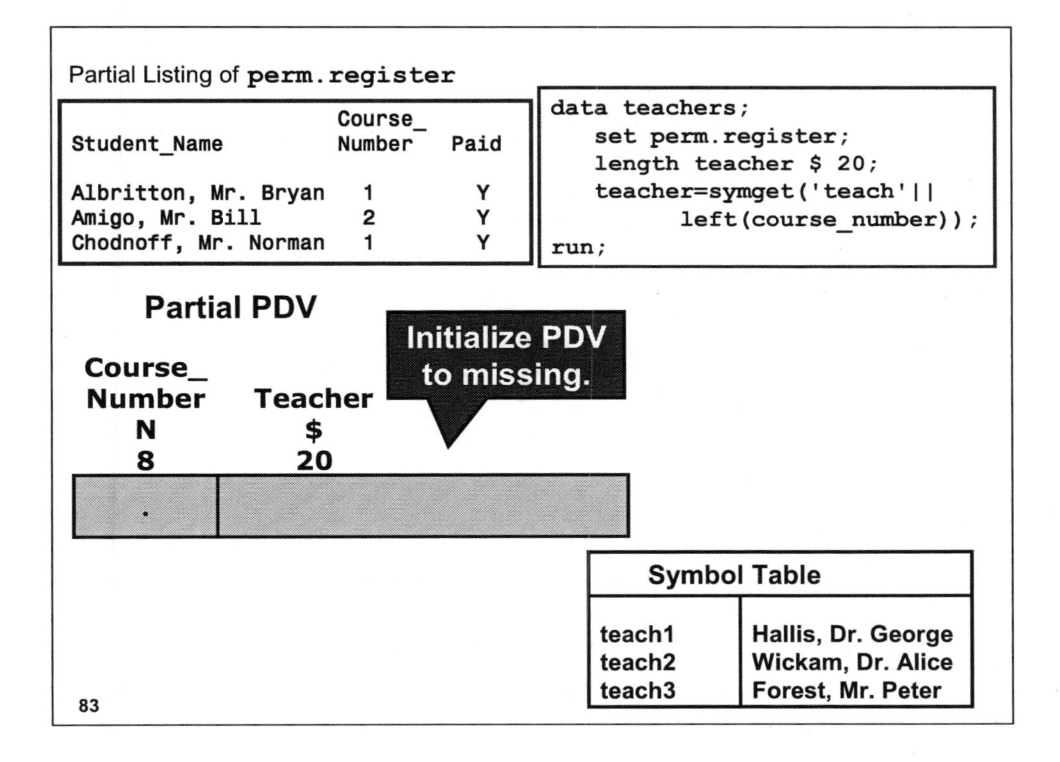
Partial Listing of perm.register
Student_Name
Course_ Number
Paid
Albritton, Mr. Bryan 1 Y
Amigo, Mr. Bill 2 Y
Chodnoff, Mr. Norman 1 Y
data teachers;
set perm.register;
length teacher $ 20;
teacher=symget('teach'||
left(course_number));
run;
Partial PDV
Course_ Number
N
8
Teacher
$
20
Initialize PDV to missing.
Symbol Table
teach1
teach2
teach3
Hallis, Dr. George
Wickam, Dr. Alice
Forest, Mr. Peter
83

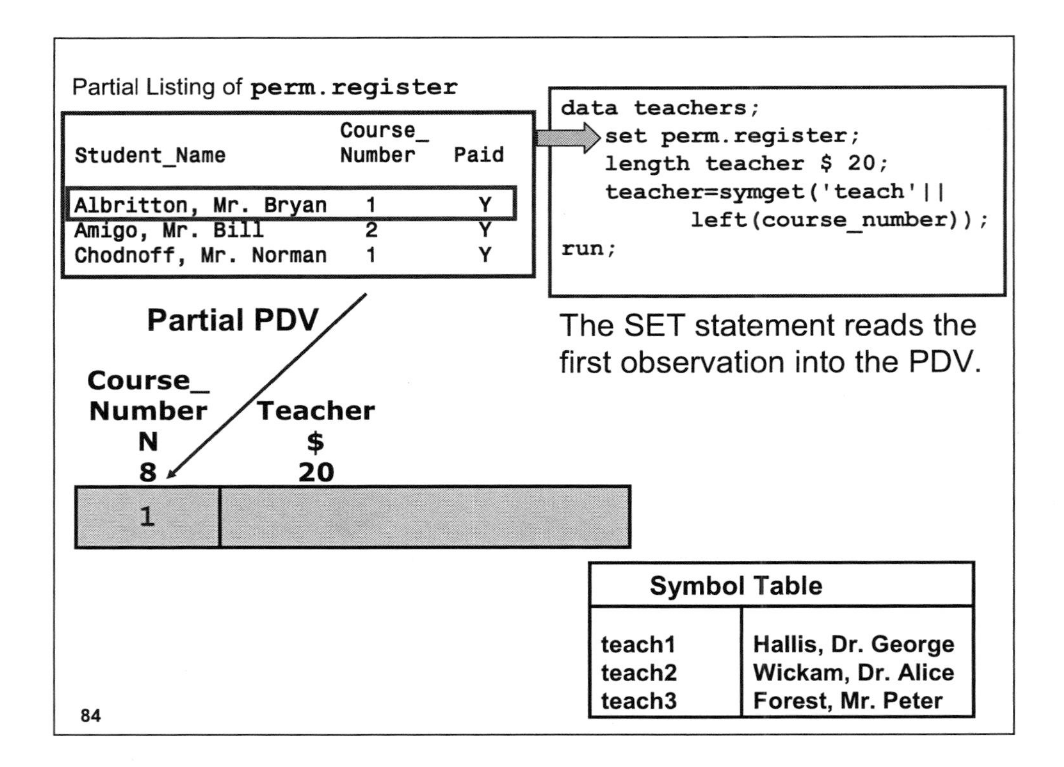
Partial Listing of perm.register
Student_Name Course_ Number Paid
Albritton, Mr. Bryan 1 Y
Amigo, Mr. Bill 2 Y
Chodnoff, Mr. Norman 1 Y
data teachers;
set perm.register;
length teacher $ 20;
teacher=symget('teach'||
left(course_number));
run;
Partial PDV
Course_ Number N 8
Teacher $ 20
1
The SET statement reads the first observation into the PDV.
Symbol Table
teach1 Hallis, Dr. George
teach2 Wickam, Dr. Alice
teach3 Forest, Mr. Peter
84

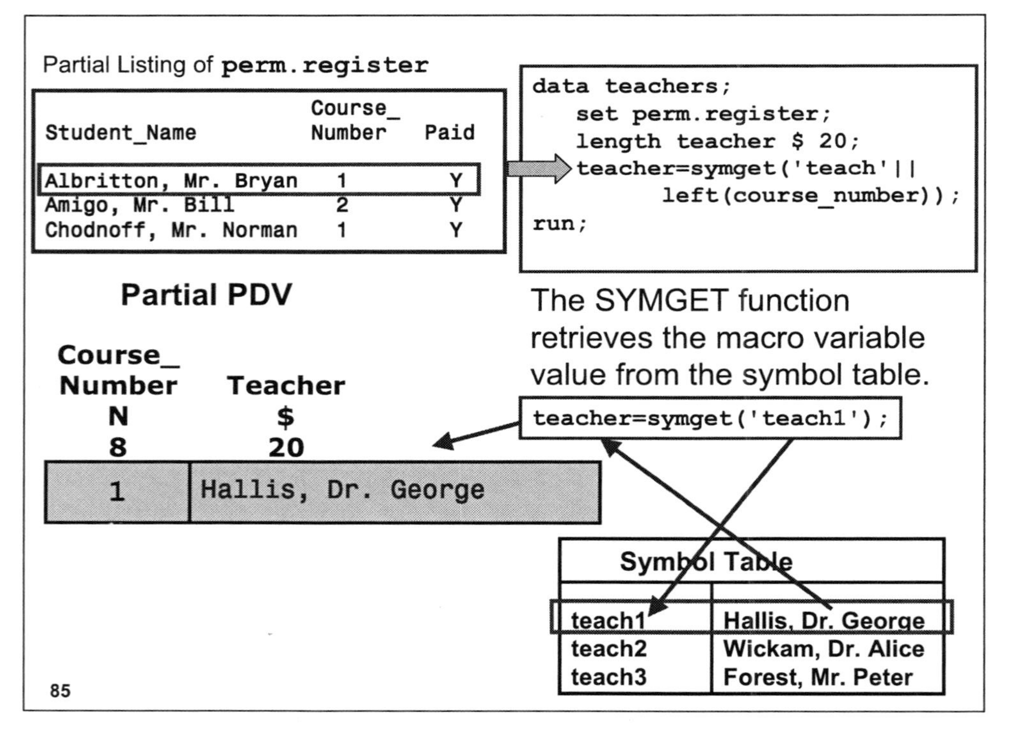
Partial Listing of perm.register
Student_Name Course_ Number Paid
Albritton, Mr. Bryan 1 Y
Amigo, Mr. Bill 2 Y
Chodnoff, Mr. Norman 1 Y
data teachers;
set perm.register;
length teacher $ 20;
teacher=symget('teach'||
left(course_number));
run;
Partial PDV
Course_ Number N 8
Teacher $ 20
1 Hallis, Dr. George
The SYMGET function retrieves the macro variable value from the symbol table.
teacher=symget('teach1');
Symbol Table
teach1 Hallis, Dr. George
teach2 Wickam, Dr. Alice
teach3 Forest, Mr. Peter
85

Partial Listing of **perm.register**

| Student_Name | Course_ Number | Paid |
|---|---|---|
| Albritton, Mr. Bryan | 1 | Y |
| Amigo, Mr. Bill | 2 | Y |
| Chodnoff, Mr. Norman | 1 | Y |

```
data teachers;
   set perm.register;
   length teacher $ 20;
   teacher=symget('teach'||
         left(course_number));
run;
```

**Automatic output**

**Partial PDV**

| Course_ Number N 8 | Teacher $ 20 |
|---|---|
| 1 | Hallis, Dr. George |

At the bottom of the step, SAS automatically outputs the observation to the new data set **work.teachers**.

| Symbol Table | |
|---|---|
| teach1 | Hallis, Dr. George |
| teach2 | Wickam, Dr. Alice |
| teach3 | Forest, Mr. Peter |

86

Partial Listing of **perm.register**

| Student_Name | Course_ Number | Paid |
|---|---|---|
| Albritton, Mr. Bryan | 1 | Y |
| Amigo, Mr. Bill | 2 | Y |
| Chodnoff, Mr. Norman | 1 | Y |

**Automatic return**

```
data teachers;
   set perm.register;
   length teacher $ 20;
   teacher=symget('teach'||
         left(course_number));
run;
```

**Partial PDV**

| Course_ Number N 8 | Teacher $ 20 |
|---|---|
| 1 | |

At the bottom of the step, SAS automatically returns to the top of the step. The PDV is reinitialized.

| Symbol Table | |
|---|---|
| teach1 | Hallis, Dr. George |
| teach2 | Wickam, Dr. Alice |
| teach3 | Forest, Mr. Peter |

87

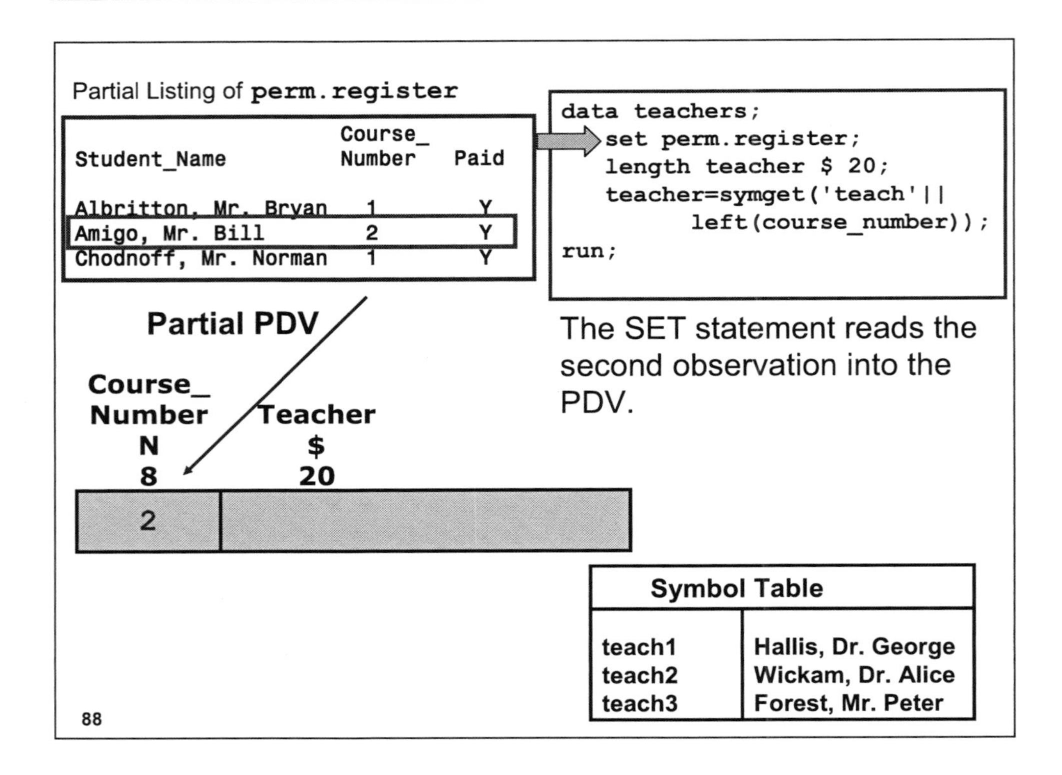
Partial Listing of perm.register
Student_Name
Course_ Number
Paid
Albritton, Mr. Bryan 1 Y
Amigo, Mr. Bill 2 Y
Chodnoff, Mr. Norman 1 Y
data teachers;
set perm.register;
length teacher $ 20;
teacher=symget('teach'||
left(course_number));
run;
Partial PDV
Course_ Number N 8
Teacher $ 20
2
The SET statement reads the second observation into the PDV.
Symbol Table
teach1 Hallis, Dr. George
teach2 Wickam, Dr. Alice
teach3 Forest, Mr. Peter
88

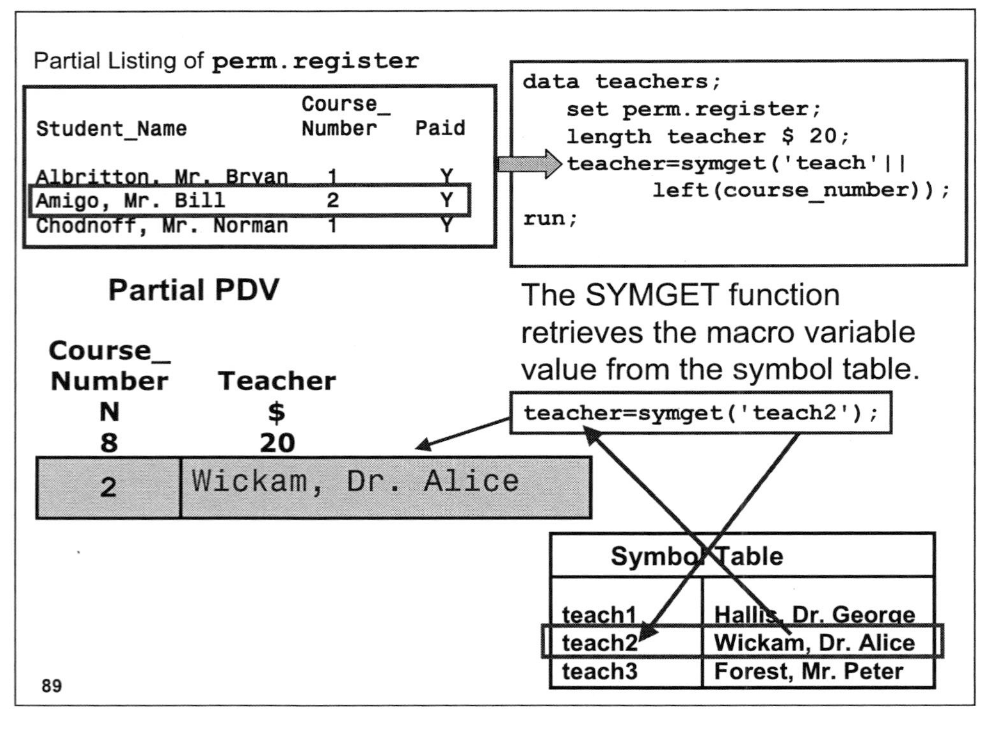
Partial Listing of perm.register
Student_Name
Course_ Number
Paid
Albritton, Mr. Bryan 1 Y
Amigo, Mr. Bill 2 Y
Chodnoff, Mr. Norman 1 Y
data teachers;
set perm.register;
length teacher $ 20;
teacher=symget('teach'||
left(course_number));
run;
Partial PDV
Course_ Number N 8
Teacher $ 20
2
Wickam, Dr. Alice
The SYMGET function retrieves the macro variable value from the symbol table.
teacher=symget('teach2');
Symbol Table
teach1 Hallis, Dr. George
teach2 Wickam, Dr. Alice
teach3 Forest, Mr. Peter
89

Partial Listing of **perm.register**

```
                          Course_
Student_Name              Number    Paid

Albritton, Mr. Bryan      1         Y
Amigo, Mr. Bill           2         Y
Chodnoff, Mr. Norman      1         Y
```

```
data teachers;
   set perm.register;
   length teacher $ 20;
   teacher=symget('teach'||
         left(course_number));
run;
```

**Partial PDV**

| Course_ Number N 8 | Teacher $ 20 |
|---|---|
| | |

Processing continues until SAS has read all rows in the **perm.register** data set.

| Symbol Table | |
|---|---|
| teach1 | Hallis, Dr. George |
| teach2 | Wickam, Dr. Alice |
| teach3 | Forest, Mr. Peter |

90

## The SYMGET Function

```
title1 "Teacher for Each Registered Student";
proc print data=teachers;
   var student_name course_number teacher;
run;
```

SYMGET1

Partial SAS Output

```
                 Teacher for Each Registered Student

                                            Course_
    Obs    Student_Name                     Number          teacher

      1    Albritton, Mr. Bryan                1        Hallis, Dr. George
      2    Amigo, Mr. Bill                     2        Wickam, Dr. Alice
      3    Chodnoff, Mr. Norman                1        Hallis, Dr. George
```

91

## Exercises

### 3. Resolving Macro Variables with the SYMGET Function

Retrieve the **starts** program shown below and submit it to create a series of macro variables containing the starting date for each course.

```
data _null_;
   set perm.schedule;
   call symput('start'||trim(left(course_number)),
      put(begin_date,mmddyy10.));
run;
```

**a.** Display the values of the newly created macro variables in the SAS log.

**b.** Create a temporary data set named **outstand** containing the students in the **perm.register** data set who have not yet paid their registration fee. Create a new variable that indicates the starting date for the corresponding course number. Print the **outstand** data set.

The INPUT function is needed to convert character values of macro variables retrieved by the SYMGET function into numeric SAS data values.

**4. Macro Variable Storage and Resolution (Optional)**

Determine the type, length, and value of the DATA step variables in the program below.

```
%let var1=cat;
%let var2=3;
data test;
   length s1 s4 s5 $ 3;
   call symput('var3','dog');
   r1="&var1";
   r2=&var2;
   r3="&var3";
   s1=symget('var1');
   s2=symget('var2');
   s3=input(symget('var2'),2.);
   s4=symget('var3');
   s5=symget('var'||left(r2));
run;
```

| Name | Type | Length | Value |
|---|---|---|---|
| R1 | | | |
| R2 | | | |
| R3 | | | |
| S1 | | | |
| S2 | | | |
| S3 | | | |
| S4 | | | |
| S5 | | | |

Hint: Mimic the behavior of SAS by making three passes through the program: word scanning, compilation, and execution.

Hint: Draw a symbol table, updating it as each macro variable is created and assigned a value.

# Solutions to Exercises

## 3. Resolving Macro Variables with the SYMGET Function

a. The _USER_ argument in the %PUT statement displays all user-created macro variables.

```
%put _user_;
```

Partial SAS Log

```
GLOBAL START17 02/28/2006
GLOBAL START16 01/24/2006
GLOBAL DSN perm.courses
GLOBAL VARS days fee
GLOBAL START8 06/14/2005
GLOBAL START18 03/28/2006
GLOBAL START9 07/19/2005
GLOBAL CRSNUM 3
GLOBAL DATE 01/11/2005
GLOBAL START4 01/25/2005
GLOBAL START5 03/01/2005
GLOBAL START6 04/05/2005
GLOBAL NUMPAID 14
GLOBAL START7 05/24/2005
GLOBAL START11 09/20/2005
GLOBAL NUMSTU 20
GLOBAL CRSNAME Local Area Networks
GLOBAL DUE $3,900
GLOBAL START10 08/16/2005
GLOBAL NUM 8
GLOBAL START1 10/26/2004
GLOBAL START13 11/15/2005
GLOBAL START2 12/07/2004
GLOBAL START12 10/04/2005
GLOBAL START3 01/11/2005
GLOBAL START15 01/10/2006
GLOBAL START14 12/06/2005
```

The order in which the macro variables are displayed may differ from the order in which they were created.

**b.** The correct date can be obtained by appending the value of the **course_number** variable as a suffix to START to identify the corresponding macro variable name. The retrieved (character) value should be converted to a numeric SAS date value with a permanently assigned format.

```
data outstand;
   set perm.register;
   where paid='N';
   begin=input(symget('start'||
         left(course_number)),mmddyy10.);
   format begin date9.;
run;

proc print data=outstand;
   var student_name course_number begin;
   title1 "Class Dates for Students";
   title2 "with Outstanding Fees";
run;
```

Partial SAS Output

```
                          Class Dates for Students
                               with Outstanding Fees

                                      Course_
 Obs    Student_Name                  Number          begin

   1    Amigo, Mr. Bill                  1        26OCT2004
   2    Edwards, Mr. Charles             1        26OCT2004
   3    Haubold, Ms. Ann                 1        26OCT2004
   4    Hodge, Ms. Rita                  1        26OCT2004
   5    McGillivray, Ms. Kathy           1        26OCT2004
   6    Pancoast, Ms. Jane               1        26OCT2004
   7    Divjak, Ms. Theresa              2        07DEC2004
   8    Gandy, Dr. David                 2        07DEC2004
   9    Harrell, Mr. Ken                 2        07DEC2004
  10    Hill, Mr. Paul                   2        07DEC2004
  11    Lewanwowski, Mr. Dale R.         2        07DEC2004
  12    Nandy, Ms. Brenda                2        07DEC2004
  13    Ng, Mr. John                     2        07DEC2004
  14    Williams, Mr. Gene               2        07DEC2004
  15    Chevarley, Ms. Arlene            3        11JAN2005
```

## 4. Macro Variable Storage and Resolution (Optional)

### Word Scanning

Substitutions based on macro variable references using & occur during word scanning.

**R1** and **R2** Macro variables VAR1 and VAR2 exist so both substitutions occur.

**R3** Macro variable VAR3 does not exist until the CALL SYMPUT statement executes, so no substitution is made.

```
data test:
length s1 s4 s5 $ 3;
call symput('var3','dog');
r1="cat";
r2=3;
r3="&var3";
s1=symget('var1');
s2=symget('var2');
s3=input(symget('var2'),2.);
s4=symget('var3');
s5=symget('var'||left(r2));
run;
```

**Compilation**

The attributes of each variable are determined during compilation of the resulting DATA step program:

```
data test:
length s1 s4 s5 $ 3;
call symput('var3','dog');
r1="cat";
r2=3;
r3="&var3";
s1=symget('var1');
s2=symget('var2');
s3=input(symget('var2'),2.);
s4=symget('var3');
s5=symget('var'||left(r2));
run;
```

| | |
|---|---|
| `S1`, `S4`, `S5` | Explicit definition as character variables with length 3. |
| `R2` | Lack of quotes around the assigned value indicates a numeric variable. Default length for numeric variables is 8. |
| `R1` and `R3` | Quotes around the assigned value indicate a character variable. The number of characters inside the quotes determines the length. |
| `S2` | Assignment from the SYMGET function indicates a character variable. No explicitly assigned length defaults to 200; the compile does not know what value will be in the symbol table during execution, the 200 bytes is allocated. |
| `S3` | Assignment from the INPUT function with a numeric informat indicates a numeric variable. Default length for numeric variables is 8. |

### Execution

The values of each variable are determined during execution of the program. It is at this time that the CALL SYMPUT statement creates the macro variable VAR3 so that its value is available for retrieval by the SYMGET function later in the DATA step.

| | |
|---|---|
| **R1** and **R2** | Hardcoded values are assigned. |
| **R3** | The reference &VAR3 is a text string during execution, so this is also a hardcoded value. |
| **S1** | Value obtained from the symbol table. |
| **S2** | Value obtained from the symbol tables does not fill allotment of 200 characters; there are 199 trailing blanks. |
| **S3** | The first two characters obtained from the symbol table are converted into a numeric value using the 2. informat. |
| **S4** and **S5** | Same value obtained from the symbol table since each SYMGET argument results in the character string `var3`. Macro variable VAR3 was created earlier in the execution of the DATA step. |

| **Name** | **Type** | **Length** | **Value** |
|---|---|---|---|
| R1 | Char | 3 | cat |
| R2 | Num | 8 | 3 |
| R3 | Char | 5 | &var3 |
| S1 | Char | 3 | cat |
| S2 | Char | 200 | 3 |
| S3 | Num | 8 | 3 |
| S4 | Char | 3 | dog |
| S5 | Char | 3 | dog |

# 4.4 Creating Macro Variables in SQL

## Objectives

- Create macro variables during PROC SQL execution.
- Store several values in one macro variable using the SQL procedure.

94

## The SQL Procedure INTO Clause

The SQL procedure INTO clause can create or update macro variables.

General form of the SQL procedure INTO clause:

```
SELECT col1, col2, . . . INTO :mvar1, :mvar2,...
      FROM table-expression
      WHERE where-expression
      other clauses;
```

This form of the INTO clause does not trim leading or trailing blanks.

95

## The SQL Procedure INTO Clause

Example: Create a macro variable that contains the total of all course fees.

```
proc sql noprint; Suppress the print result
   select sum(fee) format=dollar10.
      into :totfee Capture the sum(fee).
      from perm.all;
quit;
```

SQL1

Partial SAS Log

```
13   %let totfee=&totfee;
14   %put totfee=&totfee;
totfee=$354,380
```

The %LET statement removes leading and trailing blanks from TOTFEE.

96

## The SQL Procedure INTO Clause

The INTO clause can create multiple macro variables per row when multiple rows are selected.

General form of the INTO clause to create multiple macro variables per row:

> **SELECT** *col1, . . .* **INTO** *:mvar1 - :mvarn,...*
> **FROM** *table-expression*
> **WHERE** *where-expression*
> *other clauses*;

97

## The SQL Procedure INTO Clause

Example: Create macro variables from the course code and begin date from the first two rows returned by the SELECT statement from **perm.schedule**.

```
title 'SQL result';
proc sql;
  select course_code, begin_date format=mmddyy10.
  into :crsid1-:crsid2, :date1-:date2
  from perm.schedule
  where year(begin_date)=2006
  order by begin_date;
quit;
%put &crsid1, &date1;
%put &crsid2, &date2;
```

SQL2

98

## The SQL Procedure INTO Clause

SELECT statement output

Partial SAS Log

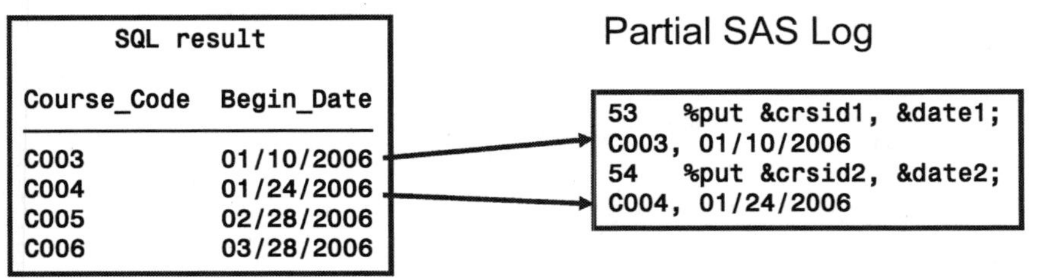

SQL result

| Course_Code | Begin_Date |
|---|---|
| C003 | 01/10/2006 |
| C004 | 01/24/2006 |
| C005 | 02/28/2006 |
| C006 | 03/28/2006 |

```
53   %put &crsid1, &date1;
C003, 01/10/2006
54   %put &crsid2, &date2;
C004, 01/24/2006
```

99

## The SQL Procedure INTO Clause (Self-Study)

The INTO clause can create macro variables for an unknown number of rows.

1. Run a query to determine the number of rows and create a macro variable NUMROWS to store that number.
2. Run a query using NUMROWS as the suffix of a numbered series of macro variables.

100

## The SQL Procedure INTO Clause (Self-Study)

SQL3

Create ranges of macro variables that contain the course code, location, and starting date of all courses scheduled in 2006.

```
proc sql noprint;
   select count(*)
      into :numrows
      from perm.schedule
      where year(begin_date)=2006;
   %let numrows=&numrows;
   %put There are &numrows courses in 2006;
   select course_code, location,
         begin_date format=mmddyy10.
      into :crsid1-:crsid&numrows,
           :place1-:place&numrows,
           :date1-:date&numrows
      from perm.schedule
      where year(begin_date)=2006
      order by begin_date;
   %put _user_;
quit;
```

Partial SAS Log

```
20   proc sql noprint;
21      select count(*)
22         into :numrows
23         from perm.schedule
24      where year(begin_date)=2006;
25      %let numrows=&numrows;
26      %put There are &numrows courses in 2006;
There are 4 courses in 2006
27      select course_code, location,
28             begin_date format=mmddyy10.
29         into :crsid1-:crsid&numrows,
30              :place1-:place&numrows,
31              :date1-:date&numrows
32         from perm.schedule
33      where year(begin_date)=2006
34      order by begin_date;
35      %put _user_;
GLOBAL SQLOBS 4
GLOBAL CRSID2 C004
GLOBAL SQLOOPS 22
GLOBAL CRSID3 C005
GLOBAL DATE4 03/28/2006
GLOBAL PLACE1 Dallas
GLOBAL CRSID1 C003
GLOBAL PLACE2 Boston
GLOBAL PLACE3 Seattle
GLOBAL DATE1 01/10/2006
GLOBAL CRSID4 C006
GLOBAL TOTFEE $354,380
GLOBAL DATE2 01/24/2006
GLOBAL DATE3 02/28/2006
GLOBAL SQLRC 0
GLOBAL NUMROWS 4
GLOBAL PLACE4 Dallas
```

## The SQL Procedure INTO Clause

The INTO clause can store all unique values of a specified column into a single macro variable.

General form of the INTO clause to create a list of unique values in one macro variable:

**SELECT** *col1*, . . .
  **INTO :***mvar* SEPARATED BY '*delimiter*', . . .
  **FROM** *table-expression*
  **WHERE** *where-expression*
  *other clauses*;

102

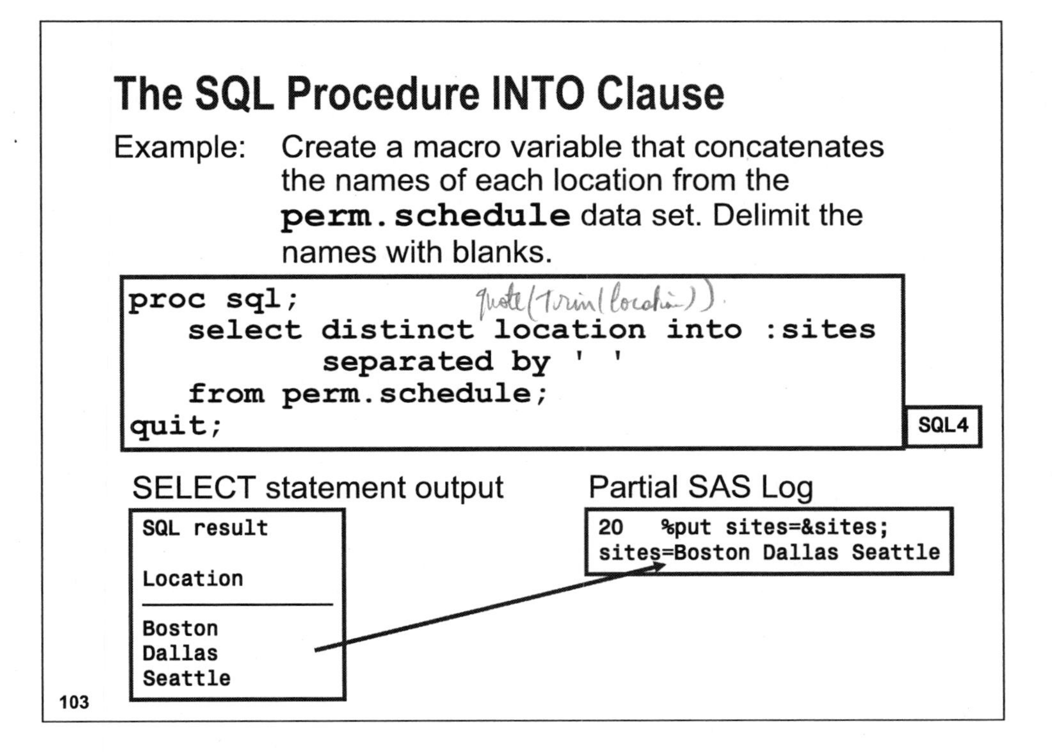

## Exercises

**5. Creating Multiple Macro Variables Using SQL**

**a.** The **perm.schedule** data set contains the variable **begin_date**, which holds the starting date of each course for 18 classes. Use the SQL procedure to create a set of macro variables named START1 through START18. The value of each START macro variable should be in MMDDYY10. format.

**b.** Open the **sqlrost** program shown below. Modify the TITLE statement so that the series of Xs are replaced with the appropriate indirect macro variable references based on the current value of NUM, which represents the course number (1 through 18). Submit the modified program.

```
%let num=4;
proc print data=perm.all noobs n;
   where course_number=&num;
   var student_name student_company;
   title "Roster for Course &num Beginning on XXXXXX";
run;
```

**c. (Optional)**
Complete parts **a** and **b** of this exercise without the explicit knowledge of the number of classes in the **perm.schedule** data set.

# Solutions to Exercises

## 5. Creating Multiple Macro Variables Using SQL

**a.** A special form of the INTO clause is useful for creating series of macro variables from multiple rows of an SQL query.

```
proc sql noprint;
   select begin_date format=mmddyy10.
         into :start1 - :start18
      from perm.schedule;
quit;
```

**b.** Because the series of macro variables has a common root (START) and a suffix that corresponds to the value of the NUM macro variable, two ampersands are used in front of the completed reference.

```
%let num=4;

proc print data=perm.all noobs n;
   where course_number=&num;
   var student_name student_company;
   title1 "Roster for Course &num Beginning on &&start&num";
run;
```

Partial Output

```
                    Roster for Course 4 Beginning on 01/25/2005

     Student_Name                Student_Company

     Bates, Ms. Ellen            Reston Railway
     Boyd, Ms. Leah              United Shoes Co.
     Chan, Mr. John              California Lawyers Assn.
     Chevarley, Ms. Arlene       Motor Communications
     Chow, Ms. Sylvia            Bostic Amplifier Inc.
     Crace, Mr. Ron              Von Crump Seafood
     Edwards, Mr. Charles        Gorman Tire Corp.
     Garza, Ms. Cheryl           Admiral Research & Development Co.
     Geatz, Mr. Patrick D.       San Juan Gas and Electric
     Keever, Ms. Linda           Crossbow of California
     Kelley, Ms. Gail            Crossbow of California
     Kendig, Mr. James           Rocks International
     Kimble, Mr. John            Alforone Chemical
     Koleff, Mr. Jim             Emulate Research
     Montgomery, Mr. Jeff        Bonstell Electronics
     Moore, Mr. John             California Dept. of Insurance
     Page, Mr. Scott             Applied Technologies
     Parker, Mr. Robert          SMASH Hardware Inc.
     Pledger, Ms. Terri          Candide Corporation
     Snell, Dr. William J.       US Treasury
     Stackhouse, Ms. Loretta     Donnelly Corp.
     Sulzbach, Mr. Bill          Sailbest Ships
     Swayze, Mr. Rodney          Reston Railway
```

c. **(Optional)** The NUMROWS macro variable stores how many records will be returned by the query. This is the same as the number of macro variables in each series.

```
proc sql noprint;
   select count(*)
      into :numrows
      from perm.schedule;
   %let numrows=&numrows;
   select begin_date format=mmddyy10.
      into :start1 - :start&numrows
      from perm.schedule;
quit;

%let num=4;
proc print data=perm.all noobs n;
   where course_number = &num;
   var student_name student_company;
   title1 "Roster for Course &num Beginning on &&start&num";
run;
```

# Chapter 5 Macro Programs

# 5.1 Conditional Processing

## Objectives

- Conditionally process SAS code within a macro program.
- Monitor macro execution.
- Insert entire steps, entire statements, and partial statements into a SAS program.

3

## The Need for Macro-Level Programming

Suppose you submit a program every day to create registration listings for courses to be held later in the current month.

Every Friday you also submit a second program to create a summary of revenue generated so far in the current month.

4

## The Need for Macro-Level Programming

Example: Automate the application so that only **one program** is required.

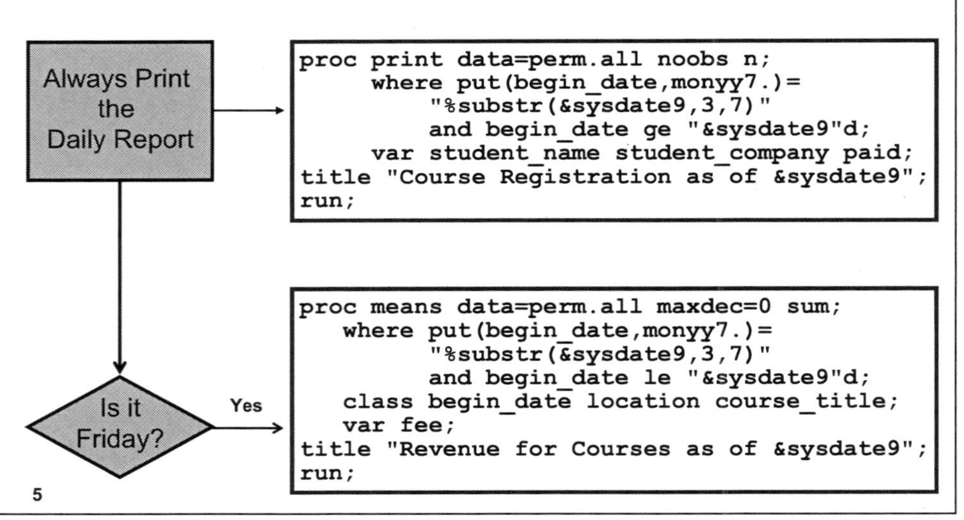


```
proc print data=perm.all noobs n;
     where put(begin_date,monyy7.)=
          "%substr(&sysdate9,3,7)"
          and begin_date ge "&sysdate9"d;
     var student_name student_company paid;
title "Course Registration as of &sysdate9";
run;
```

```
proc means data=perm.all maxdec=0 sum;
   where put(begin_date,monyy7.)=
         "%substr(&sysdate9,3,7)"
         and begin_date le "&sysdate9"d;
   class begin_date location course_title;
   var fee;
title "Revenue for Courses as of &sysdate9";
run;
```

5

## Conditional Processing

You can perform conditional execution with %IF-%THEN and %ELSE statements.

General form of %IF-%THEN and %ELSE statements:

> **%IF** *expression* **%THEN** *text*;
> **%ELSE** *text*;

*expression* can be any valid macro expression.

The %ELSE statement is optional.

These macro language statements can only be used inside a macro definition.

6

**CAUTION**

Compound expressions can be specified using the AND and OR operators. Do not precede these keywords with %.

## Conditional Processing

The text following keywords %THEN and %ELSE can be

- a macro programming statement
- constant text
- an expression
- a macro variable reference
- a macro call.

Macro language expressions are similar to DATA step expressions, except the following, which are **not** valid in the macro language:

- 1 <= &x <= 10
- special WHERE operators
- IN comparison operator (prior to SAS®9).

7 ✎ The macro IN comparison operator is new in SAS®9.

## Monitoring Macro Execution

The MLOGIC system option displays macro execution messages in the SAS log, including

- macro initialization
- parameter values
- results of arithmetic and logical operations
- macro termination.

General form of the MLOGIC|NOMLOGIC option:

> **OPTIONS** MLOGIC;
> **OPTIONS** NOMLOGIC;

The default setting is NOMLOGIC.

8

## Processing Complete Steps

Step 1: Create separate macros for the **daily** and **weekly** programs.

```
%macro daily;
   proc print data=perm.all noobs n;
      where put(begin_date,monyy7.)="%substr(&sysdate9,3,7)"
            and begin_date ge "&sysdate9"d;
      var student_name student_company paid;
      title "Course Registration as of &sysdate";
    run;
%mend daily;

%macro weekly;
   proc means data=perm.all maxdec=0 sum;
      where put(begin_date,monyy7.)="%substr(&sysdate9,3,7)"
            and begin_date le "&sysdate9"d;
      class begin_date location course_title;
      var fee;
      title "Revenue for Courses as of &sysdate9";
   run;
%mend weekly;
```

9

## Processing Complete Steps

Step 2: Write a third macro that always calls the DAILY macro and conditionally calls the WEEKLY macro.

```
%macro reports;
   %daily
   %if &sysday=Friday %then %weekly;
%mend reports;
```

COND01

implied character string => that's why doesn't have quote

10

## Monitoring Macro Execution

Example: Use the MLOGIC option to monitor the REPORTS macro.

Partial SAS Log

```
494  %macro reports;
495     %daily
496     %if &sysday=Friday %then %weekly;
497  %mend reports;
498
499  options mlogic;
500  %reports
MLOGIC(REPORTS):  Beginning execution.
MLOGIC(DAILY):  Beginning execution.
MLOGIC(DAILY):  Ending execution.
MLOGIC(REPORTS):  %IF condition &sysday=Friday is TRUE
MLOGIC(WEEKLY):  Beginning execution.
MLOGIC(WEEKLY):  Ending execution.
MLOGIC(REPORTS):  Ending execution.
```

11

## Macro Syntax Errors

If a macro definition contains macro language syntax errors, error messages are written to the SAS log and a nonexecutable (dummy) macro is created.

Example: Suppose the percent sign is missing from the %THEN statement.

Partial SAS Log

```
514  %macro reports;
515     %daily
516     %if &sysday=Friday then %weekly;
ERROR: Expected %THEN statement not found.  A dummy macro will be
       compiled.
517  %mend reports;
```

12

## Conditional Processing

Use %DO and %END statements following %THEN or %ELSE to generate text that contains semicolons.

**%IF** *expression* **%THEN %DO**;
    *statement*; *statement*;...
**%END**;
**%ELSE %DO**;
    *statement*; *statement*;...
**%END**;

13

## Processing Complete Steps

Example: Use a single macro to generate the daily report unconditionally and the weekly report on Friday.

```
%macro reports;
   proc print data=perm.all noobs n;
      where put(begin_date,monyy7.)="%substr(&sysdate9,3,7)"
            and begin_date ge "&sysdate9"d;
      var student_name student_company paid;
      title "Course Registration as of &sysdate";
   run;
 %if &sysday=Friday %then %do;
   proc means data=perm.all maxdec=0 sum;
      where put(begin_date,monyy7.)="%substr(&sysdate9,3,7)"
            and begin_date le "&sysdate9"d;
      class begin_date location course_title;
      var fee;
      title "Revenue for Courses as of &sysdate9";
   run;
 %end;
%mend reports;
```

14

COND02

## Processing Complete Steps

Example: Store the production SAS programs in external files and copy those files to the input stack with %INCLUDE statements.

```
%macro reports;
   %include 'c:\mypgms\daily.sas';
   %if &sysday=Friday %then %do;
        %include 'c:\mypgms\weekly.sas';
   %end;
%mend reports;
```

COND03

15

## Processing Complete Statements

Example: Insert individual statements within a PROC step.

```
%macro attend(crs,start=01jan2005,stop=31dec2005);
  proc freq data=perm.all;
     where begin_date between "&start"d and "&stop"d;
     table location / nocum;
     title "Enrollment from &start to &stop";
     %if &crs= %then %do;
         title2 "For all Courses";
     %end;
     %else %do;
         title2 "For Course &crs only";
         where also course_code="&crs";
     %end;
  run;
%mend;
options mprint mlogic;
%attend(start=01jul2005)
%attend(C003)
```

COND04

16

## Processing Complete Statements

SAS log from macro call %attend(start=01jul2005)

```
71   %attend(start=01jul2005)
MLOGIC(ATTEND):  Beginning execution.
MLOGIC(ATTEND):  Parameter START has value 01jul2005
MLOGIC(ATTEND):  Parameter CRS has value
MLOGIC(ATTEND):  Parameter STOP has value 31dec2005
MPRINT(ATTEND):   proc freq data=perm.all;
MPRINT(ATTEND):   where begin_date between "01jul2005"d and "31dec2005"d;
MPRINT(ATTEND):   table location / nocum;
MPRINT(ATTEND):   title "Enrollment from 01jul2005 to 31dec2005";
MLOGIC(ATTEND):  %IF condition &crs= is TRUE
MPRINT(ATTEND):   title2 "For all Courses";
MPRINT(ATTEND):   run;

NOTE: There were 162 observations read from the data set PERM.ALL.
      WHERE (begin_date>='01JUL2005'D and begin_date<='31DEC2005'D);

MLOGIC(ATTEND):  Ending execution.
```

17

## Processing Complete Statements

SAS log from macro call %attend(C003)

```
72   %attend(C003)
MLOGIC(ATTEND):  Beginning execution.
MLOGIC(ATTEND):  Parameter CRS has value C003
MLOGIC(ATTEND):  Parameter START has value 01jan2005
MLOGIC(ATTEND):  Parameter STOP has value 31dec2005
MPRINT(ATTEND):   proc freq data=perm.all;
MPRINT(ATTEND):   where begin_date between "01jan2005"d and "31dec2005"d;
MPRINT(ATTEND):   table location / nocum;
MPRINT(ATTEND):   title "Enrollment from 01jan2005 to 31dec2005";
MLOGIC(ATTEND):  %IF condition &crs= is FALSE
MPRINT(ATTEND):   title2 "For Course C003 only";
MPRINT(ATTEND):   where also course_code="C003";
NOTE: Where clause has been augmented.
MPRINT(ATTEND):   run;

NOTE: There were 50 observations read from the data set PERM.ALL.
      WHERE (begin_date>='01JAN2005'D and begin_date<='31DEC2005'D) and
      (course_code='C003');

MLOGIC(ATTEND):  Ending execution.
```

18

## Processing Complete Statements

Example: Insert individual statements within a DATA step.

```
%macro choice(status);
  data fees;
    set perm.all;
    %if %upcase(&status)=PAID %then %do;
        where paid = 'Y';
        keep student_name course_code
             begin_date totalfee;
    %end;
    %else %do;
        where paid = 'N';
        keep student_name course_code
              begin_date totalfee latechg;
        latechg=fee*1.10;
    %end;
    if      location='Boston'  then totalfee=fee*1.06;
    else if location='Seattle' then totalfee=fee*1.025;
    else if location='Dallas'  then totalfee=fee*1.05;
  run;
%mend choice;
%choice(PAID)
%choice(OWED)
```

COND05

Macro comparisons are case sensitive.

19

## Processing Complete Statements

Partial SAS Log

```
744  %choice(PAID)
MLOGIC(CHOICE):  Beginning execution.
MLOGIC(CHOICE):  Parameter STATUS has value PAID
MPRINT(CHOICE):   data fees;
MPRINT(CHOICE):   set perm.all;
MLOGIC(CHOICE):  %IF condition %upcase(&status)=PAID is TRUE
MPRINT(CHOICE):   where paid = 'Y';
MPRINT(CHOICE):   keep student_name course_code begin_date totalfee;
MPRINT(CHOICE):   if location='Boston' then totalfee=fee*1.06;
MPRINT(CHOICE):   else if location='Seattle' then
totalfee=fee*1.025;
MPRINT(CHOICE):   else if location='Dallas' then totalfee=fee*1.05;
MPRINT(CHOICE):   run;

NOTE: There were 327 observations read from the data set PERM.ALL.
      WHERE paid='Y';
NOTE: The data set WORK.FEES has 327 observations and 4 variables.
NOTE: DATA statement used (Total process time):
      real time           0.02 seconds
      cpu time            0.02 seconds
```

20

# Processing Complete Statements

Partial SAS Log

```
745  %choice(OWED)
MLOGIC(CHOICE):  Beginning execution.
MLOGIC(CHOICE):  Parameter STATUS has value OWED
MPRINT(CHOICE):   data fees;
MPRINT(CHOICE):   set perm.all;
MLOGIC(CHOICE):  %IF condition %upcase(&status)=PAID is FALSE
MPRINT(CHOICE):   where paid = 'N';
MPRINT(CHOICE):   keep student_name course_code begin_date totalfee
latechg;
MPRINT(CHOICE):   latechg=fee*1.10;
MPRINT(CHOICE):   if location='Boston' then totalfee=fee*1.06;
MPRINT(CHOICE):   else if location='Seattle' then
totalfee=fee*1.025;
MPRINT(CHOICE):   else if location='Dallas' then totalfee=fee*1.05;
MPRINT(CHOICE):   run;

NOTE: There were 107 observations read from the data set PERM.ALL.
      WHERE paid='N';
NOTE: The data set WORK.FEES has 107 observations and 5 variables.
NOTE: DATA statement used (Total process time):
      real time           0.02 seconds
      cpu time            0.02 seconds
```

21

## Processing Partial Statements

Conditionally insert text into the middle of a statement.

Example: Generate either a one-way or two-way frequency table, depending on a parameter value.

```
%macro counts (cols=_character_, rows=);
    proc freq data=perm.all;
      tables
      %if &rows ne  %then &rows *;
         &cols
      ;
    run;
%mend counts;
options mprint mlogic;
%counts(cols=paid)
%counts(cols=paid, rows=course_number)
```

COND06

22

The abbreviated variable list `_character_` stands for all character variables in a data set.

## Processing Partial Statements

Partial SAS Log

```
633  %counts(cols=paid)
MPRINT(COUNTS):   proc freq data=perm.all;
MPRINT(COUNTS):   tables paid ;
MPRINT(COUNTS):   run;

NOTE: There were 434 observations read from the data set PERM.ALL.
NOTE: PROCEDURE FREQ used (Total process time):
      real time           0.00 seconds
      cpu time            0.01 seconds

634  %counts(cols=paid, rows=course_number)
MPRINT(COUNTS):   proc freq data=perm.all;
MPRINT(COUNTS):   tables course_number * paid ;
MPRINT(COUNTS):   run;

NOTE: There were 434 observations read from the data set PERM.ALL.
NOTE: PROCEDURE FREQ used (Total process time):
      real time           0.01 seconds
      cpu time            0.02 seconds
```

23

## Parameter Validation

Example: Validate a parameter value before generating SAS code based on that value.

```
%macro courses(site);
   %let site=%upcase(&site);
   %if &site=DALLAS
    or &site=SEATTLE
    or &site=BOSTON %then %do;
       proc print data=perm.schedule;
          where upcase(location)="&site";
          title "COURSES OFFERED AT &site";
       run;
   %end;
   %else %put Sorry, no courses taught at &site..;
%mend courses;
```

COND07

24

## Parameter Validation

Example: Validate a parameter value before generating SAS code based on that value.

```
%macro courses(site);
   %let site=%upcase(&site);
   %if &site in DALLAS SEATTLE BOSTON %then %do;
       proc print data=perm.schedule;
          where upcase(location)="&site";
          title "COURSES OFFERED AT &site";
       run;
   %end;
   %else %put Sorry, no courses taught at &site..;
%mend courses;
```

COND08

The IN operator is new in SAS®9. The list of values is not enclosed in parentheses.

25

The IN operator is not available in SAS 9.1.2 and 9.1.3, but will return in SAS 9.2.

# Parameter Validation

Partial SAS Log

```
788  %courses(Dallas)
MPRINT(COURSES):   proc print data=perm.schedule;
MPRINT(COURSES):   where upcase(location)="DALLAS";
MPRINT(COURSES):   title "COURSES OFFERED AT DALLAS";
MPRINT(COURSES):   run;
NOTE: There were 6 observations read from the data set
      PERM.SCHEDULE.
      WHERE UPCASE(location)='DALLAS';
NOTE: PROCEDURE PRINT used (Total process time):
      real time           0.00 seconds
      cpu time            0.00 seconds


789  %courses(LA)
Sorry, no courses taught at LA.
```

26

## Parameter Validation

Use the %INDEX function to check the value of a macro variable against a list of valid values.

General form of the %INDEX function:

```
%INDEX(argument1, argument2)
```

The %INDEX function

- searches *argument1* for the first occurrence of *argument2*
- returns an integer representing the position in *argument1* of the first character of *argument2* if there is an exact match
- returns 0 if there is no match.

27

## Parameter Validation

```
%INDEX(argument1, argument2)
```

*argument1* and *argument2* can be

- constant text
- macro variable references
- macro functions
- macro calls.

28

## Parameter Validation

Example: Parameter validation with the %INDEX function.

```
%macro courses(site);
   %let site=%upcase(&site);
   %let sitelist=*DALLAS*SEATTLE*BOSTON*;
   %if %index(&sitelist,*&site*) > 0 %then %do;
      proc print data=perm.schedule;
         where upcase(location)="&site";
         title "COURSES OFFERED AT &site";
      run;
   %end;
   %else %do;
      %put Sorry, no courses taught at &site..;
      %put Valid locations are: &sitelist..;
   %end;
%mend courses;
```

COND09

29

## Parameter Validation

Partial SAS Log

```
762  %courses(Dallas)
MPRINT(COURSES):   proc print data=perm.schedule;
MPRINT(COURSES):   where upcase(location)="DALLAS";
MPRINT(COURSES):   title "COURSES OFFERED AT DALLAS";
MPRINT(COURSES):   run;
NOTE: There were 6 observations read from the data set
      PERM.SCHEDULE.
      WHERE UPCASE(location)='DALLAS';
NOTE: PROCEDURE PRINT used (Total process time):
      real time           0.00 seconds
      cpu time            0.00 seconds

763  %courses(LA)
Sorry, no courses taught at LA.
Valid locations are: *DALLAS*SEATTLE*BOSTON*.
```

30

## Parameter Validation

Example: Modify the previous program so that the macro variable SITELIST is data-driven.

```
%macro courses(site);
   %let site=%upcase(&site);
   proc sql noprint;
      select distinct upcase(location)
         into :sitelist separated by '*'
      from perm.schedule;
     quit;
   %if %index(*&sitelist*,*&site*) > 0
   %then %do;
     . . .
```

COND10

31

## Developing Macro-Based Applications

If a macro-based application generates SAS code, use a four-step development approach.

1. Write and debug the SAS program without any macro coding.
2. Generalize the program by replacing hardcoded constants with macro variable references. Initialize the macro variables with %LET statements.
3. Create a macro definition by placing %MACRO and %MEND statements around your program. Convert %LET statements to macro parameters as appropriate.
4. Add macro-level programming statements such as %IF-%THEN.

32

## Exercises

### 1. Validating Macro Parameters

**a.** Open the **paidstat** program shown below into the Editor window and submit it.

```
%macro paid(crsnum);
   proc print data=perm.register label n noobs;
      var student_name paid;
      where course_number=&crsnum;
      title "Fee Status for Course &crsnum";
   run;
%mend paid;

%paid(2)
```

**b.** Modify the macro so it submits the PROC PRINT step only if the CRSNUM parameter has a value between 1 and 18. If the CRSNUM value is out of range, the macro should write this message to the SAS log:

```
Course Number must be between 1 and 18.
          Supplied value was: x
```

The value of x is the CRSNUM parameter.

**c.** Resubmit the macro definition and call the macro using both valid and invalid parameter values.

**d.** Modify the macro to support a second positional parameter named STATUS. Add this statement after the WHERE statement:

```
where also paid="&status";
```

At the beginning of the macro, extract the first character of STATUS and store it in uppercase. Alter the macro so that the PROC PRINT step can be submitted only when the STATUS parameter begins with Y or N. Write a message to the log when the STATUS parameter is invalid.

Resubmit the macro definition and call the macro using both valid and invalid values for STATUS.

## 2. Defining, Executing, and Debugging a Macro (Optional)

**a.** If you have the SAS windowing environment active, exit SAS and then start a new SAS session. Remember to assign the **perm** libref in the new SAS session.

Open the **printit** program shown below into the Editor window and submit it.

```
%macro printit;
   %if &syslast = _NULL_ %then %do;
      proc print data=_last_(obs=5);
         title "Listing of data set &syslast";
      run;
   end;
%mend;
```

**b.** Use the SAS log to diagnose the compilation error. Fix the syntax error and resubmit the macro definition.

**c.** Submit a call to the PRINTIT macro. An error message appears.

Activate system options that print information in the SAS log to help you diagnose the error. Call the PRINTIT macro again and examine the SAS log.

Fix the logic error in the program. Resubmit the macro definition and call the macro. If no SAS code is submitted when the macro is called, you have repaired the error.

**d.** Alter the macro definition by writing a message to the SAS log whenever the %IF expression is false:

```
%put No SAS data set has been created.;
```

Recompile the macro and call it. The text from the %PUT statement should appear in the SAS log.

**e.** Submit this program:

```
proc sort data=perm.students
          out=business(keep=student_company) nodupkey;
   by student_company;
run;
```

Make a call to the PRINTIT macro. You should get a listing of the **business** data set.

## Solutions to Exercises

### 1. Validating Macro Parameters

a. Open the program **paidstat** shown below into the Editor window and submit it.

```
%macro paid(crsnum);
   proc print data=perm.register label n noobs;
      var student_name paid;
      where course_number=&crsnum;
      title "Fee Status for Course &crsnum";
   run;
%mend paid;

%paid(2)
```

b. To define a valid range, the %IF expression must contain two comparisons connected with the AND operator. Each message line requires a separate %PUT statement.

```
%macro paid(crsnum);
   %if &crsnum >=1 and &crsnum <= 18 %then %do;
      proc print data=perm.register label noobs n;
         where course_number=&crsnum;
         title "Fee Status for Course &crsnum";
      run;
   %end;
   %else %do;
      %put Course Number must be between 1 and 18;
      %put Supplied Value was: &crsnum;
   %end;
%mend paid;

%paid(2)
%paid(20)
```

c. Resubmit the macro definition and call the macro.

Partial SAS Log

```
MLOGIC(PAID):  Ending execution.
222  %paid(20)
MLOGIC(PAID):  Beginning execution.
MLOGIC(PAID):  Parameter CRSNUM has value 20
MLOGIC(PAID):  %IF condition &crsnum >=1 and &crsnum <= 18 is FALSE
MLOGIC(PAID):  %PUT Course Number must be between 1 and 18
Course Number must be between 1 and 18
MLOGIC(PAID):  %PUT Supplied Value was: &crsnum
Supplied Value was: 20
MLOGIC(PAID):  Ending execution.
```

**d.** The %UPCASE and %SUBSTR functions are used to extract the first character of the parameter value and translate it to uppercase. The additional condition based on STATUS can be implemented using the AND operator with the previous CRSNUM validation expression or with nested %IF-%THEN statements.

```
%macro paid(crsnum,status);
   %let status1=%upcase(%substr(&status,1,1));
   %if &status1=Y or &status1=N %then %do;
      %if &crsnum >= 1 and &crsnum <= 18 %then %do;
         proc print data=perm.register label n noobs;
            var student_name paid;
            where course_number=&crsnum;
            where also paid="&status1";
            title "Fee Status for Course &crsnum";
         run;
      %end;
      %else %do;
         %put Course Number must be between 1 and 18;
         %put Supplied Value was:  &crsnum;
      %end;
   %end;
   %else %do;
      %put Status must begin with Y or N;
      %put Supplied value was:  &status;
   %end;
%mend paid;

%paid(2,Y)
%paid(2,no)
%paid(2,?)
```

*; '; *"; %mend; run;
%put ok;

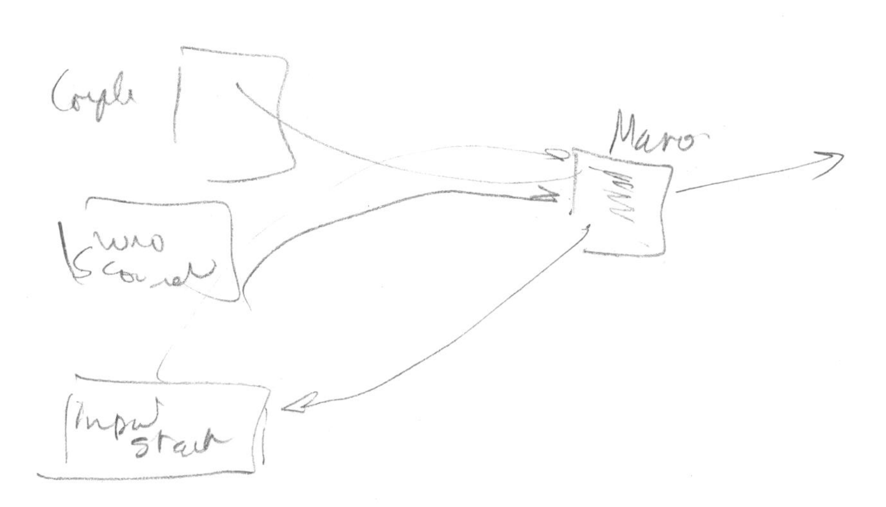

Partial SAS Log

```
246  %paid(2,no)
MLOGIC(PAID):  Beginning execution.
MLOGIC(PAID):  Parameter CRSNUM has value 2
MLOGIC(PAID):  Parameter STATUS has value no
MLOGIC(PAID):  %LET (variable name is STATUS1)
MLOGIC(PAID):  %IF condition &status1=Y or &status1=N is TRUE
MLOGIC(PAID):  %IF condition &crsnum >= 1 and &crsnum <= 18 is TRUE
MPRINT(PAID):   proc print data=perm.register label n noobs;
MPRINT(PAID):   var student_name paid;
MPRINT(PAID):   where course_number=2;
MPRINT(PAID):   where also paid="N";
NOTE: Where clause has been augmented.
MPRINT(PAID):   title "Fee Status for Course 2";
MPRINT(PAID):   run;
NOTE: There were 8 observations read from the dataset PERM.REGISTER.
      WHERE (course_number=2) and (paid='N');
NOTE: PROCEDURE PRINT used:
      real time           2.40 seconds
      cpu time            0.03 seconds


MLOGIC(PAID):  Ending execution.
247  %paid(2,?)
MLOGIC(PAID):  Beginning execution.
MLOGIC(PAID):  Parameter CRSNUM has value 2
MLOGIC(PAID):  Parameter STATUS has value ?
MLOGIC(PAID):  %LET (variable name is STATUS1)
MLOGIC(PAID):  %IF condition &status1=Y or &status1=N is FALSE
MLOGIC(PAID):  %PUT Status must begin with Y or N
Status must begin with Y or N
MLOGIC(PAID):  %PUT Supplied value was:  &status
Supplied value was:  ?
MLOGIC(PAID):  Ending execution
```

**2. Defining, Executing, and Debugging a Macro (Optional)**

**a.** If you have the SAS windowing environment active, exit SAS and then start a new SAS session. Assign the **perm** libref in the new SAS session.

Include the program **printit** shown below into the Program Editor window and submit it.

```
%macro printit;
   %if &syslast = _NULL_ %then %do;
      proc print data=_last_(obs=5);
         title "Listing of data set &syslast";
      run;
   end;
%mend;
```

**b.** The missing percent sign in the % END statement causes the compilation error.

**c.** The %PRINTIT macro call generates an error message in the SAS log.

Partial SAS Log

```
25   %printit
ERROR: There is not a default input data set (_LAST_ is _NULL_).

NOTE: The SAS System stopped processing this step because of errors.
```

Activating the MPRINT, MLOGIC, and SYMBOLGEN options before calling the macro again provides additional information to assist in debugging the problem.

```
options mprint mlogic symbolgen;

%printit
```

Partial SAS Log

```
35   %printit
MLOGIC(PRINTIT):  Beginning execution.
SYMBOLGEN:  Macro variable SYSLAST resolves to _NULL_
MLOGIC(PRINTIT):  %IF condition &syslast = _NULL_ is TRUE
MPRINT(PRINTIT):   proc print data=_last_(obs=5);
ERROR: There is not a default input data set (_LAST_ is _NULL_).
SYMBOLGEN:  Macro variable SYSLAST resolves to _NULL_
MPRINT(PRINTIT):   title "Listing of data set _NULL_";
MPRINT(PRINTIT):   run;

NOTE: The SAS System stopped processing this step because of errors.
NOTE: PROCEDURE PRINT used:
      real time           0.01 seconds
      cpu time            0.01 seconds

MLOGIC(PRINTIT):  Ending execution.
```

The PROC PRINT step is generated when there is not a previously created data set. When there is no data set, the automatic macro variable SYSLAST has the value `_NULL_`. Therefore, the operator used with the %IF statement should be NE, not =.

```
%macro printit;
   %if &syslast ne _NULL_ %then %do;
      proc print data=_last_(obs=5);
         title "Listing of data set &syslast";
      run;
   %end;
%mend printit;
```

**d.** The message can be written to the SAS log using the %PUT statement within the %ELSE portion of the conditional logic.

```
%macro printit;
   %if &syslast ne _NULL_ %then %do;
      proc print data=_last_(obs=5);
         title "Listing of data set &syslast";
      run;
   %end;
   %else %put No SAS data set has been created.;
%mend;
```

In another approach, the message could be generated based on the main condition and the report generated as the alternative.

```
%macro printit;
  %if &syslast =_NULL_
    %then %put No SAS data set has been created.;
  %else %do;
     proc print data=_last_(obs=5);
        title "Listing of data set &syslast";
     run;
  %end;
%mend;
%printit
```

Partial SAS Log

```
115  %macro printit;
116    %if &syslast =_NULL_
117      %then %put No SAS data set has been created.;
118    %else %do;
119       proc print data=_last_(obs=5);
120          title "Listing of data set &syslast";
121       run;
122    %end;
123  %mend;
124  options mlogic mprint symbolgen;
125  %printit
MLOGIC(PRINTIT):  Beginning execution.
SYMBOLGEN:  Macro variable SYSLAST resolves to _NULL_
MLOGIC(PRINTIT):  %IF condition &syslast =_NULL_ is TRUE
MLOGIC(PRINTIT):  %PUT No SAS data set has been created.
No SAS data set has been created.
MLOGIC(PRINTIT):  Ending execution.
```

e. After creating a data set, the PRINTIT macro generates a PROC PRINT step to display it.

```
proc sort data=perm.students
     out=business(keep=student_company) nodupkey;
   by student_company;
run;
```

Partial SAS Log

```
148  %printit
MLOGIC(PRINTIT):  Beginning execution.
MLOGIC(PRINTIT):  %IF condition &syslast =_NULL_ is FALSE
MPRINT(PRINTIT):   proc print data=_last_(obs=5);
MPRINT(PRINTIT):   title "Listing of data set WORK.BUSINESS
           ";
MPRINT(PRINTIT):   run;

NOTE: There were 5 observations read from the dataset WORK.BUSINESS.
NOTE: PROCEDURE PRINT used:
      real time           0.02 seconds
      cpu time            0.02 seconds


MLOGIC(PRINTIT):  Ending execution.
```

SAS Output

```
      Listing of data set WORK.BUSINESS

               Obs    Student_Company

                 1    ABC, Inc.
                 2    ACDD
                 3    Admiral Research & Development Co.
                 4    Al's Discount Clothing
                 5    Alforone Chemical
```

## 5.2 Iterative Processing

### Objectives

- Execute macro language statements iteratively.
- Generate SAS code iteratively.

35

### Simple Loops

Many macro applications require iterative processing.

The iterative %DO statement can repeatedly

- execute macro language statements
- generate SAS code.

General form of the iterative %DO statement:

**%DO** *index-variable=start* **%TO** *stop* <**%BY** *increment*>;<br>
    *text*<br>
**%END**;

36

## Simple Loops

- %DO and %END statements are valid only inside a macro definition.
- *Index-variable* is a macro variable.
- *Index-variable* is created in the local symbol table if it does not already exist in an existing symbol table.
- *Start*, *stop*, and *increment* values can be any valid macro expressions that resolve to integers.
- %BY clause is optional (default *increment* is 1).

37

## Simple Loops

*Text* can be

- constant text
- macro variables or expressions
- macro statements
- macro calls.

38

## Simple Loops

Example: Create a numbered series of macro variables. Display each macro variable in the SAS log by repeatedly executing %PUT within a macro loop.

```
data _null_;
  set perm.schedule end=no_more;
  call symputx('teach'||left(_n_),teacher);
  if no_more then call symputx('count',_n_);
run;

%macro putloop;
  %do i=1 %to &count;
      %put TEACH&i is &&teach&i;
  %end;
%mend putloop;
```

LOOP1

39

No code is sent to the compiler when the macro executes. The %PUT statements are executed by the macro processor.

## Simple Loops

Partial SAS Log

```
12   %putloop
TEACH1 is Hallis, Dr. George
TEACH2 is Wickam, Dr. Alice
TEACH3 is Forest, Mr. Peter
TEACH4 is Tally, Ms. Julia
TEACH5 is Hallis, Dr. George
TEACH6 is Berthan, Ms. Judy
TEACH7 is Hallis, Dr. George
TEACH8 is Wickam, Dr. Alice
TEACH9 is Forest, Mr. Peter
TEACH10 is Tally, Ms. Julia
TEACH11 is Tally, Ms. Julia
TEACH12 is Berthan, Ms. Judy
TEACH13 is Hallis, Dr. George
TEACH14 is Wickam, Dr. Alice
TEACH15 is Forest, Mr. Peter
TEACH16 is Tally, Ms. Julia
TEACH17 is Hallis, Dr. George
TEACH18 is Berthan, Ms. Judy
```

40

# Generating Complete Steps

Example: Iteratively generate complete SAS steps.

```
%macro readraw(first=2000,last=2006);
  %do year=&first %to &last;
      data year&year;
        infile "raw&year..dat";
        input course_code $4.
              location    $15.
              begin_date  date9.
              teacher     $25.;
      run;
      proc print data=year&year;
      title "Scheduled classes for &year";
      run;
  %end;
%mend readraw;
%readraw(first=2000,last=2002)
```

LOOP2

41

# Generating Complete Steps

Partial SAS Log

```
MLOGIC(READRAW):  %DO loop index variable YEAR is now 2001; loop will iterate again.
MPRINT(READRAW):   data year2001;
MPRINT(READRAW):   infile "raw2001.dat";
MPRINT(READRAW):   input course_code $4. location $15. begin_date date9. teacher $25.;
MPRINT(READRAW):   run;

NOTE: The infile "raw2001.dat" is:
      File Name=C:\workshop\winsas\macr\raw2001.dat,
      RECFM=V,LRECL=256

NOTE: 12 records were read from the infile "raw2001.dat".
      The minimum record length was 53.
      The maximum record length was 53.
NOTE: The data set WORK.YEAR2001 has 12 observations and 4 variables.

MPRINT(READRAW):   proc print data=year2001;
MPRINT(READRAW):   title "Scheduled classes for 2001";
MPRINT(READRAW):   run;

NOTE: There were 12 observations read from the data set WORK.YEAR2001.

MLOGIC(READRAW):  %DO loop index variable YEAR is now 2002; loop will  iterate again.
MPRINT(READRAW):   data year2002;
MPRINT(READRAW):   infile "raw2002.dat";
MPRINT(READRAW):   input course_code $4. location $15. begin_date date9. teacher $25.;
MPRINT(READRAW):   run;
```

42

## Generating Data-Dependent Steps

Example: Print all data sets in a SAS data library.

Data set information is available in the dynamic view **vstabvw** in the **sashelp** library.

```
proc print data=sashelp.vstabvw;
   where libname="PERM";
   title "sashelp.vstabvw";
run;
```

→view table give an information about the library.

→dictionary table.
→contains information about SAS system.

PROC PRINT Output

sashelp.vstabvw

| Obs | libname | memname | memtype |
|---|---|---|---|
| 3480 | PERM | ALL | DATA |
| 3481 | PERM | COURSES | DATA |
| 3482 | PERM | REGISTER | DATA |
| 3483 | PERM | SCHEDULE | DATA |
| 3484 | PERM | STUDENTS | DATA |

43

## Generating Data-Dependent Steps

Store data set names in macro variables.

```
data _null_;
   set sashelp.vstabvw end=final;
   where libname="PERM";
   call symputx('dsn'||left(_n_),memname);
   if final then call symputx('totaldsn',_n_);
run;
%put _user_;
```

Partial SAS Log

```
7      %put _user_;
GLOBAL DSN1 ALL
GLOBAL DSN2 COURSES
GLOBAL DSN3 REGISTER
GLOBAL DSN4 SCHEDULE
GLOBAL DSN5 STUDENTS
GLOBAL TOTALDSN 5
```

44

## Generating Data-Dependent Steps

Use a macro loop to print every data set in the library.

```
%macro printlib(lib=WORK,obs=5);
  %let lib=%upcase(&lib);
  data _null_;
    set sashelp.vstabvw end=final;
    where libname="&lib";
    call symputx('dsn'||left(_n_),memname);
    if final then call symputx('totaldsn',_n_);
  run;
  %do i=1 %to &totaldsn;
    proc print data=&lib..&&dsn&i(obs=&obs);
       title "&lib..&&dsn&i Data Set";
    run;
  %end;
%mend printlib;
%printlib(lib=PERM)
```

LOOP3

45

## Generating Data-Dependent Steps

Partial SAS Log

```
MPRINT(PRINTLIB):   proc print data=PERM.ALL(obs=5);
MPRINT(PRINTLIB):   title "PERM.ALL Data Set";
MPRINT(PRINTLIB):   run;
NOTE: There were 5 observations read from the data set PERM.ALL.

MPRINT(PRINTLIB):   proc print data=PERM.COURSES(obs=5);
MPRINT(PRINTLIB):   title "PERM.COURSES Data Set";
MPRINT(PRINTLIB):   run;
NOTE: There were 5 observations read from the data set PERM.COURSES.

MPRINT(PRINTLIB):   proc print data=PERM.REGISTER(obs=5);
MPRINT(PRINTLIB):   title "PERM.REGISTER Data Set";
MPRINT(PRINTLIB):   run;
NOTE: There were 5 observations read from the data set PERM.REGISTER.

MPRINT(PRINTLIB):   proc print data=PERM.SCHEDULE(obs=5);
MPRINT(PRINTLIB):   title "PERM.SCHEDULE Data Set";
MPRINT(PRINTLIB):   run;
NOTE: There were 5 observations read from the data set PERM.SCHEDULE.
```

46

# Generating Data-Dependent Steps

Example: Create a separate data set for each value of a selected variable in a selected data set. Use the variable **location** in **perm.schedule**.

Listing of PERM.SCHEDULE

| Obs | Course_ Number | Course_ Code | Location | Begin_ Date | Teacher |
|---|---|---|---|---|---|
| 1 | 1 | C001 | Seattle | 26OCT2004 | Hallis, Dr. George |
| 2 | 2 | C002 | Dallas | 07DEC2004 | Wickam, Dr. Alice |
| 3 | 3 | C003 | Boston | 11JAN2005 | Forest, Mr. Peter |
| 4 | 4 | C004 | Seattle | 25JAN2005 | Tally, Ms. Julia |
| 5 | 5 | C005 | Dallas | 01MAR2005 | Hallis, Dr. George |
| 6 | 6 | C006 | Boston | 05APR2005 | Berthan, Ms. Judy |
| 7 | 7 | C001 | Dallas | 24MAY2005 | Hallis, Dr. George |
| 8 | 8 | C002 | Boston | 14JUN2005 | Wickam, Dr. Alice |
| 9 | 9 | C003 | Seattle | 19JUL2005 | Forest, Mr. Peter |
| 10 | 10 | C004 | Dallas | 16AUG2005 | Tally, Ms. Julia |
| 11 | 11 | C005 | Boston | 20SEP2005 | Tally, Ms. Julia |
| 12 | 12 | C006 | Seattle | 04OCT2005 | Berthan, Ms. Judy |
| 13 | 13 | C001 | Boston | 15NOV2005 | Hallis, Dr. George |
| 14 | 14 | C002 | Seattle | 06DEC2005 | Wickam, Dr. Alice |
| 15 | 15 | C003 | Dallas | 10JAN2006 | Forest, Mr. Peter |
| 16 | 16 | C004 | Boston | 24JAN2006 | Tally, Ms. Julia |
| 17 | 17 | C005 | Seattle | 28FEB2006 | Hallis, Dr. George |
| 18 | 18 | C006 | Dallas | 28MAR2006 | Berthan, Ms. Judy |

47

# Generating Data-Dependent Steps

SAS Program and Log

```
MPRINT(SITES):   data Boston Dallas Seattle ;
MPRINT(SITES):   set perm.schedule;
MPRINT(SITES):   select(location);
MPRINT(SITES):   when("Boston") output Boston;
MPRINT(SITES):   when("Dallas") output Dallas;
MPRINT(SITES):   when("Seattle") output Seattle;
MPRINT(SITES):   otherwise;
MPRINT(SITES):   end;
MPRINT(SITES):   run;

NOTE: There were 18 observations read from the data set PERM.SCHEDULE.
NOTE: The data set WORK.BOSTON has 6 observations and 5 variables.
NOTE: The data set WORK.DALLAS has 6 observations and 5 variables.
NOTE: The data set WORK.SEATTLE has 6 observations and 5 variables.
```

48

## Generating Data-Dependent Steps

Store data values in macro variables.

```
%macro sites (data=, var=);
  proc sort data=&data(keep=&var)
       out=values nodupkey;
    by &var;
  run;
  data _null_;
    set values end=last;
    call symputx('site'||left(_n_),&var);
    if last then call symputx('count',_n_);
  run;
  %put _local_;
```

LOOP4

*continued...*

49

## Generating Data-Dependent Steps

Partial SAS log with result of %put _local_;

```
SITES DATA perm.schedule
SITES I
SITES COUNT 3
SITES VAR location
SITES SITE3 Seattle
SITES SITE2 Dallas
SITES SITE1 Boston
```

The **_local_** argument of the **%PUT** statement lists the name and value of macro variables local to the currently executing macro.

50

## Generating Data-Dependent Steps

Generate the DATA step, using macro loops for iterative substitution. Call the macro.

```
data
  %do i=1 %to &count;
    &&site&i
  %end;
  ;
  set &data;
  select(&var);
    %do i=1 %to &count;
      when("&&site&i") output &&site&i;
    %end;
    otherwise;
  end;
run;
%mend sites;
%sites(data=perm.schedule, var=location)
```

LOOP4

51

## Generating Data-Dependent Steps

Partial SAS Log

```
MPRINT(SITES):   data Boston Dallas Seattle ;
MPRINT(SITES):   set perm.schedule;
MPRINT(SITES):   select(location);
MPRINT(SITES):   when("Boston") output Boston;
MPRINT(SITES):   when("Dallas") output Dallas;
MPRINT(SITES):   when("Seattle") output Seattle;
MPRINT(SITES):   otherwise;
MPRINT(SITES):   end;
MPRINT(SITES):   run;

NOTE: There were 18 observations read from the data set PERM.SCHEDULE.
NOTE: The data set WORK.BOSTON has 6 observations and 5 variables.
NOTE: The data set WORK.DALLAS has 6 observations and 5 variables.
NOTE: The data set WORK.SEATTLE has 6 observations and 5 variables.
```

52

## Conditional Iteration (Self-Study)

You can perform conditional iteration in macros with %DO %WHILE and %DO %UNTIL statements.

General form of the %DO %WHILE statement:

```
%DO %WHILE(expression);
    text
%END;
```

A %DO %WHILE loop

- evaluates *expression* at the top of the loop before the loop executes
- executes repetitively while expression is true.

53

## Conditional Iteration (Self-Study)

General form of the %DO %UNTIL statement:

```
%DO %UNTIL(expression);
    text
%END;
```

*expression* can be any valid macro expression.

A %DO %UNTIL loop

- evaluates *expression* at the bottom of the loop after the loop executes
- executes repetitively until expression is true
- executes at least once.

54

## Conditional Iteration (Self-Study)

Review: Create a macro variable with a delimited list of values.

```
573  proc sql noprint;
574     select distinct upcase(location)
575        into :sitelist separated by '*'
576        from perm.schedule;
577  quit;

578  %put sitelist=&sitelist;
sitelist=BOSTON*DALLAS*SEATTLE
```

55

## Conditional Iteration (Self-Study)

Example: Execute macro language statements within a **%DO %WHILE** loop.

```
%macro values(text,delim=*);
   %let i=1;
   %let value=%scan(&text,&i,&delim);
   %if &value= %then %put Text is blank.;
   %else %do %while (&value ne );
      %put Value &i is: &value;
      %let i=%eval(&i+1);
      %let value=%scan(&text,&i,&delim);
   %end;
   %mend values;
%values(&sitelist)
```

LOOP5

56

## Conditional Iteration (Self-Study)

Example: Execute macro language statements within a **%DO %UNTIL** loop.

```
%macro values(text,delim=*);
   %let i=1;
   %let value=%scan(&text,&i,&delim);
   %if &value= %then %put Text is blank.;
   %else %do %until (&value= );
      %put Value &i is: &value;
      %let i=%eval(&i+1);
      %let value=%scan(&text,&i,&delim);
   %end;
%mend values;
%values(&sitelist)
```

LOOP6

57

## Conditional Iteration (Self-Study)

Result of macro call.

Partial SAS Log

```
572  %values(&sitelist)
Value 1 is: BOSTON
Value 2 is: DALLAS
Value 3 is: SEATTLE
```

58

## Exercises

### 3. Using Macro Loops

Open the **printnum** program shown below into the Editor window.

```
proc print data=perm.all label noobs n;
   where course_number=3;
   var student_name student_company;
   title "Enrollment for Course 3";
run;
```

Define a macro program that generates a separate listing for each of the courses in the **perm.all** data set. The values of COURSE_NUMBER range from 1 to 18.

### 4. Generating Data-Dependent Steps (Optional)

**a.** Define a macro that can print a series of reports, each report containing observations having a particular value for a selected variable. For example, because the **perm.schedule** data set contains six distinct values for COURSE_CODE, the macro should produce six reports, one for each distinct value of COURSE_CODE.

Parameters for the macro are

- data set to be printed
- variables used for subsetting
- type of variable (CHAR, NUM).

**b.** Use the macro to generate a separate report for each training location in **perm.schedule** data set.

**c.** Use the macro to generate a separate report for each class duration in the **perm.courses** data set.

# Solutions to Exercises

### 3. Using Macro Loops

A simple macro loop with an index variable starting at 1 and stopping at 18 will produce the reports.

```
%macro prtrost;
   %do num=1 %to 18;
      proc print data=perm.all label noobs n;
         where course_number=&num;
         var student_name student_company;
         title1 "Enrollment for Course &num";
      run;
   %end;
%mend prtrost;

options mprint nomlogic;

%prtrost
```

Partial SAS Log

```
MPRINT(PRTROST):   proc print data=perm.all label noobs n;
MPRINT(PRTROST):   where course_number=1;
MPRINT(PRTROST):   var student_name student_company;
MPRINT(PRTROST):   title1 "Enrollment for Course 1";
MPRINT(PRTROST):   run;
NOTE: There were 23 observations read from the dataset PERM.ALL.
      WHERE course_number=1;
NOTE: PROCEDURE PRINT used:
      real time           0.07 seconds
      cpu time            0.07 seconds
```

## 4. Generating Data-Dependent Steps (Optional)

a. The SORT procedure can produce a list of distinct values for a given variable. These values can be placed into a series of macro variables. Using a macro loop, the series of macro variables can be processed to produce one report for each original data value. The type of variable parameter controls whether quotes are placed around data in the WHERE statement.

```
%macro printall(dsn,var,type=CHAR);
   %let dsn=%upcase(&dsn);
   %let var=%upcase(&var);
   %let type=%upcase(&type);
   proc sort data=&dsn(keep=&var) out=unique nodupkey;
      by &var;
   run;

   data _null_;
      set unique end=final;
      call symput('value'||left(_n_),
           trim(left(&var)));
      if final then call symput('count',_n_);
   run;

   %do i=1 %to &count;
      proc print data=&dsn;
         %if &type=CHAR %then %do;
             where &var="&&value&I";
         %end;
         %else %do;
            where &var=&&value&i;
         %end;
         title1 "Listing of &dsn Data Set";
         title2 "for &var=&&value&I";
      run;
   %end;
%mend printall;
```

**b.** The macro call to generate a separate report for each training center location in the **perm.schedule** data set is

```
%printall(perm.schedule,location)
```

Partial SAS Log

```
MPRINT(PRINTALL):   proc print data=PERM.SCHEDULE;
MPRINT(PRINTALL):   where LOCATION="Boston";
MPRINT(PRINTALL):   title1 "Listing of PERM.SCHEDULE Data Set";
MPRINT(PRINTALL):   title2 "for LOCATION=Boston";
MPRINT(PRINTALL):   run;
NOTE: There were 6 observations read from the dataset PERM.SCHEDULE.
      WHERE LOCATION='Boston';
NOTE: PROCEDURE PRINT used:
      real time           1.96 seconds
      cpu time            0.01 seconds


MPRINT(PRINTALL):   proc print data=PERM.SCHEDULE;
MPRINT(PRINTALL):   where LOCATION="Dallas";
MPRINT(PRINTALL):   title1 "Listing of PERM.SCHEDULE Data Set";
MPRINT(PRINTALL):   title2 "for LOCATION=Dallas";
MPRINT(PRINTALL):   run;
NOTE: There were 6 observations read from the dataset PERM.SCHEDULE.
      WHERE LOCATION='Dallas';
NOTE: PROCEDURE PRINT used:
      real time           2.03 seconds
      cpu time            0.04 seconds


MPRINT(PRINTALL):   proc print data=PERM.SCHEDULE;
MPRINT(PRINTALL):   where LOCATION="Seattle";
MPRINT(PRINTALL):   title1 "Listing of PERM.SCHEDULE Data Set";
MPRINT(PRINTALL):   title2 "for LOCATION=Seattle";
MPRINT(PRINTALL):   run;
NOTE: There were 6 observations read from the dataset PERM.SCHEDULE.
      WHERE LOCATION='Seattle';
NOTE: PROCEDURE PRINT used:
      real time           1.97 seconds
      cpu time            0.01 seconds
```

**c.** The macro call to generate a separate report for each class duration in the **perm.courses** data set.

```
%printall(perm.courses,days,type=num)
```

Partial SAS Log

```
MPRINT(PRINTALL):   proc print data=PERM.COURSES;
MPRINT(PRINTALL):   where DAYS=2;
MPRINT(PRINTALL):   title1 "Listing of PERM.COURSES Data Set";
MPRINT(PRINTALL):   title2 "for DAYS=2";
MPRINT(PRINTALL):   run;
NOTE: There were 2 observations read from the dataset PERM.COURSES.
      WHERE DAYS=2;
NOTE: PROCEDURE PRINT used:
      real time           1.46 seconds
      cpu time            0.02 seconds


MPRINT(PRINTALL):   proc print data=PERM.COURSES;
MPRINT(PRINTALL):   where DAYS=3;
MPRINT(PRINTALL):   title1 "Listing of PERM.COURSES Data Set";
MPRINT(PRINTALL):   title2 "for DAYS=3";
MPRINT(PRINTALL):   run;
NOTE: There were 2 observations read from the dataset PERM.COURSES.
      WHERE DAYS=3;
NOTE: PROCEDURE PRINT used:
      real time           1.51 seconds
      cpu time            0.05 seconds


MPRINT(PRINTALL):   proc print data=PERM.COURSES;
MPRINT(PRINTALL):   where DAYS=4;
MPRINT(PRINTALL):   title1 "Listing of PERM.COURSES Data Set";
MPRINT(PRINTALL):   title2 "for DAYS=4";
MPRINT(PRINTALL):   run;
NOTE: There were 1 observations read from the dataset PERM.COURSES.
      WHERE DAYS=4;
NOTE: PROCEDURE PRINT used:
      real time           1.44 seconds
      cpu time            0.02 seconds


MPRINT(PRINTALL):   proc print data=PERM.COURSES;
MPRINT(PRINTALL):   where DAYS=5;
MPRINT(PRINTALL):   title1 "Listing of PERM.COURSES Data Set";
MPRINT(PRINTALL):   title2 "for DAYS=5";
MPRINT(PRINTALL):   run;
NOTE: There were 1 observations read from the dataset PERM.COURSES.
      WHERE DAYS=5;
NOTE: PROCEDURE PRINT used:
      real time           1.46 seconds
      cpu time            0.03 seconds
```

# 5.3 Global and Local Symbol Tables

## Objectives

- Explain the difference between global and local symbol tables.
- Describe how the macro processor decides which symbol table to use.
- Describe the concept of nested macros and the hierarchy of symbol tables.

61

## The Global Symbol Table

The *global symbol table* is

- created during the initialization of a SAS session or noninteractive execution
- initialized with automatic or system-defined macro variables
- deleted at the end of the session.

62

## The Global Symbol Table

Macro variables in the global symbol table

- are available anytime during the session
- can be created by your program
- have values that can be changed during the session (except some automatic macro variables).

63

## The Global Symbol Table

Global Symbol Table

| Variable | Value |
|---|---|
| SYSDATE | **23FEB04** |
| SYSDAY | **Monday** |
| SYSVER | **9.1** |
| . | . |
| . | . |
| . | . |
| uservar1 | **value1** |
| uservar2 | **value2** |

64

## The Global Symbol Table

You can create a global macro variable with a

- %LET statement (used outside a macro definition)
- DATA step containing a SYMPUT routine
- SELECT statement containing an INTO clause in PROC SQL
- %GLOBAL statement.

65

## The Global Symbol Table

General form of the %GLOBAL statement:

```
%GLOBAL macrovar1 macrovar2 . . . ;
```

The %GLOBAL statement

changing the scope of that macro variable => no effect already in the global variable.

- creates one or more macro variables in the global symbol table and assigns them null values
- can be used inside or outside a macro definition
- has no effect on variables already in the global table.

66

## The Local Symbol Table

A *local symbol table* is

- created when a macro with a parameter list is called or a local macro variable is created during macro execution
- deleted when the macro finishes execution.

A local table is not created unless and until a request is made to create a local variable. Macros that do not create local variables do not have a local table.

67

## The Local Symbol Table

Local macro variables can be

- created and initialized at macro invocation (macro parameters)
- created during macro execution
- updated during macro execution
- referenced anywhere within the macro.

68

## The Local Symbol Table

The memory used by a local table can be reused when the table is deleted after macro execution. Therefore, use local variables instead of global variables whenever possible.

Local Symbol Table

| Variable | Value |
|---|---|
| parameter1 | **value1** |
| parameter2 | **value2** |
| . | . |
| . | . |
| . | . |
| uservar1 | **value1** |
| uservar2 | **value2** |

69

## The Local Symbol Table

In addition to macro parameters, you can create local macro variables with any of the following methods used **inside** a macro definition:

- %LET statement
- DATA step containing a SYMPUT routine
- SELECT statement containing an INTO clause in PROC SQL
- %LOCAL statement.

The SYMPUT routine creates local variables only if a local table already exists.

70

## The %LOCAL Statement

General form of %LOCAL statement:

**%LOCAL** *macrovar1 macrovar2* . . . ;

The %LOCAL statement

- can appear only inside a macro definition
- creates one or more macro variables in the local symbol table and assigns them null values
- has no effect on variables already in the local table.

71

## The %LOCAL Statement

Declare the index variable of a macro loop as a local variable to prevent the accidental contamination of macro variables of the same name in the global table or other local tables.

```
%macro putloop;
  %local i;
  %do i=1 %to &count;
      %put TEACH&i is &&teach&i;
  %end;
%mend putloop;
```

72

## The SYMPUTX Routine

The optional *scope* argument of the SYMPUTX routine specifies where to store the macro variable:

```
CALL SYMPUTX(macro-variable, text <,scope>);
```

- G specifies the global symbol table.
- L specifies the most local of **existing** symbol tables, which might be the global symbol table if no local symbol table exists.

✎ The SYMPUTX routine is new in SAS®9.

73

## Rules for Creating and Updating Variables

When the macro processor receives a request to create or update a macro variable during macro execution, the macro processor follows these rules:

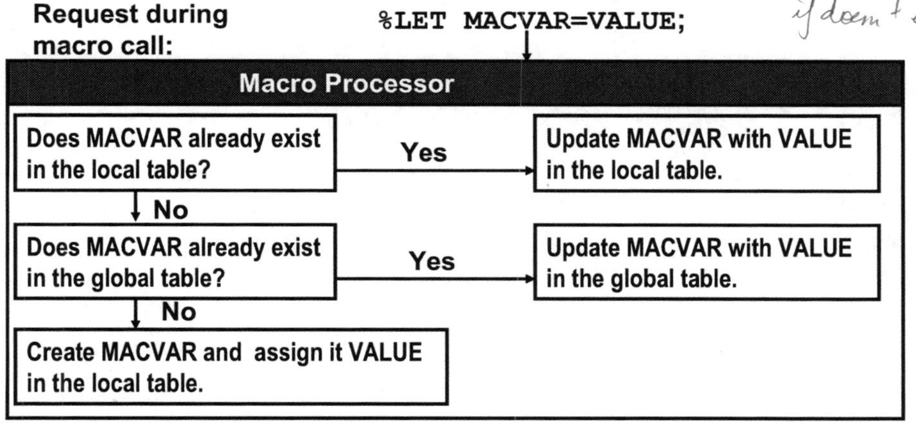


74

## Rules for Resolving Variables

To resolve a macro variable reference during macro execution, the macro processor follows these rules:

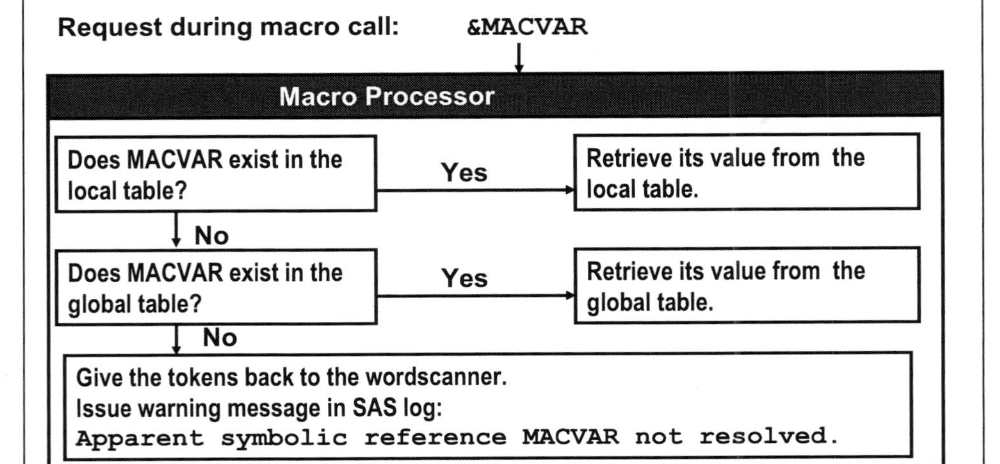


## Multiple Local Tables

Multiple local tables can exist concurrently during macro execution.

Example: Define two macros. One calls the other.

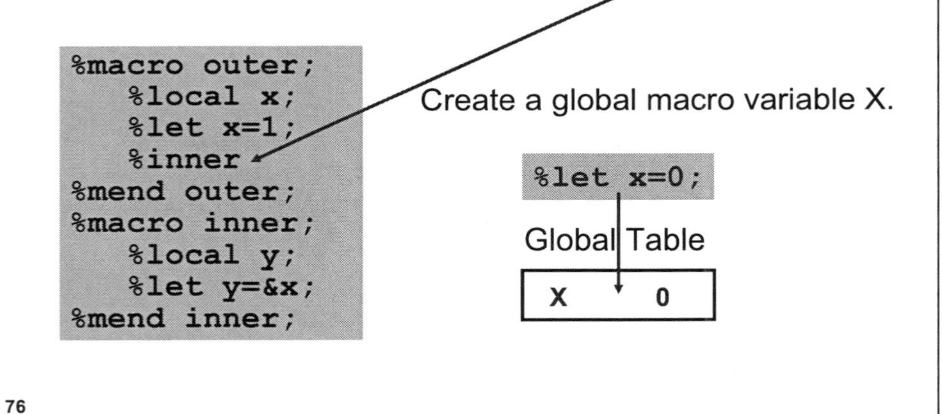


76

## Multiple Local Tables

Call the OUTER macro. When the %LOCAL statement executes, a local table is created.

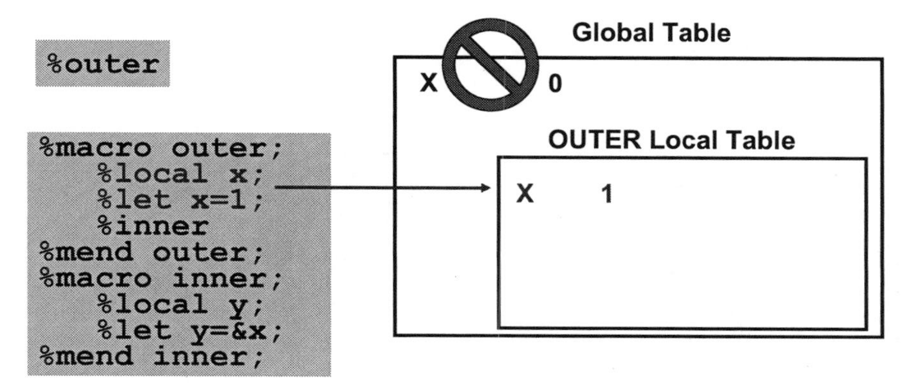


What happens if the %LOCAL statement in the OUTER macro is omitted?

77

## Multiple Local Tables

A nested macro call can create its own local symbol table in addition to any other tables that may currently exist.

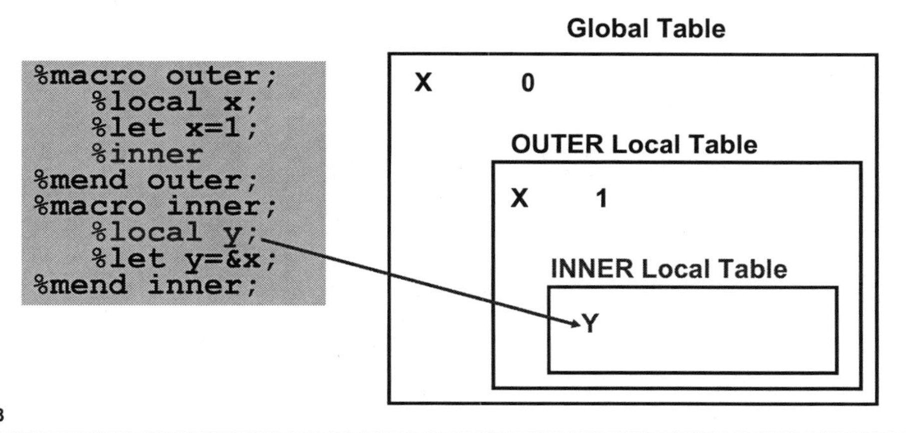


78

## Multiple Local Tables

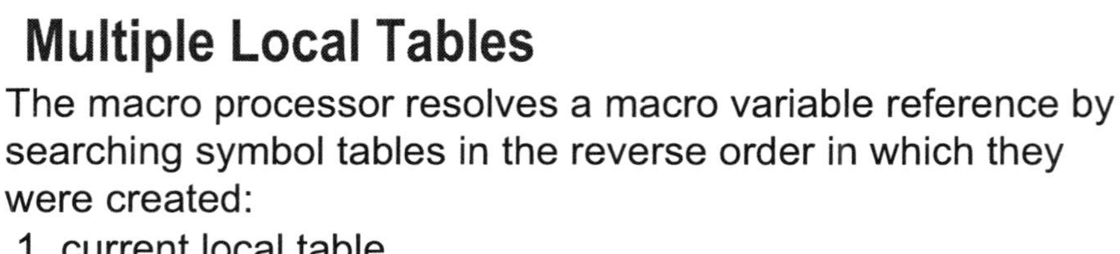

The macro processor resolves a macro variable reference by searching symbol tables in the reverse order in which they were created:

1. current local table
2. previously created local tables
3. global table.

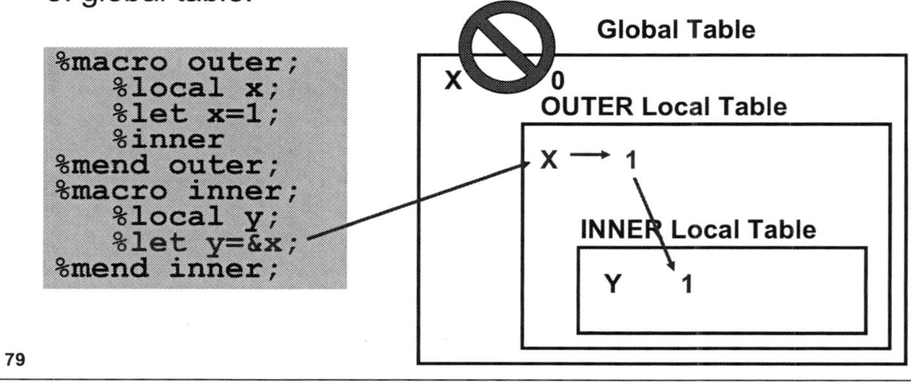

```
%macro outer;
   %local x;
   %let x=1;
   %inner
%mend outer;
%macro inner;
   %local y;
   %let y=&x;
%mend inner;
```



79

The global variable X is **not** available to the INNER macro.

## Multiple Local Tables

When the INNER macro finishes execution, its local table is deleted. Control passes back to the OUTER macro.

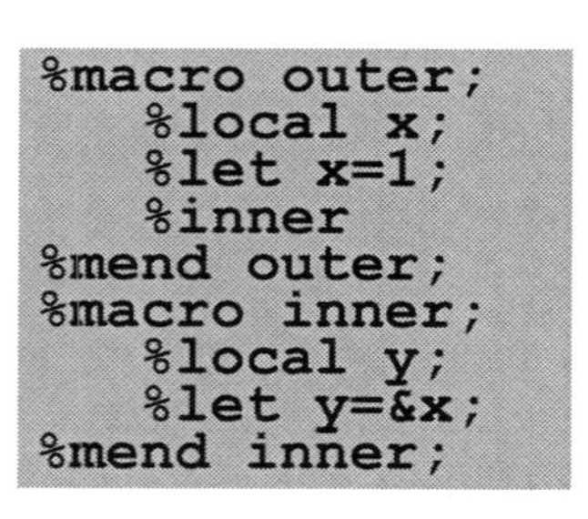

```
%macro outer;
   %local x;
   %let x=1;
   %inner
%mend outer;
%macro inner;
   %local y;
   %let y=&x;
%mend inner;
```

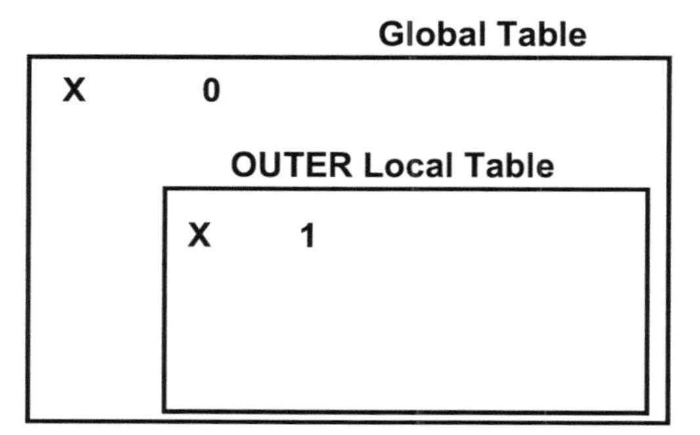



80

## Multiple Local Tables

When the OUTER macro finishes execution, its local table is removed. Only the GLOBAL table remains.

```
%macro outer;
   %local x;
   %let x=1;
   %inner
%mend outer;
%macro inner;
   %local y;
   %let y=&x;
%mend inner;
```

**Global Table**

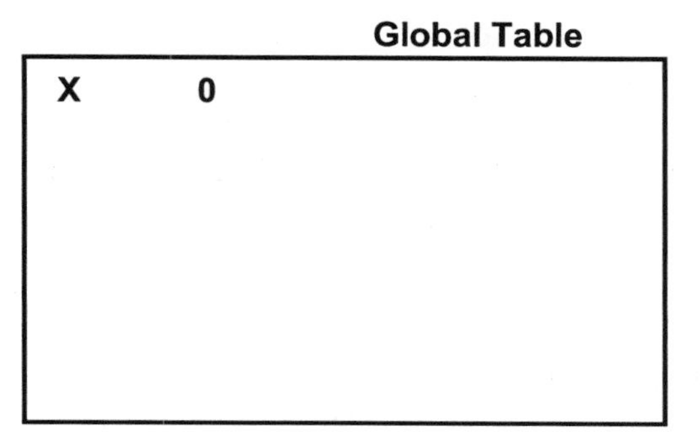


81

## Multiple Local Tables

Example: Call the NUMOBS macro within the CHECK macro to find the number of observations in a subset of the `perm.students` data set.

Conditionally execute additional SAS code if the subset contains any observations.

Call the macro to list students from different companies.

82

## Multiple Local Tables

```
%macro numobs(lib,dsn);
  %global num;
  %let num=0;
  proc sql noprint;
    select (nobs-delobs) into :num
        from dictionary.tables
        where libname="%upcase(&lib)"
            and memname="%upcase(&dsn)";
  quit;
  %let num=&num;
%mend numobs;
%macro check(comp);
  data subset;
    set perm.students;
    where student_company="&comp";
  run;
  %numobs(work,subset)
  %if &num>0 %then %do;
    proc print data=subset noobs;
       var student_name city_state;
       title "&num Students from &comp";
    run;
  %end;
  %else %put No students from &comp..;
%mend check;
```

**Why is NUM declared *global* in the NUMOBS macro? Is there another solution?**

SYMBOL1

83

```
%macro check(comp);
  data subset;
    set perm.students;
    where student_company="&comp";
  run;
  %numobs(work,subset)
  %if &num>0 %then %do;
    proc print data=subset noobs;
       var student_name city_state;
       title "&num Students from &comp";
    run;
  %end;
  %else %put No students from &comp..;
%mend check;
%check(Reston Railway)
```

**Global Table**

check Local Table

| comp | Reston Railway |
|---|---|

84

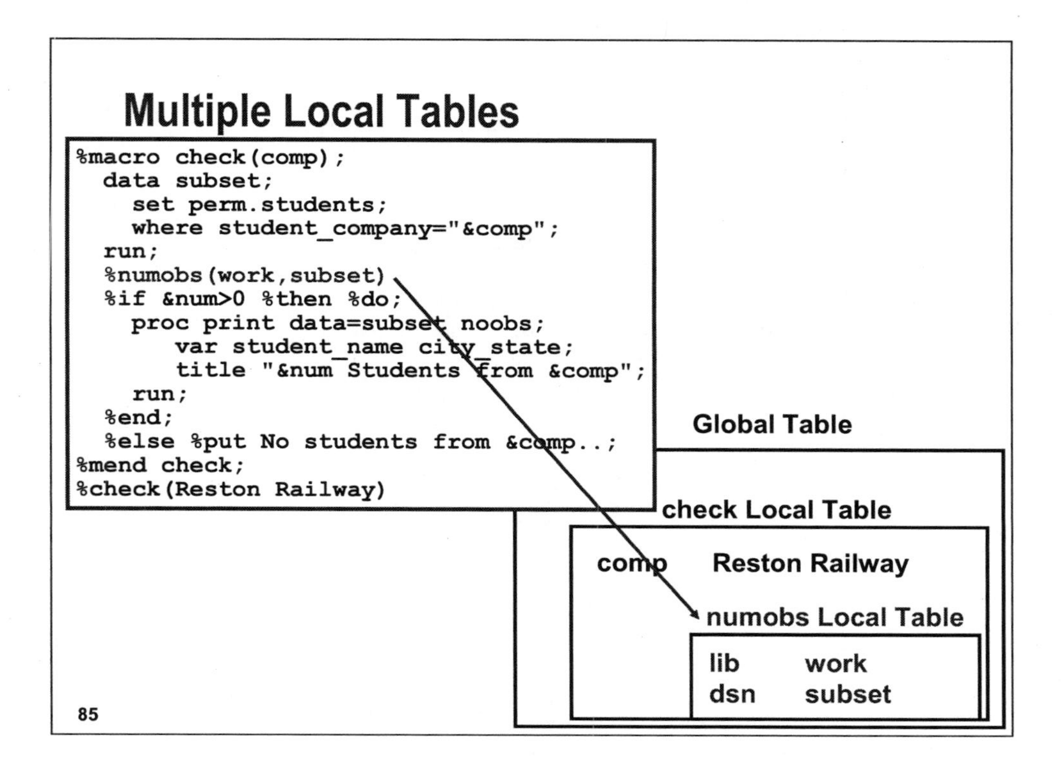
Multiple Local Tables
%macro check(comp);
data subset;
set perm.students;
where student_company="&comp";
run;
%numobs(work,subset)
%if &num>0 %then %do;
proc print data=subset noobs;
var student_name city_state;
title "&num Students from &comp";
run;
%end;
%else %put No students from &comp..;
%mend check;
%check(Reston Railway)
Global Table
check Local Table
comp Reston Railway
numobs Local Table
lib work
dsn subset
85

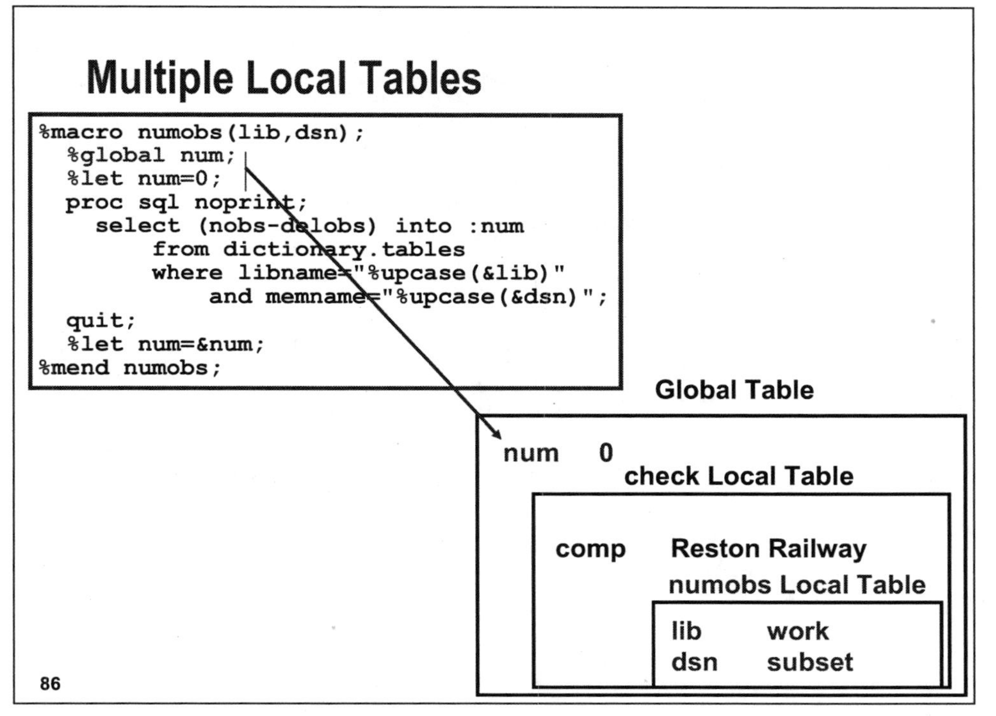
Multiple Local Tables
%macro numobs(lib,dsn);
%global num;
%let num=0;
proc sql noprint;
select (nobs-delobs) into :num
from dictionary.tables
where libname="%upcase(&lib)"
and memname="%upcase(&dsn)";
quit;
%let num=#
%mend numobs;
Global Table
num 0
check Local Table
comp Reston Railway
numobs Local Table
lib work
dsn subset
86

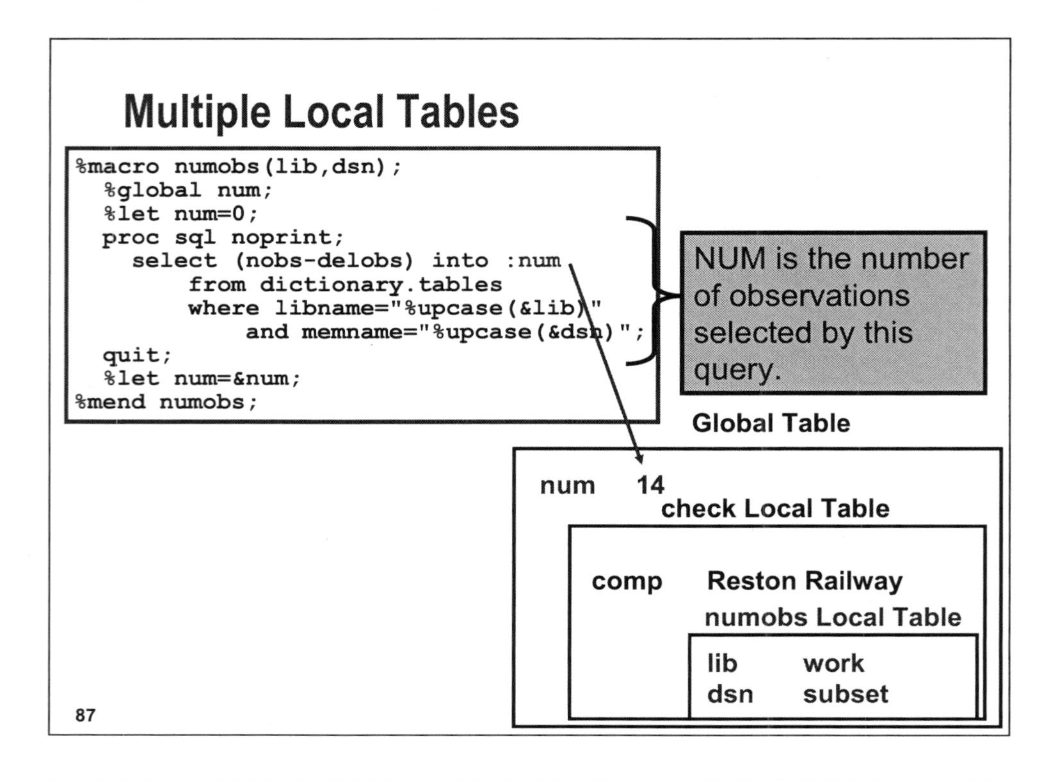
Multiple Local Tables
%macro numobs(lib,dsn);
%global num;
%let num=0;
proc sql noprint;
select (nobs-delobs) into :num
from dictionary.tables
where libname="%upcase(&lib)"
and memname="%upcase(&dsn)";
quit;
%let num=#
%mend numobs;
NUM is the number of observations selected by this query.
Global Table
num 14
check Local Table
comp Reston Railway
numobs Local Table
lib work
dsn subset
87

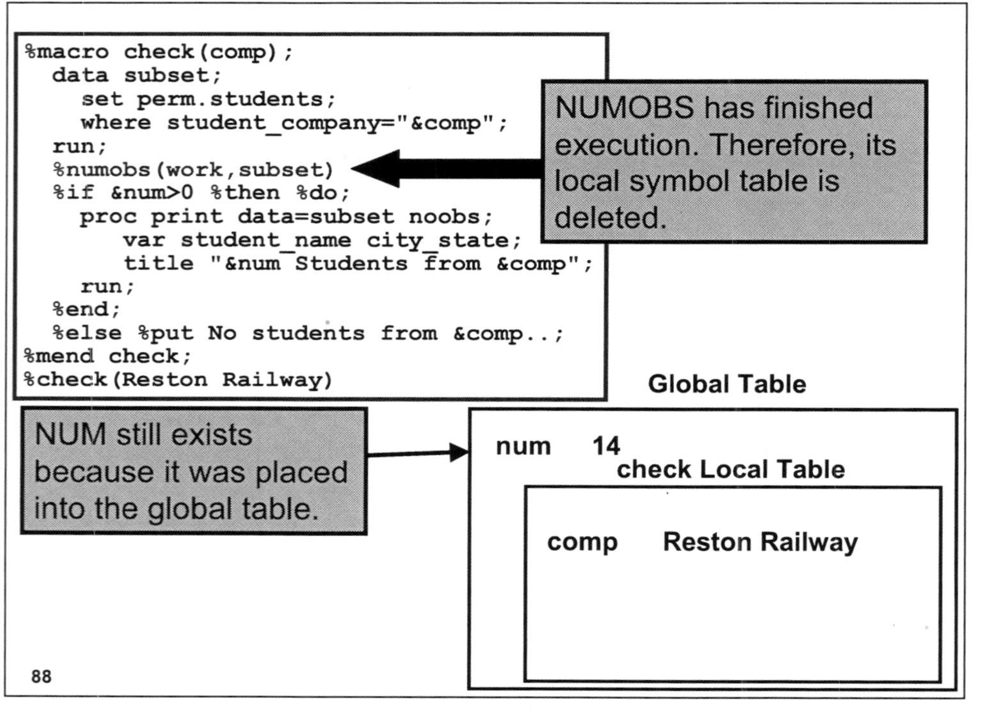
%macro check(comp);
data subset;
set perm.students;
where student_company="&comp";
run;
%numobs(work,subset)
%if &num>0 %then %do;
proc print data=subset noobs;
var student_name city_state;
title "&num Students from &comp";
run;
%end;
%else %put No students from &comp..;
%mend check;
%check(Reston Railway)
NUMOBS has finished execution. Therefore, its local symbol table is deleted.
NUM still exists because it was placed into the global table.
Global Table
num 14
check Local Table
comp Reston Railway
88

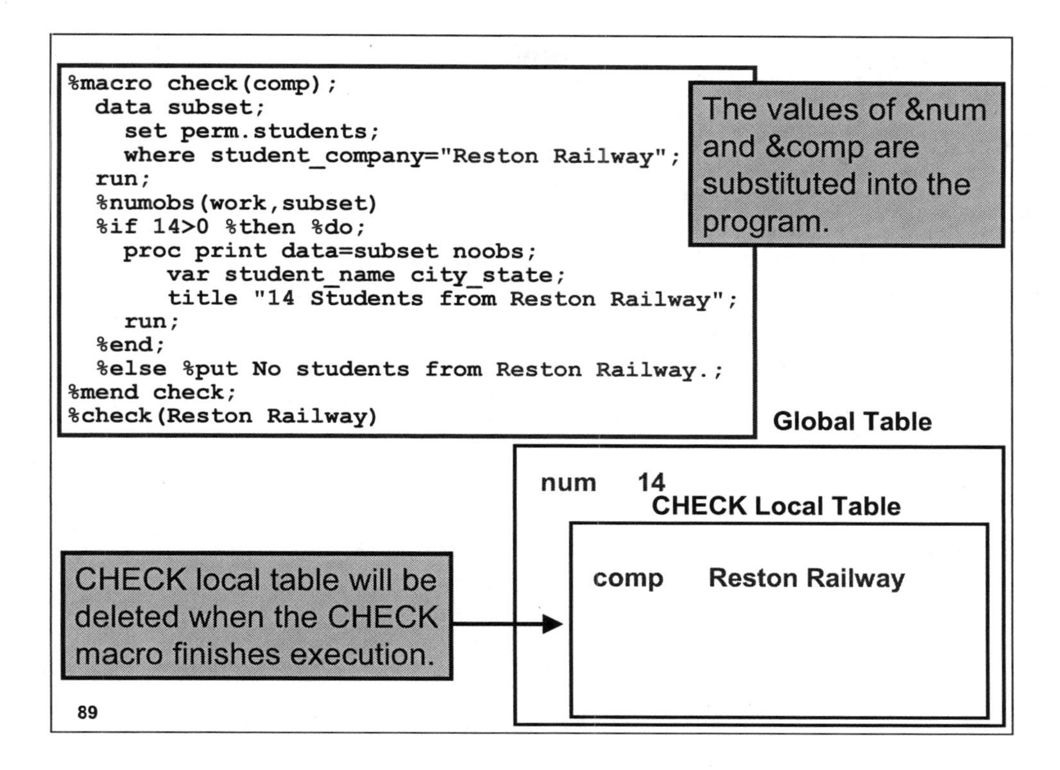


## Multiple Local Tables

Partial SAS Log

```
174  %check(Reston Railway)

NOTE: There were 14 observations read from the data set PERM.STUDENTS.
      WHERE student_company='Reston Railway';
NOTE: The data set WORK.SUBSET has 14 observations and 3 variables.
NOTE: DATA statement used (Total process time):
      real time           0.00 seconds
      cpu time            0.01 seconds

NOTE: PROCEDURE SQL used (Total process time):
      real time           0.00 seconds
      cpu time            0.01 seconds

NOTE: There were 14 observations read from the data set WORK.SUBSET.
NOTE: PROCEDURE PRINT used (Total process time):
      real time           0.00 seconds
      cpu time            0.00 seconds
```

90

# Multiple Local Tables

Partial SAS Log

```
175  %check(Raston Railway)

NOTE: There were 0 observations read from the data set PERM.STUDENTS.
      WHERE student_company='Raston Railway';
NOTE: The data set WORK.SUBSET has 0 observations and 3 variables.
NOTE: DATA statement used (Total process time):
      real time           0.01 seconds
      cpu time            0.01 seconds

NOTE: PROCEDURE SQL used (Total process time):
      real time           0.00 seconds
      cpu time            0.00 seconds

No students from Raston Railway.
```

91

## Exercises

### 5. Creating Multiple Symbol Tables

**a.** Open the **nested** program shown below into the Editor window.

```
%macro prtrost(num=1);
   data _null_;
      call symput('today',
           trim(left(put(today(),mmddyy10.))));
   run;

   proc print data=perm.all label noobs n;
      where course_number=&num;
      var student_name student_company city_state;
      title1 "Enrollment for Course &num as  of &today";
   run;
%mend prtrost;
%prtrost(num=8)
```

**b.** Move the DATA step into a separate macro named DATEMVAR with one parameter corresponding to the format used in the PUT function. Make DATE9. the default value of this parameter.

**c.** Place a call to the new macro before the PROC PRINT step (where the DATA step had been). Use the value MMDDYY10. instead of the default value for the macro's parameter. Submit the revised program.

**d.** Make certain that the reference to &TODAY in the title resolves to the formatted value of today's date.

# Solutions to Exercises

## 5. Creating Multiple Symbol Tables

When the DATA step is moved outside the original macro, and the new macro has parameters, the macro variable TODAY is placed in the local table for the new macro unless it is explicitly made available to the original macro.

This can be done by making TODAY

- a global variable, or
- a local variable for the original macro, which can be updated within the new macro as the macro processor traverses through the separate local tables in the reverse order that they were created.

```
%macro datemvar(fmt=date9.);
   data _null_;
      call symput('today',
      trim(left(put(today(),&fmt))));
   run;
%mend datemvar;

%macro prtrost(num=1);
   %local today;
   %datemvar(fmt=mmddyy10.);
   proc print data=perm.all label noobs n;
      where course_number=&num;
      var student_name student_company city_state;
      title1 "Enrollment for Course &num as of &today";
   run;
%mend prtrost;

%prtrost(num=8)
```

# Chapter 6 Learning More

# 6.1 SAS Resources

## Objectives

- Explore other services and resources available to all SAS users.

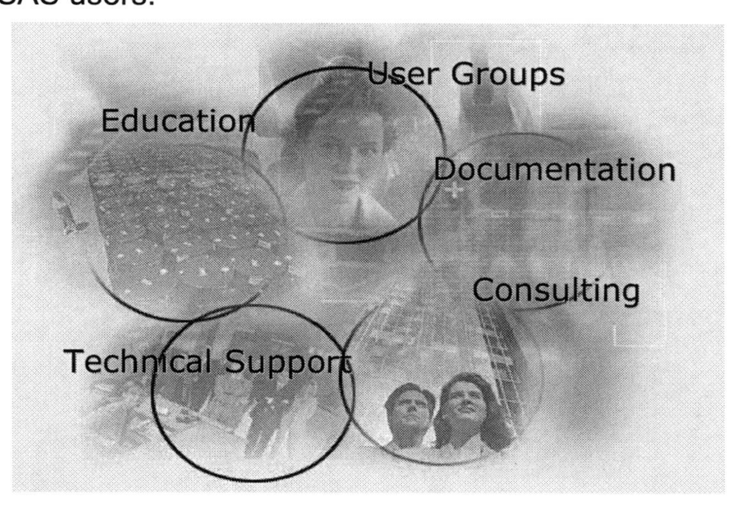


3

## SAS Services

SAS is a full-service company that provides

- Training — instructor-based and online training options
- Certification — global certification program to assess knowledge of SAS software and earn industry-recognized credentials
- Online Help — a comprehensive online Help system to address many information needs
- Documentation — extensive online and hardcopy reference information.

4

# SAS Customer Support Center

Access the SAS Customer Support Center to learn more about available services and resources.

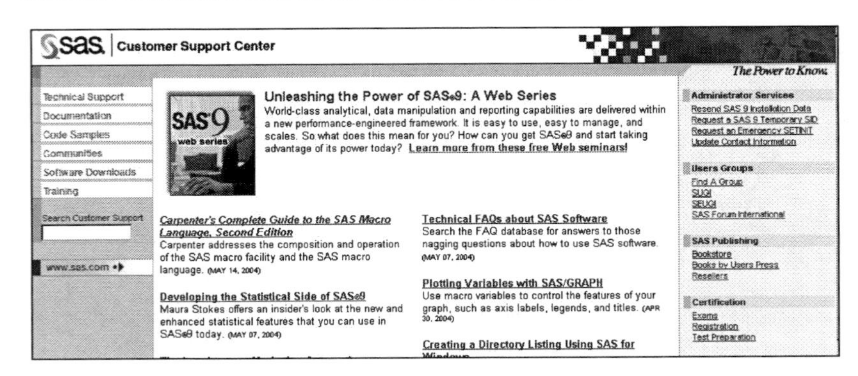


**support.sas.com/**

5

You can use the SAS Web site to

- read about software, either by application or by industry
- learn about upcoming worldwide events, such as industry trade shows
- report problems to the Technical Support Division
- learn about consulting services
- identify the most appropriate learning path and register for courses online
- review the list of certification exams designed to assess knowledge of SAS software; identify test preparation options; and register online for a certification exam
- browse and order from the online version of the *SAS® Publications* catalog
- access online versions of SAS publications.

## SAS Training

SAS provides comprehensive training services.

- Instructor-based training (public and onsite)
- Business Knowledge Series seminars (led by industry experts)
- E-Learning (self-paced and Live Web)

For additional information, visit the SAS Training Web site.

**support.sas.com/training/**

6

## Training Services

SAS offers training services to help you achieve business and professional goals. Whether you are a beginning or an accomplished SAS software user, training services are available to help you increase your skills and expand your knowledge.

**Instructor-based training** offers both public and on-site courses that encompass the breadth of SAS solutions and software including

- the SAS programming language
- report writing
- applications development
- data warehousing
- client/server strategies
- structured query language (SQL)
- financial consolidation and reporting
- database access
- statistical analysis.

**Seminars led by industry experts** are also available through the Business Knowledge Series to provide you with expertise in the latest business developments.

**e-Learning** is an optimal choice when time and distance are an issue. SAS offers Live Web classes and self-paced e-learning to help you get the training you need while accommodating your busy schedule. The benefits of e-learning include the following:

- Bring SAS software or JMP training directly to your desktop and learn at your own pace anytime, anywhere.
- Learn at your convenience.
- Personalize your training.
- Practice in your own SAS session.
- Enhance what you learn in the classroom.

For more information about training services, visit the Web at http://support.sas.com/training and order the complimentary *SAS® Training* catalog (http://support.sas.com/training/us/catalog.html). Published biannually, the *SAS® Training* catalog contains detailed course descriptions, course fees, and suggested learning paths, as well as information on discounts and special offers.

Additional learning paths include

- Data Presentation
- Data Mining
- SAS IT Resource Management
- SAS Human Capital Management
- Statistical Analysis
- JMP
- StatView.

## SAS Technology Conferences

SAS holds an annual Data Mining conference where you can learn the latest developments in the data mining field.

**www.sas.com/events/dmconf/**

7

## SAS Certified Professional Program

Consider taking a certification exam to assess your knowledge of SAS software. For a current listing of certification exams and registration information, visit the SAS Certification Web site.

**support.sas.com/certify/**

8

# Online Help

SAS features an extensive online Help system built into the software.

9

# SAS Documentation

The Documentation section of the Customer Support Center is designed to give you quick and easy access to the documentation provided by SAS.

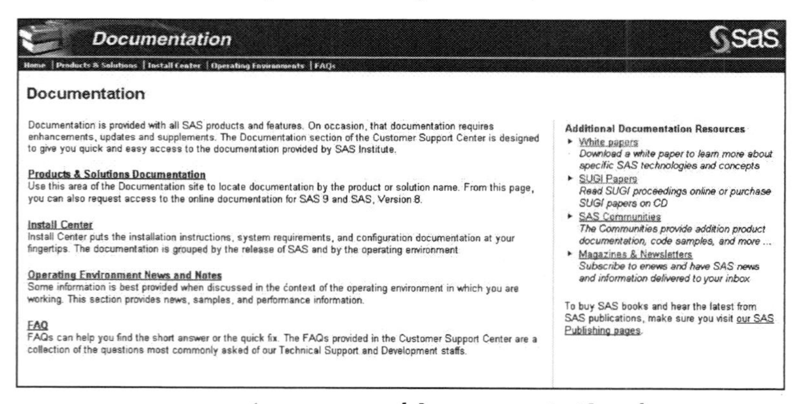


**support.sas.com/documentation/**

10

# Online Documentation

You can access SAS OnlineDoc, which provides you with SAS reference documentation.

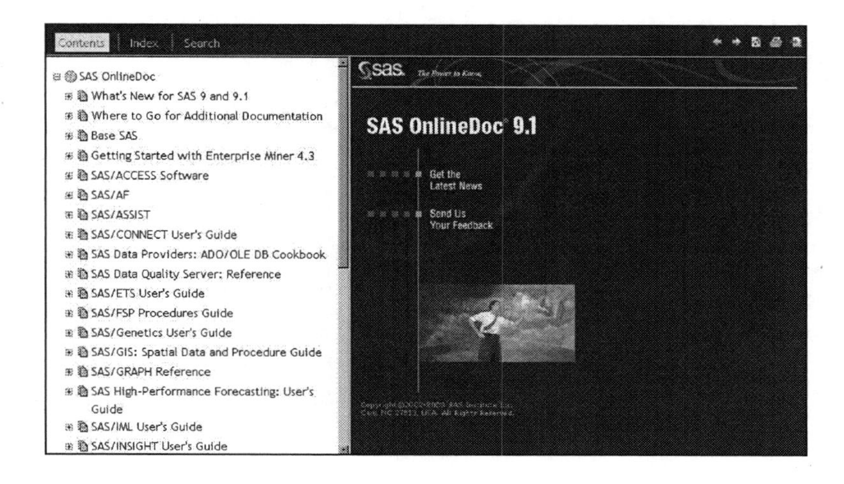


11

# Hardcopy Documentation

Some SAS documentation is available in hardcopy.

For more information, visit the SAS Publishing Web site.

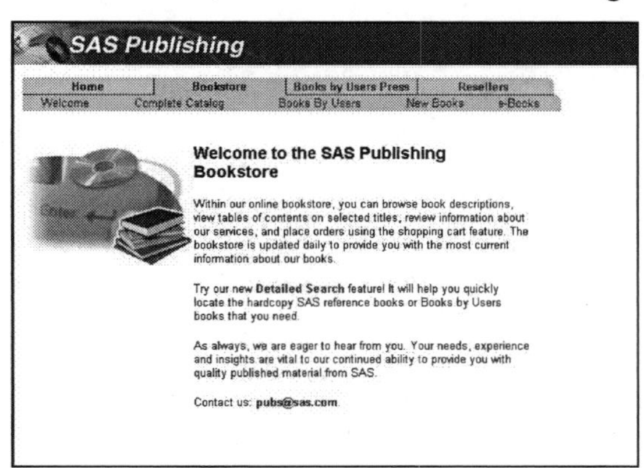


**support.sas.com/publishing/**

12

## Publications Services

For a complete list of documentation available in online and hardcopy form, access the SAS Publications Web site at http://support.sas.com/publishing .

You can order documentation using the Publications Catalog through the SAS Publications Web site or by calling **1-800-727-3228.**

Online and printed documentation includes

- Getting Started Guides, which provide an introduction to selected features of SAS
- Reference Guides, which cover the SAS language
- User's Guides, which show applications of SAS features
- Companions, which explain the implementation of SAS features in specific operating environments
- Changes and Enhancements, which describe "What's New" in each release of SAS software
- Books by Users, written by expert SAS software users on a variety of topics
- Proceedings from SAS Users Group conferences.

SAS publishes a number of magazines and newsletters. To view these periodicals, access the SAS Publications Web site.

### Additional SAS Services

SAS also provides

- Sample Programs — online code samples, technical tips, how-to advice
- Online Communities — resources related to specific subject areas
- Technical Support — specialists for all SAS software products and supported operating systems.
- Consulting Services — short- or long-term services to meet business needs.

13

# Code Samples

Sample programs and technical tips from SAS developers, SAS technical support consultants, and longtime SAS users are available online.

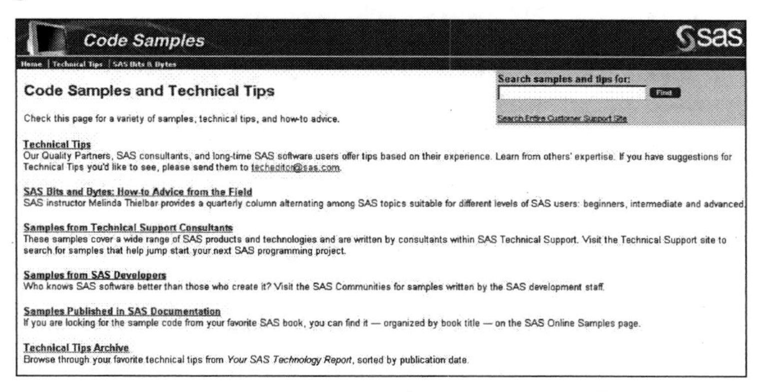


**support.sas.com/sassamples/**

14

# Online Communities

SAS communities offer quick online access to information related to many subject areas.

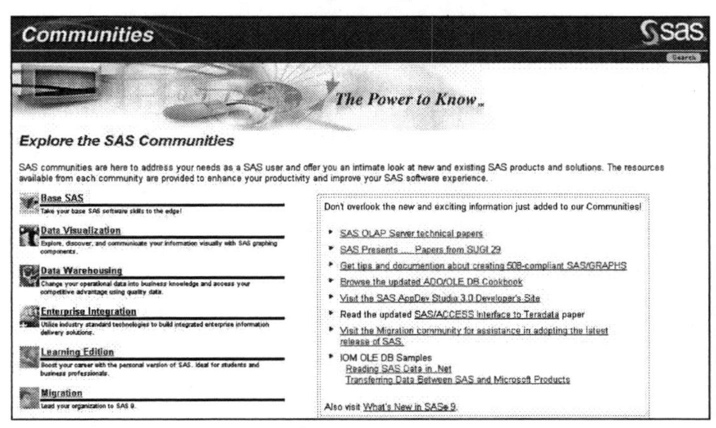


**support.sas.com/rnd/**

15

## Technical Support

**Goals:**

- Provide support to our users to solve any problems they encounter when using SAS software.
- Free unlimited support.
- Local support at each site - designated SAS consultant.

**World Wide Web Services:**

- Report/resolve problems
- Frequently asked questions
- SASware Ballot suggestions/results
- Download zaps/fixes/patches
- Upload code/data
- Search SAS notes
- Alert notes.

16

## Contacting Technical Support

**Web:** **support.sas.com/techsup/**

**E-mail:** support@sas.com - report problems
suggest@sas.com - software suggestions

**Telephone (North America):**
9:00 a.m. until 8:00 p.m. Eastern Time, Monday-Friday
(919) 677-8008

17

 Customers outside North America should contact their local SAS office for telephone support.

## Technical Support Services

Technical Support provides you with the resources to answer questions or solve problems that you encounter when you use SAS software. You have access to a variety of tools to solve problems on your own and a variety of ways to contact Technical Support when you need help.

- **Free, Unlimited Support**

  Free technical support is available to all sites that license software from SAS. This includes unlimited telephone support for customers in North America by calling **1-919-677-8008**. Customers outside North America can contact their local SAS Institute office. There is also an e-mail interface and FTP site.

- **Reported Problems**

  Although SAS software is recognized as a leader in reliability, SAS realizes that no software is problem free. We do our best to let you know about bugs or problems that have been reported to Technical Support. Information about reported problems is available in the SAS Notes and SAS/C Compiler Usage Notes, which are distributed with the software, and can also be searched via the Web interface. We also inform you about more serious problems through Alert Notes and the TSNEWS-L list server.

- **Local Support at Your Site**

  To provide the most effective response to your questions and problems, one or more persons at your site are designated as local SAS support personnel. These are knowledgeable SAS users who are provided with additional resources to assist all SAS users at your site. You can often get a quick answer to your SAS questions by contacting your local SAS consultant before calling SAS Technical Support.

To use SAS Technical Support, you must know your SAS System site number. Your site number can be found at the top of the log. The site number can also be easily obtained using the SETINIT procedure, which displays information about your SAS installation in the log.

```
PROC SETINIT NOALIAS;
RUN;
```

## Consulting Services

Services provided:

- knowledge transfer
- application development
- analytical consulting
- implement business solutions.

18

## Consulting Services

SAS offers flexible consulting options to meet short- or long-term business needs. Services such as installation, needs assessment, project scoping, prototyping, or short-term technical assistance help you to reap the benefits of SAS software as quickly as possible.

Consultants provide expertise in areas such as

- data warehousing
- data mining
- business intelligence
- Web-enablement tasks
- analytical solutions
- business solutions
- custom applications
- client/server technology
- systems-related issues.

## Other SAS Users

SAS users can share their experiences through

- SAS Users Groups
- the SAS-L Internet mail list
- the COMP.SOFT-SYS.SAS newsgroup

19

## SAS Users Groups

SAS Users Groups offer the opportunity to

- enhance your understanding of SAS software and services
- exchange ideas about using your software and hardware most productively
- learn of new SAS products and services as soon as they become available
- have more influence over the direction of SAS software and services.

20

## International Users Groups

SUGI (pronounced soo-gee)

SAS Users Group International. Annual conference held March or April in North America.

SAS Forum International (formerly SEUGI)

Annual conference held May or June in Europe.

SUGA (SAS Users Group of Australia)

Annual Conference held August or September in Australia.

21

## U.S. Regional User Groups

| | |
|---|---|
| SESUG | SouthEast SAS Users Group |
| NESUG | NorthEast SAS Users Group |
| MWSUG | MidWest SAS Users Group |
| SCSUG | South-Central SAS Users Group |
| WUSS | Western Users of SAS Software |
| PNWSUG | Pacific Northwest SAS Users Group |

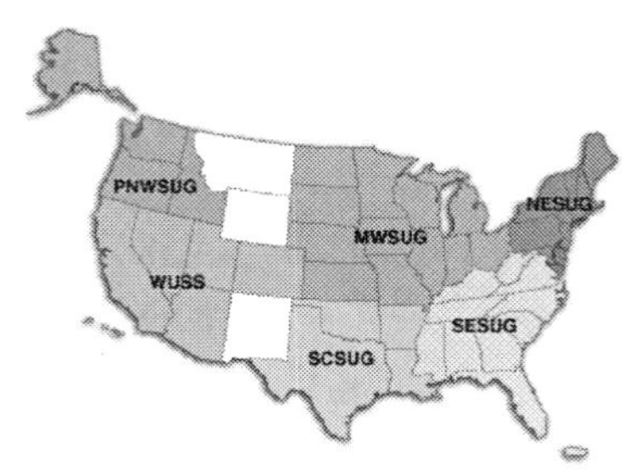


22

## Other Users Groups

| | |
|---|---|
| **Local** | City or area user group. Often hold multiple meetings per year. |
| **Special Interest** | Industry-specific user groups. |
| **In-house** | Single organization or company user group. |
| **Worldwide** | Most countries have their own users groups. |

**support.sas.com/usergroups/**

23

## SAS-L Internet Mail List

**SAS-L** is a user-run Internet mail list (LISTSERV) devoted to issues relating to SAS software products.

You can use SAS-L to exchange information (and opinions) about SAS software, or to post questions about SAS software and get responses from SAS users around the world.

SAS-L is sponsored by the University of Georgia.

SAS-L is neither moderated nor supported by SAS.

24

## Subscribing to SAS-L

To subscribe to the SAS-L mail list, send a message to listserv@listserv.uga.edu.

The subject line is ignored and the body should contain SUBSCRIBE SAS-L *your name here*

.

For example, SUBSCRIBE SAS-L Tom Smith is how Tom Smith would subscribe.

You can also manage your subscription through the SAS-L Web site:

**listserv.uga.edu/archives/sas-l.html**

25

## COMP.SOFT-SYS.SAS Newsgroup

The **COMP.SOFT-SYS.SAS** Usenet newsgroup mirrors the SAS-L mail list.

To view this newsgroup, use a newsgroup viewer such as **groups.google.com**.

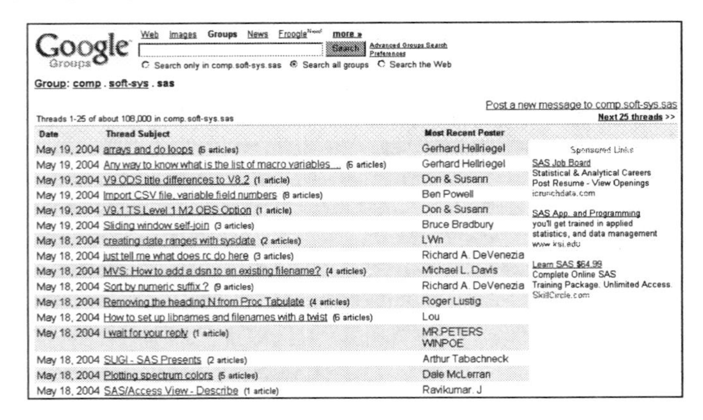


26

# Additional Information

Access the SAS Web site to learn more about available SAS software, support, and services.

**www.sas.com**

# 6.2 What's Next After SAS® Macro Language

## Objectives

- Explore which SAS training courses are appropriate after you complete SAS® Macro Language.

29

## Additional SAS Training Courses

SAS® Macro Language is part of the Accessing and Manipulating Data learning path of the SAS curriculum:

30

Additional learning paths include

- SAS Enterprise Guide
- Business Intelligence
- Data Presentation and Reporting
- Application Development
- Statistical Analysis
- Data Mining
- Activity-Based Management
- Supplier Relationship Management and Risk Management
- Warranty Analysis
- Financial Management, IT Management, and Strategic Performance Management
- Customer Intelligence
- Pharmaceutical/Health Care
- Scientific Discovery
- JMP.

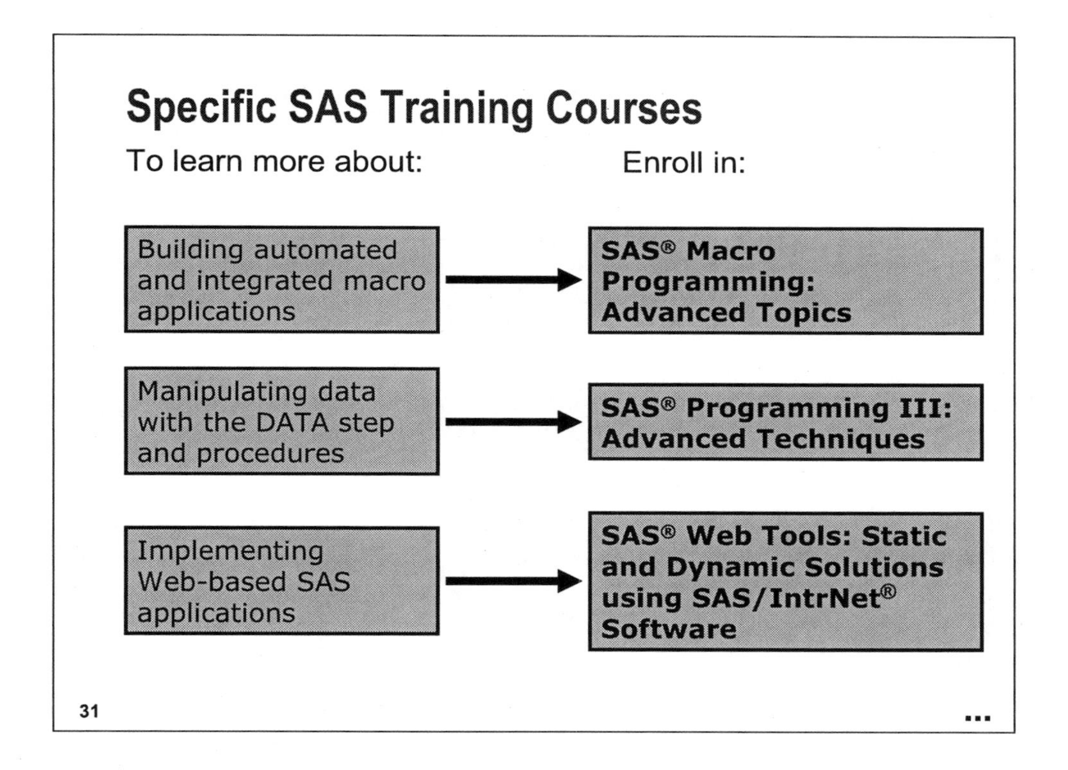

## Before You Leave...

Do not forget to

- fill out your evaluation
- make a copy of the course data (if desired)
- pick up your diploma
- deposit your name badge in the container provided by your course coordinator.

32

## Thank You...

for attending SAS® Macro Language.

We hope that the topics you have learned in this course will enhance your ability to build more flexible SAS applications and reduce your effort in creating and maintaining those applications.

33

# Appendix A Flow Diagram



% sysfunc (today (), format )

# A.1 Program Flow

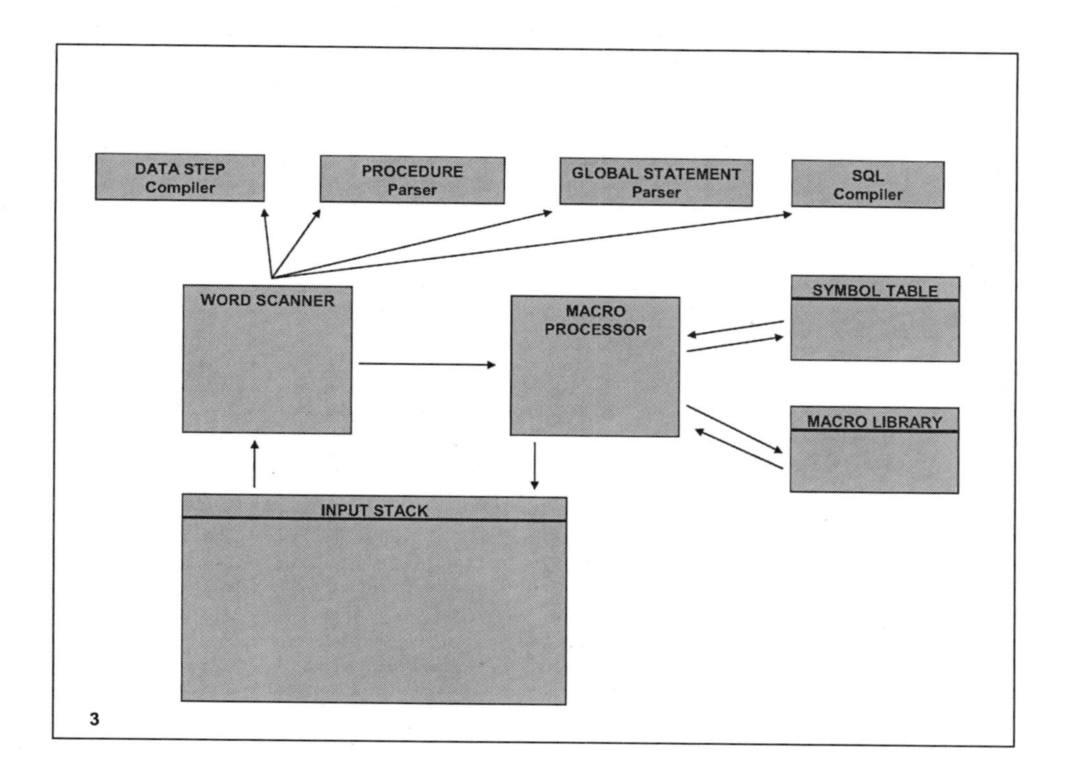

# Appendix B Index